The Cooperative Edge

Beyond Globalism: Remaking American Foreign Economic Policy (1989), with Raymond Vernon

Iron Triangles and Revolving Doors: Cases in U.S. Foreign and Economic Policymaking (1991), with Raymond Vernon and Glenn Tobin

The Cooperative Edge

THE INTERNAL POLITICS OF INTERNATIONAL CARTELS

DEBORA L. SPAR

CORNELL UNIVERSITY PRESS

Ithaca and London

First published 1994 by Cornell University Press.

This book is a volume in the series
Cornell Studies in Political Economy,
edited by Peter J. Katzenstein.

Library of Congress Cataloging-in-Publication Data

Spar, Debora L.
    The cooperative edge : the internal politics of international cartels /
Debora L. Spar.
       p.   cm.—(Cornell studies in political economy)
    Includes bibliographical references and index.
    ISBN 0-8014-2658-8 (alk. paper)
    1. Cartels.   2. International economic relations.   I. Title.   II. Series.
HD2757.5.S68   1994
338.8'7—dc20   93-34801

Printed in the United States of America

⊗ The paper in this book meets the minimum requirements
of the American National Standard for Information Sciences—
Permanence of Paper for Printed Library Materials, ANSI Z39.48-1984.

To Miltos

Contents

The meek shall inherit the earth, but not its mineral resources.

—John Paul Getty

Preface

In the five years since it began, this book has gone through several incarnations. It originated as a study of the Soviet oil industry, expanded to include natural gas, and then settled into a project on Soviet commodity trade in general. At the outset, my goal was to examine how the Soviets sold their natural resources on world markets and how they manipulated this trade in pursuit of political gain.

The problem, though, was that I could not find any evidence that the Soviets were in fact using trade as a political weapon. Instead, in all the markets I examined, they appeared to be acting as perfectly rational sellers, "playing the market" as well as if not better than their capitalist competitors. And so I started over, formulating a new project to examine why the Soviets were not using any of the economic weapons that, theoretically at least, were at their disposal. But here again I stopped. Very quickly I realized that the real puzzle was not why the Soviets were not competing more vigorously but rather why they were cooperating so effectively. In particular, I discovered that in several commodity markets the Soviets were actively colluding with their South African counterparts, joining forces to stabilize prices and boost their long-term returns. Why, I wondered, were the Soviets—passionate crusaders against capitalism and apartheid—cooperating with the South Africans? What could possibly be keeping these strangest of bedfellows together? And what broader lessons lay buried in their collusion?

And so I started over once again. I abandoned oil, energy, and resource wars and turned entirely to the question of cooperation in international commodity markets—the question of cartels. I wanted to understand how competing producers could learn to work together, how they could overcome the constant pressures to compete, and how they could sustain their cooperation during economic downturns and political strife. Logically I knew that cartels almost always made economic sense. But empirically I also knew that they usually failed. The puzzle I gave myself was to explain this contradiction and to understand why the Soviets and South Africans had somehow managed to get around it. And the answer, I discovered, was largely a factor of internal structure and organization. Some producers, I argue, are simply better equipped than others to cooperate. Even under the same external conditions, certain *kinds* of players are more apt to succeed at the cooperative game. Describing these players and the conditions that facilitate their cooperation is thus the central mission of this book.

Substantively, the book is about markets, producers, and cartels. Theoretically, though, it is concerned with cooperation. I am interested in cartels not for their own sake but rather for what they can teach us about the politics and processes of international cooperation. In the course of this project, I have spent many months reviewing the economic literature on cartels. At some point, I have summarized the most relevant aspects of this literature and incorporated it into the text. And always, at some later point, I have removed these discussions from the manuscript or relegated them to a handful of footnotes. Thus while the economics of cartels underlie this study, they are not integral to it. I hope economists will read this book. I hope they will enjoy it, argue with it, and perhaps even learn something from it. But it is still not a book about the economics of cartels. Rather, this is a book about cooperation and about the internal forces that shape, constrain, and define the cooperative process. And in this regard, I hope it will be of interest not just to political scientists but also to businesspeople, policymakers, and anyone else concerned with the practical, as well as the theoretical, issues of cooperation.

As this book has gone through its many lives, it has also benefited from the encouragement and guidance of many people. Stanley

Hoffmann was a source of constant support and encouragement. Always, he provided gentle criticism, a sense of perspective, and inspiration whenever the halls of academia looked particularly bleak. Ray Vernon was, as usual, an indefatigable yet cheerful critic. His ability to spot flaws in logic, theory, fact, and grammar is legendary; his care and concern in doing so are truly remarkable. Stephan Haggard had an unfailing capacity to restructure my arguments and an uncanny way of predicting the problems that would arise. To these three advisers, I am most grateful.

In addition, I am indebted to the score of people who shared with me the knowledge of their industries, markets, and trading patterns. Because they spoke on condition of anonymity, I unfortunately cannot thank them by name. Still, I wish to include a silent note of gratitude to the individuals in the uranium, silver, gold, and diamond markets who were so generous with their time. Two others I can mention by name—Gordon Austin of the Bureau of Mines and John Lutley of the Gold and Silver Institute—were extremely helpful in the initial stages of my work. I am also grateful to the Pew Charitable Trusts for sponsoring some of my early research into the international diamond cartel. A version of this research was published as a series of teaching cases for the Kennedy School of Government at Harvard University. Subsequent research and writing were funded by the Division of Research at the Harvard Business School.

At various stages in the project, friends and colleagues have cheerfully served as sounding boards for my ideas. I am grateful on this score to Laura Hastings, Heather Hazard, Kelly Jackson, Kalypso Nicolaidis, Louis Pauly, Gordon Silverstein, Patricia Small, Glenn Tobin, David Welch, and Melissa Williams. Willis Emmons, John Goodman, Lisa Martin, Steve Solnick, Richard Tedlow, and Dick Vietor read the manuscript in its final stages and helped me rearrange and strengthen my arguments. I owe a particular debt of gratitude to Thomas McCraw, who not only pulled large sections of the manuscript apart but also masterfully suggested how I might put them together again. I also thank Angela Stent and Daniel Yergin for suggesting several years ago that I look at commodities other than oil and gas. Peter Katzenstein has been an outstanding reader, critic, and supporter of this book, and Roger Haydon a tremendous editor. Violet Crowe kept up with all the terrible last-minute details, and Allegra Young, Julia Kou, and Michael Stevenson provided invaluable research assistance.

My greatest debts are on the home front. I could not have completed this book without Irene Saavedra, who kept everything else under control while I was writing. My parents, Martin and Judith Spar, have always provided comfort and encouragement. My sons, Daniel and Andrew Catomeris, kindly timed their births to coincide with successive drafts of the manuscript. And most of all I am grateful to my husband, Miltos Catomeris, who knows far more about cartels than any architect should.

Debora L. Spar

Boston, Massachusetts

The Cooperative Edge

CHAPTER ONE

Of Cooperation, Competition, and Cartels

Cooperation is a ubiquitous problem. Everywhere we find situations where cooperation makes sense and where it should be relatively easy to achieve. There is always some way for workers and management to resolve their differences without resorting to strikes or layoffs, some way for states to avoid the high costs of conflict, and some prospect that firms will choose to divide their market shares rather than engage in ruinous price competition. Yet all too frequently these cooperative solutions go unheeded. Workers strike, states retaliate, and firms compete heatedly. Even when the benefits of cooperation are obvious, they are still often infuriatingly difficult to obtain. Plagued by uncertainty and distrust, the would-be participants pull back from the cooperative endeavor. As they retreat, cooperation falters and competition resumes.

But occasionally competition does give way to cooperation, and onetime adversaries somehow find a way to manage their rivalry and pursue their joint objectives. The puzzle, then, lies in distinguishing the differences. Why does cooperation emerge in some cases and not others? Why can some competitors abandon their battles and work together? And what separates those few enterprises that succeed from the mass that fail? These are the questions that drive this inquiry.

Ultimately, this book is most concerned with the question of international cooperation. It seeks to explain why states cooperate and how they can build institutions to nourish and sustain their cooperation. To answer these questions, the book uses an empirical study of cartels to generate hypotheses about cooperation between states. The analogy is not perfect, of course. Cartels are a particular form of cooperation and contain some characteristics that are not shared by other cooperative endeavors. Still, in many ways, cartels do epitomize the larger phenomenon of cooperation.

As with cooperation in general, cartels emerge from competition.[1] They arise because the competitors realize that they can advance their own self-interest by working with each other. Together, they can dominate the market and dictate the price that consumers must pay. By refraining from competition, cartel members reap the rewards of greater stability and higher long-term profits. The difficulty, though, lies in maintaining this cooperation, for once an arrangement is in place, any single firm can increase its own short-term profits by defecting. Thus any cartel carries the seeds of its own dissolution. This central risk of cartels is also the central dilemma of cooperation.

Recognizing the strong parallels between cartels and cooperation, many political scientists have already translated the phenomenon of cartelization into an implicit model of international cooperation.[2] Starting with the cartel analogy and the payoff structures it suggests, scholars have examined the means by which the competitive game can be modified or manipulated so as to increase the likelihood of cooperation. Drawing on the neoclassical framework of most cartel studies, they have focused on the external connections between cartels and cooperation and have built models of cooperation that rest implicitly on assumptions about how cartels work.

This book takes a different tack. Rather than refer to deductive models of cartel behavior, I go back to the markets themselves, looking to identify the concrete factors that shaped or constrained the

[1] I share here Robert O. Keohane's distinction between cooperation and harmony. Cooperation assumes that there is competition among the participants and requires that this competition be constantly and consciously restrained. See Keohane, *After Hegemony: Cooperation and Discord in the World Political Economy* (Princeton: Princeton University Press, 1984), pp. 51–55; and Kenneth A. Oye, "Explaining Cooperation under Anarchy: Hypotheses and Strategies," in Oye, ed., *Cooperation under Anarchy* (Princeton: Princeton University Press, 1986), p. 6.

[2] For example, see Duncan Snidal, "The Game *Theory* of International Politics," *World Politics* 38 (October 1985): 25–27; and Robert Gilpin, *War and Change in World Politics* (Cambridge: Cambridge University Press, 1981), p. 87.

formation of cartels. I take as my starting point the economists' conception of structure. The four markets that I examine—diamonds, uranium, gold, and silver—possess similar structural characteristics. Theoretically, they should be similarly amenable to the formation of a cartel. Instead, cooperation varies widely across the markets. There is a highly sophisticated cartel in the diamond market, an informal collaboration between the two largest producers in the gold market, a failed cartel in uranium, and no cooperation at all in the silver market. And so without denying the utility of external or structural explanations, I argue that they are not sufficient to describe the success or failure of cooperation. Something else is at work in the market.

Specifically, I focus on the internal organization of the competitors themselves. Some competitors, it appears, are simply better equipped to deal with the rigors of cooperation. They are able to threaten, punish, and commit themselves credibly at the international level. Internally, they possess certain characteristics that give them a cooperative edge. These characteristics—which I label and describe as the autonomy of the competitor, the shadow of the competitor, the pockets of the competitor, and the capacity to punish—are not necessarily desirable. They entail a degree of centralized power and organizational control that may be unacceptable to some competitors. But they may also be necessary if these competitors are to bind themselves to a cooperative agreement and resist the constant temptation to defect.

Thus, although structural factors may define the conditions under which cooperation is most likely to occur, they still do not go far enough in describing when cooperation will in fact emerge and what sorts of competitors will be best able to resolve the dilemma of cooperation. To understand cooperation more fully, we need to look not just at markets and systems but also at firms and states. If we are to explain what makes cooperation work, we need to examine what makes the competitors work.

EXPLAINING COOPERATION

Many of the most common and powerful theories of cooperation are grounded squarely in a structural, or systemic, approach. In

3

both economics and international relations, these structural theories treat cooperation as a phenomenon of the broader system in which it occurs. They take the system itself as the unit of analysis and the structure of this system as its ordering or defining characteristic. Structure in this sense refers to the overall distribution of resources within the system and the allocation of these resources among the individual units. Accordingly, structural theories of cooperation try to define the structural configurations of a system that are most likely to induce cooperation among its constituent parts.

Theories of Cartels

In the specific context of cartels, the structural approach has pushed analysts to treat cooperation among competing producers as a puzzle of market structure. Beginning with the premise that market structure determines market behavior, economists have examined the cartel problem from the outside in, looking to identify the precise structural characteristics that make markets particularly susceptible to cartelization.[3] Their central focus has been the environment in which the individual firm finds itself, and their central concern has been to specify how this external environment shapes the prospects for cooperation. To explain cartels, they have looked to the structure of oligopolistic markets.

Working in this vein, economists have identified five structural factors that appear most important in determining the formation of producer cartels: high concentration of production, high barriers to entry, a small fringe,[1] nonsubstitutability, and nondifferentiation.

---

[3] The structural approach to cartels has produced a rich and voluminous literature, most of which falls considerably beyond the scope of this book. Some of the most important works include Joe S. Bain, *Barriers to New Competition* (Cambridge: Harvard University Press, 1956); F. M. Scherer, *Industrial Market Structure and Economic Performance*, 2d ed. (Chicago: Rand-McNally, 1980); Roger Sherman, *Oligopoly: An Empirical Approach* (Lexington, Mass.: Lexington Books, 1972); and Almarin Phillips, *Market Structure, Organization, and Performance* (Cambridge: Harvard University Press, 1962). Two of the most important recent works are Jean Tirole, *The Theory of Industrial Organization* (Cambridge: MIT Press, 1990); and Richard Schmalensee and Robert D. Willig, eds., *Handbook of Industrial Organization* (Amsterdam: Elsevier, 1989).

[1] "Fringe" refers to the number of significant outside producers, that is, producers who are not large enough to be considered members of the cartel but who nevertheless contribute a not insignificant portion of the total market production.

Empirically and theoretically, these factors make sense. For instance, a high concentration of production implies that the "number problem" has been alleviated—that the fewer producers there are in a market, the easier it will be for them to come together in any joint endeavor. A small fringe reduces the possibility that outside producers will be able to impede cartelization by reducing their own prices on any significant scale. High barriers to entry lessen the likelihood that new entrants to the market will be able to disrupt the cartel by pushing prices down, and nonsubstitutability reduces the risk that consumers will find substitutes as prices rise. Finally, nondifferentiation means that the producers cannot engage in nonprice competition while still maintaining noncompetitively high prices.

Taken together, these structural factors go a long way in describing the conditions under which cartels are likely to emerge and be sustained. In particular, concentration of production remains a powerful and parsimonious predictor of cartels: the fewer the producers, the more likely they are to come together in some sort of price-fixing or market allocation scheme. The problem, though, is that the structural theories still do not explain the whole story of cartels. First, they simply do not correspond that well to the evolving empirical record of cartels. Cartels have formed in markets that bear few of the suggested structural criteria and have floundered in some of the supposedly ideal markets.[5] Second, and more important for my purposes, they do not describe the cooperative *process* and the behavior that facilitates it. Structural theories define the conditions that are conducive to a cooperative outcome, but they tell us little

[5] In the tin market, for example, a series of international agreements was signed but never proved capable of moderating the sharp cyclical downswings that plague the international market for tin. In an effort to tighten control, the Association of Tin Producing Countries was created in 1983, but even this only exacerbated the "tin crisis" of 1985, brought on in large part by financial mistakes made by the Tin Council itself. The International Natural Rubber Agreement (INRA) of 1979 fared only slightly better; after declining for three years following the agreement's signing, natural rubber prices finally began to settle in 1983, and the INRA limped on. In the coffee, cocoa, and sugar markets, nominal commodity agreements remain in effect, but all three are entirely dependent on cooperation and financial support from the Western consuming nations, and all three have broken down repeatedly as a result of internal conflict. For a thorough study of these markets, see Jock A. Finlayson and Mark W. Zacher, *Managing International Markets: Developing Countries and the Commodity Trade Regime* (New York: Columbia University Press, 1988). For other studies of cartel failure, see L. N. Rangarajan, *Commodity Conflict: The Political Economy of International*

about the means by which this outcome is achieved. They rightly inform us that unitary producers will be most successful in forming cartels but say nothing about how any given producer is able to act as a unitary actor. Thus although these theories may be perfectly adequate for an economist interested in linking inputs to outcomes, they are less satisfying when one is trying to understand the process by which a cartel is formed and sustained.[6]

Theories of Cooperation

Meanwhile, though, the structural approach remains a powerful force in the political science literature on cooperation. The two dominant explanations of international cooperation—the realist and institutionalist models—both borrow to some degree the basic assumptions of the structural economists. In particular, they both assert that the emergence of cooperation depends largely on the structure of the international system and the distribution of power within it. Cooperation is the result not just of compatible political ideologies or the preferences of the states themselves but also of the structure by which these states are arranged.[7]

Commodity Negotiations (Ithaca: Cornell University Press, 1978); Jere R. Behrman, International Commodity Agreements: An Evaluation of the UNCTAD [United Nations Conference on Trade and Development] Integrated Commodity Programme, Overseas Development Council, NIEO (New International Economic Order) Series, Monograph No. 9, October 1977; and Paul Leo Eckbo, The Future of World Oil (Cambridge, Mass.: Ballinger, 1976).

[6] Even the structural theorists themselves have recently begun to question the sufficiency of structural explanations. F. M. Scherer, for instance, wrote: "It is clear that under conditions favorable to the exercise of monopoly power, prices may be held substantially above competitive levels for extended periods of time. Still this result does not follow automatically from the mere existence of a concentrated market structure" (Industrial Market Structure, p. 266, emphasis added). Likewise, Arthur G. Fraas and Douglas F. Greer concluded that "to a large degree, none of these [structural] factors taken singly appears to be a sufficient condition nor, with the possible exception of the numbers of participants, even a necessary condition for effective collusion; instead, the emergence of an effective coalition seems to depend on some broad combination of these conditions." Fraas and Greer, "Market Structure and Price Collusion: An Empirical Analysis," Journal of Industrial Economics 26 (September 1977): 21. On this point, see also Richard Schmalensee, "Inter-Industry Studies of Structure and Performance," in Schmalensee and Willig, eds., Handbook of Industrial Organization.

[7] Kenneth N. Waltz, for instance, finds that cooperation is most likely under conditions of bipolarity; Stephen M. Walt argues that alliances are more likely to form

The realist explanation focuses almost exclusively on the structure of the international system and the role played by the hegemon, or most powerful state. Realists describe a world defined by anarchy and characterized by a constant struggle among states. In this world, cooperation can emerge only when there is one state with sufficient power to create and enforce it. If a cooperative international system serves the interests of the hegemon, then the hegemon will bear whatever costs are necessary, including the costs of coercion, to perpetuate cooperation. Thus, hegemony as Robert Keohane and Joseph Nye define it creates a situation in which "one state is powerful enough to maintain the essential rules governing interstate relations, and willing to do so."[8]

Inherently, realism is based on two key *structural* assumptions. The first is that the hegemon itself can emerge only when the international system is configured so that one state wields a preponderant amount of power. The second assumption is that cooperation is due not to the benevolence or coercion of the hegemon but rather to the fact that its power resolves the "problem of collective action,"[9] that is, just as the leader of a cartel can induce cooperation by establishing and abiding by prices and quotas, so too can a hegemon break the entropic tendencies of a group of states by providing them with public goods and thus with a disincentive to defect.[10] Hegemonic stability, therefore, provides a simple and parsimonious explanation for cooperation between competing states. States will cooperate whenever a dominant power in the system sees a stable world order as

---

under certain structural conditions. See Waltz, *Theory of International Politics* (New York: Random House, 1979); and Walt, *The Origins of Alliances* (Ithaca: Cornell University Press, 1987).

[8] Robert O. Keohane and Joseph S. Nye, *Power and Interdependence: World Politics in Transition* (Boston: Little, Brown, 1977), p. 44.

[9] The problem of collective action is discussed at length in Mancur Olson, *The Logic of Collective Action* (Cambridge: Harvard University Press, 1971). Although Charles Kindleberger did not present his original argument in these terms, he later addressed the connection between his concept of leadership and the notion of public goods. See Kindleberger, "International Public Goods without International Leadership," *American Economic Review* 76 (March 1986): 1–13.

[10] In its most extreme form, the theory predicts that cooperation is impossible without a hegemon. See Robert Gilpin, *U.S. Power and the Multinational Corporation* (New York: Basic Books, 1975), p. 85; and Keohane, *After Hegemony*, p. 34.

serving its own interests and has the power to command, or coerce, weaker members of the system.

By contrast, institutional explanations of cooperation emphasize the underlying interdependence between competitors and the demand for institutions that emerges as a result. Drawing in particular on the insights generated by the Prisoners' Dilemma (PD) game, institutional theorists assert that the major obstacle to cooperation is the threat of defection. The key to cooperation thus rests with the ability to prevent defection by ensuring iteration and inducing credible commitments.[11] If states know that the game will be repeated, they will value the future more highly and be more willing to commit themselves to cooperation. Likewise, if states know that defection will be punished, they will be less tempted by it. Cooperation will be facilitated, therefore, under three conditions: when future interactions are guaranteed, when defectors are regularly punished, and when states can commit themselves to cooperate. The way to encourage cooperation is through a system of regularized interaction and formal rules, that is, through an institution.[12]

Both the realist and the institutional models provide powerful explanations of international cooperation and of the forces that sustain it. Taken together, the two approaches can be used to describe a wide range of cooperative behavior. Both models also fall short, however, in two respects. They fail to explain the full variety of cooperation that we actually see in the real world, and they fail to describe the *process* by which cooperative arrangements are created, maintained, and occasionally dissolved. Like structural theories of cartels, the dominant theories of cooperation do a perfectly adequate job of specifying the systemic conditions under which cooperation is most likely to prevail, but that is where they stop. They cannot explain why these conducive factors—the existence of a hegemon or a rich institutional environment—sometimes will lead to a cooperative outcome and sometimes will not. They cannot explain why

[11] On the use of PD in institutional theory, see Robert Axelrod, *The Evolution of Cooperation* (New York: Basic Books, 1984), p. 7; Keohane, *After Hegemony*, pp. 66–69; and Arthur A. Stein, "Coordination and Collaboration: Regimes in an Anarchic World," in Stephen D. Krasner, ed., *International Regimes* (Ithaca: Cornell University Press, 1983), pp. 120–24.

[12] As Keohane writes, "When we think about cooperation after hegemony, we need to think about institutions" (*After Hegemony*, p. 246).

some cooperative arrangements work better than others. And they cannot describe the actual process by which competitors become cooperative.

Theories of hegemonic stability, for example, simply do not offer a complete and persuasive explanation of the empirical record. Although some instances of international cooperation can be attributed to the presence of a hegemon, in many other instances no hegemon existed. Likewise, there seems to be no guarantee that the mere emergence of a hegemon can ensure cooperation in the international system and no evidence that the stability created by the hegemon benefits all states in the system.[13] As a host of neoliberal thinkers have therefore argued, cooperation cannot be solely a product of hegemonic stability. It must be the product of other, heretofore unidentified, forces.[14]

Moreover, by concentrating on the behavior of the hegemon, the theory of hegemonic stability gives us no way to understand how the other competitors respond and never explains *why* and in what manner they decide to cooperate. This omission is critical. By overlooking the internal motivations that drive the other states to cooperate rather than to act as free riders, the theory forecloses any form of international cooperation other than the broad systemic cooperation engendered by the hegemon. Thus it ignores the theoretical and empirical proof that conflict between individual and collective action does not always ensure the failure of nonhegemonic cooperation and that, in fact, collective action among the atomistic members of a group is always possible.[15]

Finally, the theory of hegemonic stability offers no convincing explanation of the process by which international cooperation actually occurs and thus no causal link between hegemony and cooperation. Bluntly, the theory never tells us what hegemonic leaders *do* when they are being hegemonic.[16] For instance, the theory tends to blur

---

[13] Duncan Snidal, "The Limits of Hegemonic Stability Theory," *International Organization* 39 (Autumn 1985): 582.

[14] See, for instance, Keohane, *After Hegemony*, pp. 31–32.

[15] See Snidal, "Limits of Hegemonic Stability," p. 598. See also Olson, *The Logic of Collective Action*; and Russell Hardin, *Collective Action* (Baltimore: Johns Hopkins University Press for Resources for the Future, 1982).

[16] See Scott C. James and David A. Lake, "The Second Face of Hegemony: Britain's Repeal of the Corn Laws and the American Walker Tariff of 1846," *International Organization* 43 (Winter 1989): 1–29. The authors go on, however, to argue in favor of a modified form of hegemonic stability theory.

9

the distinction between benevolent and coercive hegemons, even though the two versions would logically require wholly different enforcement measures. It assumes that the hegemon's power is fungible across issue areas and that the maintenance of cooperation is a problem perpetually amenable to power politics. It does not demonstrate what, other than force, compels states to cooperate and how the allocation of costs and benefits is figured. It does not explain how these processes may change over time and how states readjust their positions within the international hierarchy. In short, the hegemonic theory of cooperation tells us little about the process of cooperation or the changing motives that compel and constrain it.

Nor do institutional theories fully explain the process of cooperation. Even when interdependence is marked, payoffs to cooperation are high, and formal arrangements have been contemplated, cooperation does not necessarily result. And when cooperation does emerge, it proves to be far more ephemeral in some instances than in others. At the level of particulars, moreover, some of the institutionalists' claims do not quite fit the empirical record. Although institutional theories stress the importance of commitment, they do not explain why some competitors are able to make commitments more credibly than others. Likewise, while emphasizing the importance of punishment as a disincentive to defection, they do not explore why some competitors can punish their rivals—or at least threaten to punish them—more effectively than can others.

Overall, then, although realism and institutionalism both tell us something about the external conditions under which states or firms are most likely to cooperate, they tell us little about *how* states or firms are able to take advantage of these conditions or about *which* states or firms will be able to do so.

By contrast, the picture of cooperation that I paint here stands somewhere between the two models and combines elements of each. It suggests that cooperation can be maintained by a combination of force and commitment. That is, even when institutions exist and the benefits of reciprocity and mutual gains are evident, the success of an agreement may nevertheless depend on the coercive capacities of its individual members—on their ability to punish, to threaten, to retaliate. What emerges from my case studies, therefore, is not a situation in which institutions persist in the wake of hegemony but rather one in which hegemonic tactics cement cooperation within an institutional setting. In that context, I describe a hybrid of cooperative behavior that falls between the explanations provided by the realist and institutional models and that is suggested by the record of cooperation in commodity cartels.

I also assert that the explanatory gap left by the realist and institutional models can best be filled by a consideration of internal as well as structural or systemic factors. Both the realist and the institutional explanations define the prospects for cooperation primarily in structural terms and are concerned mainly with explaining cooperative *outcomes*. I look, by contrast, for evidence of cooperative *behavior* and paint a picture of cooperation that is intimately connected to the internal characteristics of the competitors involved. Specifically, I argue that particular types of competitors are better equipped to create and maintain cooperation than are others. This is not to suggest that the nature of the competitors is the sole or even the most important determinant of cooperation. Rather, it is to argue that internal characteristics help bridge the gap that separates the conditions *conducive* to cooperation from the actual *formation* of a successful cooperative agreement.

LOOKING WITHIN: DEFINING AN APPROACH

Organization matters.[17] Whether one looks at firms or states or universities, it is clear that the way an institution is organized affects the way it acts. Japanese firms, with their penchant for flat pyramids and lifetime employment, are said to be able to take a longer-term perspective than their American counterparts. Parliamentary democracies behave differently from presidential ones. And institutions run by personal fiat tend to react faster and more decisively than those run by committee. At all levels, the organizational structure and culture of an institution will affect what it can do in the outside world and how successful it is likely to be. Perhaps that is

---

[17] Apparently this is still a contentious claim. Recently, Joseph E. Stiglitz noted that "somewhat surprisingly, most economists have traditionally relegated the study of organizations to business schools, or worse still, to sociologists." See Stiglitz, "Symposium on Organizations and Economics," *Journal of Economic Perspectives* 5 (Spring 1991): 15.

why external difficulties are often met by efforts to "restructure" or "reorganize."

Organization matters particularly, it seems, in the kinds of competitive situations that concern us here. When the competitors are small in number and large in size, then the internal organization of each one becomes especially relevant. If one of Smith's grocers was organized in an inefficient or noncompetitive way, then he would simply be driven out of the market, and no one would really notice or be affected. By contrast, an organizational change in one of the Seven Sisters oil companies, for example, or one of the Big Three American car manufacturers can have a dramatic impact not just on the firm directly involved but also on the other firms with which it is involved in a long-term relationship. Markets may affect the internal organization of the firm, but a firm's internal organization also affects the market. A similar logic applies to the state system. Domestic changes—especially in the more powerful states—can have dramatic global consequences.

When we look at cooperation in the international arena, therefore, we should look not at models of perfect competition, free markets, and rational actors but rather at models of oligopolies, cartels, and complex organizations. Thus, once again we are looking not just at the external structures of competition but also at the internal characteristics of the competitors. The difficulty is to figure out how internal organization and characteristics matter. What types of internal structures lead to particular external results? How can one separate the organization of an institution from the institution itself?[18]

Questions like these have tended to make scholars wary of an internally focused approach. Because treatment of internal structures often becomes mired in idiosyncratic characteristics and "thick description," it is difficult to engage these internal structures in a rigorous, parsimonious way. Still, there are ways we can break down the overarching concept of internal organization into relatively discrete variables and analyze them rigorously.[19] Drawing on some con-

---

[18] A similar set of questions plagues efforts to develop an institutional alternative to the existing behavioral theories of politics. See, for example, James G. March and Johan P. Olsen, "The New Institutionalism: Organizational Factors in Political Life," *American Political Science Review* 78 (September 1984): 734–49.

[19] Indeed, some of the most interesting recent work in the field of comparative politics tries to do just this. See, for instance, Peter Hall, *Governing the Economy: The*

cepts that have emerged from industrial organization[20] and management theory, for instance, we can begin to identify and examine internal characteristics without abandoning entirely the goal of parsimony.

I begin here with the notion of internal hierarchies and with the assumption that any large-scale institution—be it a state or a firm—needs to be approached not as a black box of preferences and behavior but rather as a composite of diverse units and divided responsibilities.[21] In practice, after all, neither states nor firms are monolithic. States contain interest groups, legislative bodies, bureaucracies, and a host of other institutions and values. Producers in a cartel are

---

Politics of State Intervention in Britain and France (New York: Oxford University Press, 1986); and Stephan Haggard, *Pathways from the Periphery: The Politics of Growth in the Newly Industrializing Countries* (Ithaca: Cornell University Press, 1990).

[20] The terminology here gets extremely confusing. What I refer to as "industrial organization" has also been labeled the "new institutionalism" or the "economics of institutions" or the "economics of organizations." Since all these terms refer to related bodies of literature, I am treating them together and calling them collectively industrial organization. For a radical review of this literature, see William M. Dugger, *Underground Economics: A Decade of Institutionalist Dissent* (Armonk, N.Y.: M. E. Sharpe, 1992). For a more mainstream account, see Richard E. Caves, "Industrial Organization, Corporate Strategy, and Structure," *Journal of Economic Literature* 18 (March 1980): 64–92. The leading theorist in this literature is probably Oliver E. Williamson, who in turn draws on the earlier work of R. H. Coase. See Williamson, *Corporate Control and Business Behavior* (Englewood Cliffs, N.J.: Prentice Hall, 1970), *Markets and Hierarchies* (New York: Free Press, 1975), and *The Economic Institutions of Capitalism* (New York: Free Press, 1985); and Coase, "The Nature of the Firm," in Coase, *The Firm, the Market, and the Law* (Chicago: University of Chicago Press, 1988), pp. 33–55.

[21] Alfred D. Chandler, Jr., provides one of the most persuasive explorations of internal structure. Writing as a business historian, he argues that as the corporation replaced the family firm in the United States, so too did the "visible hand of management" replace Adam Smith's invisible hand of market forces. Whereas the activities of the family firm had been largely dictated by the simple need to react to market and price mechanisms, the modern corporation, with its numerous operating units and hierarchies of managers, has its activities "monitored and coordinated by salaried employees rather than market mechanisms." In other words, the internal structure of hierarchy of the firm is crucial in determining its market behavior. See Chandler, *The Visible Hand: The Managerial Revolution in American Business* (Cambridge: Belknap Press of Harvard University Press, 1977), esp. pp. 1–14. Along similar lines, numerous other scholars have tried to identify how specific organizational structures affect a firm's behavior in the market. See, for instance, Joseph L. Bower, "Managing the Resource Allocation Process: A Study of Corporate Planning and Investment" (Boston: Division of Research, Graduate School of Business Administration, Harvard University, 1970); and Richard P. Rumelt, "Strategy, Structure, and Economic Performance" (Boston: Division of Research, Graduate School of Business Administration, Harvard University, 1974).

likely to be composed of various managers, labor interests, and stockholder considerations—or as Joseph Stiglitz describes it, "managers managing managers managing managers . . . managing workers."[22] All these layers, though, are not created equal. On the contrary, virtually all institutions are structured hierarchically.[23] Responsibilities are allocated among various levels of the hierarchy, and authority is divided among separate, often competing, units. In such complex systems, control becomes more elusive. The leaders need to define themselves against the rest of the hierarchy and create mechanisms that ensure their authority over its constituent parts. The ability of the leadership to wrest and retain control thus becomes a key factor in shaping the institution's direction and performance. As Oliver Williamson explains, "If the effectiveness with which the internal compliance machinery can be exercised varies systematically with organization form . . . changes in organization form can on this account alone be expected to have significant performance consequences."[24] Thus, understanding the behavior of both firms and states becomes largely a matter of understanding their internal structures and, in particular, how these structures affect the ability of their leaders to get reliable information, communicate objectives, and implement decisions. The distribution of authority within a firm or a state can therefore be treated as a key variable for determining its external behavior.

Against this backdrop, the remainder of this chapter examines how the internal organization of competitors can affect their capacity for external cooperation. Specifically, I describe four internal characteristics that help to explain the emergence of cooperation in my cartel cases and that can potentially be generalized to other instances of cooperation among competitors. I refer to these characteristics as the autonomy of the competitor, the shadow of the competitor, the pockets of the competitor, and the capacity to punish. None of these characteristics can, by itself, determine whether coop-

---

[22] Stiglitz, "Symposium on Organizations and Economics," p. 20.

[23] Arguments on the universality of hierarchical structures appear most elegantly in the work of Herbert Simon. See especially Simon, "The Architecture of Complexity," *Proceedings of the American Philosophical Society* 106 (December 1962): 467–82, and "Organizations and Markets," *Journal of Economic Perspectives* 5 (Spring 1991): 25–44.

[24] Williamson, *Corporate Control and Business Behavior*, p. 173.

eration will emerge. Taken together, however, they begin to paint a picture of the *kinds* of internal structures that facilitate cooperation and thus of the *kinds* of competitors that are most likely to create and maintain cooperative ventures.

The Autonomy of the Competitor

Reduced to its core, the problem of cooperation is really a problem of commitment and credibility. If we presume that cooperation is indeed possible under competition, then we must also recognize that it rests on a delicate balance of perception, promises, and threats. If cooperation is ever to emerge, each competitor must convince the other that it is serious, that it will match cooperation with cooperation and defection with defection. How, though, can one demonstrate this resolve? How, when the risks of unrequited cooperation are high, can one adversary ever convince another that it is willing and able to temper competition with collaboration?

One set of possible solutions focuses on the strategic context of the cooperative game and on the structure of the payoffs. In this context, it is presumably possible to make commitment more credible by making cooperation more desirable or defection more painful. Thus, most analyses of commitment have started with Thomas Schelling's observation that credibility can be enhanced by raising the costs of defection, either by tying one's own hands or by relying on third-party enforcers.[25] The problem, though, is that changing the payoff structure is not by itself sufficient to ensure that commitments will be credible, simply because it still cannot guarantee that any of the parties will be able to deliver its commitments. Modifications made in the structure of the situation or the environment of the game can, at best, make the parties more willing to commit. Nothing that is done externally, however, can affect the actual ability of the competitors to deliver their commitments. Rather, this ability is dependent on the internal capabilities of the competitors themselves. If a competitor can demonstrate an ability to fulfill its promises and imple-

[25] See Thomas C. Schelling, *The Strategy of Conflict* (Cambridge: Harvard University Press, 1980), pp. 24–25. See also B. Curtis Eaton and Richard G. Lipsey, "Capital, Commitment, and Entry Equilibrium," *Bell Journal of Economics* 12 (Autumn 1981): 593–604.

ment its threats, then its commitments will be credible. If, however, it proves unable to follow through, then its commitments become worthless, and changes in the external structure of the game will be relatively ineffective in promoting cooperation. Or as Helen Milner has put it, "Lack of credibility in one's threats and promises is a problem *within* states; governments, political parties, and business firms all worry about their own capacity and that of others to live up to their stated commitments."[26]

At a certain point, therefore, the problem of credible commitments becomes as simple to explain in theory as it is difficult to attain in practice. Basically, it is a problem of internal autonomy and a question of whether or not a competitor can actually implement all that it has promised to do. In most analyses of cooperation, however, this central factor is rendered irrelevant by the assumption of unitary and rational behavior that political science has borrowed from neoclassical economics. I argue, however, that to understand commitment and credibility, we must discard the assumption that either states or firms can be treated as nondifferentiated units. On the contrary, if we presume that cooperation under anarchy depends on the ability to make commitments, then we must go to the level of the unit, as this ability cannot come from anything in the external system or structure of the situation. It can be determined only within the state or the producer and thus will vary across states and producers.

In this context, the first and most central observation of this book is that the ability of producers (and by analogy, states) to participate in cooperative arrangements will vary in accordance with the autonomy of the producer or state itself. Specifically, commitments will be credible only if the producer or the state can demonstrate an ability to deliver its promises. This ability, in turn, is determined in large part by the internal structures of control and coordination that shape its ability to discipline its internal factions so as to implement its external plans. When all subunits and individuals are tightly organized and centrally controlled, the people who actually represent the producer or the state at the international level will likely have little

[26] Helen Milner, "International Theories of Cooperation among Nations: Strengths and Weaknesses," *World Politics* 44 (April 1992): 481. See also Robert D. Putnam, "Diplomacy and Domestic Politics," *International Organization* 42 (Summer 1988): 427–60.

difficulty in maintaining the internal discipline needed to deliver on international commitments. Under these conditions, commitment becomes credible, and cooperation can ensue.

Commitment also appears to be facilitated in those cases where there simply are no significant internal groups and thus where the representative of the producer or the state—the "principal participant" in my terms—is truly able to behave as an autonomous competitor. If there is no dissent or at least no means by which dissent can be made effective, then the principal participant can make promises or issue threats knowing that it has the power to deliver them. By contrast, if there are independent groups and if they have different preferences with regard to the cooperative outcome, then assuring internal unity becomes a more difficult task. Any cooperation that the producer or the state wishes to undertake, therefore, becomes a bargaining game on two levels: not only does the principal participant need to act strategically at the international level, but it must also engage in a delicate balancing act at home. In pursuit of their own interests or goals, internal factions may try to block the cooperative solution or mold it to fit their own needs. They may veto it outright, disregard it, or simply refuse to implement the provisions that affect them. In the process, external promises are whittled away, and threats become inoperable. If this process is repeated over time, the ability of the state or producer to make credible commitments will be significantly weakened.

Autonomy is thus almost indispensable to effective cooperation. By "autonomy" I mean the ability of the principal participant within an organization to impose its chosen policy on the other relevant internal factions, to implement this policy internally, and to withstand opposition. Autonomy refers to the capacity of the principal participant to keep its internal factions in line, regardless of whether this control occurs through force, persuasion, or the use of side payments. It is, therefore, quite similar to Max Weber's proposition that large-scale organizations can behave coherently as long as they either centralize authority or carefully build a controlling hierarchy.

The autonomy of the competitor affects the cooperative process primarily insofar as it affects its ability to make credible commitments and issue credible threats. In any situation of cooperation among competitors, the cooperative settlement will persist only so long as all members can be persuaded not to defect and only so long as they believe that their partners have been likewise persuaded. One means of persuasion, of course, is coercion, and indeed the hegemonic model of cooperation is built on the notion that one of the group's members will have sufficient power simply to compel the others to remain within the confines of the cooperative settlement. Another means of persuasion, however, and the means described in the institutional model, is through the establishment of institutions that regularize the conduct of their members, make it more predictable, and offer a measure of security by creating the mechanisms for enforcement.

Both models thus present a convincing picture of the means by which members commit themselves to a cooperative agreement and the ways in which their commitments are facilitated at the international level. Missing from both models, though, is an analysis of how subsystemic factors affect a competitor's ability to make credible and binding commitments. A commitment at the international level, after all, is worthwhile only if it can be implemented internally. Likewise, commitments are believable only if a competitor has demonstrated over time its ability to fulfill them.

In the chapters that follow, the relationship between autonomy and commitment emerges quite clearly. The cases immediately reveal that not all markets are populated by the ideal producer described in cartel theory and not all cartels function as neatly as the theory would describe. In the first place, where international cartels are concerned, the "producers" are customarily states. This does not mean that the states are actually in the business of production but simply that they are generally involved in the international negotiations. Thus the state is the point of reference within the cartel—we speak, for instance, of the member *states* of the Organization of Petroleum Exporting Countries (OPEC). Therefore, when we describe international cartels, the state usually becomes synonymous with the producer, although in practical terms, it is only rarely the physical producer of the goods in question. Rather, the state serves as a convenient clearinghouse for all groups involved in production and connected in some way to the cartel. Often, the state also serves as the principal participant in the cartel. That is, it acts as the representative of all the other domestic groups, as the encourager or enforcer of domestic participation, and as the party responsible for actually ensuring compliance at the international level. In some cases, the task of the principal participant is easy; all the individual firms or agencies will share a common interest in the goals of an international cartel[27] and a common willingness to allow the principal participant—usually in the form of a state agency or official—to represent their interest at the international level. A similar unitary outcome is likely to occur if production in the state is controlled by a single governmental agency or a single monopolistic firm.

When a clear-cut route to consensus is lacking, however, the formation of a cartel becomes a good deal more complex. In such cases, the task of the principal participant is not only to represent the state at the international level but also to devise some means by which a domestic consensus can be forged and opposition suppressed. As long as each of the internal groups retains a unique payoff structure, a particular attitude toward international collaboration, and an ability to back its opinions with action, it will be very difficult for the state to act as an autonomous "producer" and thus very unlikely that the principal participant will ever be able to deliver the state at the international level.

Before we proceed any farther, a point of clarification is probably in order. Sometimes the members of the cartels that I examine are firms and sometimes they are states; sometimes the internal characteristics that I describe adhere mainly to the firm and, at other times, to the state. This shift of focus, however, does not in any way affect the core of the argument. At the international level, cooperation in commodity cartels includes *both* firms and states. Sometimes the cooperation (or proposed cooperation) will be among states, sometimes among firms, and at times among a combination of states and firms. In each instance both entities are involved—the state insofar as it regulates corporate behavior and sets the tone for international intercourse and the firm insofar as it controls the means and modes of production. Even when the firm and the state are one, both the governmental and the corporate aspects are involved. The focus of my

---

[27] In game theoretic terms, all the separate units have similar preference orderings.

analysis, then, is on firms *and* states and on the relationship between them and all their subordinate components.

What is truly critical in the formation of cartels is the *internal organization* of each competitor. It makes no difference whether the principal participant in the cartel is a corporate leader, a bureaucratic agency, or a top political figure. What matters, I argue, is the *position* that the principal participant holds within the overall internal framework—whether it can speak for all affected interests, whether it has the capacity to implement what it promises, and whether it can maintain discipline within its own ranks. If the principal participant at the domestic level has the authority to bring all internal factions in line—be they firms, state agencies, or concerned bureaucracies—then it will be able to make international commitments with confidence and credibility. If, on the other hand, the principal participant has little or no control over these crucial internal factions, then it faces the constant possibility that its international commitments will be modified, vetoed, or opposed from within its own ranks. The emergence of cooperation, therefore, rests to a large degree on the internal autonomy of the competitors involved and especially with their ability to maintain discipline within their own factions.

The Shadow of the Competitor

My second proposition relates to the well-rehearsed notions of iteration, time horizons, and the "shadow of the future." Here again, the evidence from the cartel cases supports the relevance of these concepts but adds a slight twist to the accepted wisdom.

Generally, it is suggested that when the shadow of the future is long, cooperation will be relatively more valuable to the competitors involved and thus easier to establish. If the competitors think they are playing a one-time game, they will be more tempted to grab all gains in the short run, confident that the long-term benefits of cooperation are negligible and that no future opportunities will arise for the other players to wreak revenge. If, on the other hand, the future casts a long shadow and the competitors know that their game will be repeated, defection in any one instance becomes less profitable, as the one-time rewards it may bring must be weighed against the costs incurred by making cooperation considerably less likely in all future meetings.[28] Thus, it is generally acknowledged that the prospects for cooperation will be increased whenever the competitors know that they are likely to be involved with each other for a long and potentially infinite period of time.[29] As Robert Axelrod argues, "What makes the emergence of cooperation possible is the possibility that interaction will continue."[30]

The logic behind this concept is undeniably sound. What it neglects to consider, however, and what emerges clearly in this book is that the shadow of the future may be less important than an individual decision maker's perception of it. Seen from a structural perspective, the shadow adheres to the overall situation of the competitors; from an internal approach, however, the relevant shadow is attached to the principal participant from each side. If the principal participant identifies completely with the organization it represents, then its shadow will indeed be determined by the overall prospects for future interaction. If, however, the principal participant has a different future, for instance, if its party is about to be turned out of office or its firm about to become the subject of a hostile takeover, then its discount rate may differ from that of a "rational" actor. Because it will not be around to reap the full benefits of cooperation, it will more likely want to maximize returns in the short run and avoid paying any of the costs of cooperation. In such cases, the principal participant may not be willing to be patient, and thus the state or producer that it represents may not be able to gain the benefits of long-term cooperation.

The key point is that decision makers' behavior will be conditioned by their *personal* time horizons and particularly by their perceptions of their own likely tenures in office. The essential discount rate is not necessarily that of the "rational" actor but rather the one that is calculated by the individual decision maker who actually serves as the principal participant in an international agreement. As John

---

[28] See, for instance, Oye, "Cooperation under Anarchy," pp. 12–18.

[29] For a discussion of the necessity of infinite repetitions in order to ensure cooperative behavior, see Robert Telsor, "A Theory of Self-enforcing Agreements," *Journal of Business* 53 (January 1980): 27–44; and R. Duncan Luce and Howard Raiffa, *Games and Decisions* (New York: Wiley, 1957), pp. 94–102.

[30] Robert Axelrod, "The Emergence of Cooperation among Egoists," *American Political Science Review* 75 (June 1981): 307.

Tilton notes, "Public officials may be more concerned about the short run than the long run because their job security may depend on visible signs of progress within a period of several years."[31] In this case, the officials will tend to discount the value of future gains in favor of more immediate rewards. From their perspective, the shadow of the future is short, if not irrelevant.[32]

All cooperative arrangements entail initial costs. If cooperation under anarchy is to occur, all competitors must be willing to accept these costs as being just payment for the long-term rewards of certainty, stability, and—in the case of cartels at least —higher profits. If the principal participant knows that she will receive the eventual benefits, she will often be willing to shoulder the costs. If, on the other hand, she fears that she will not be around to reap the benefits or collect the fame, she is not going to be nearly as eager to pay the costs, especially if she thinks that the very process of paying them may further undermine her domestic position and shorten her tenure. As Norman Frohlich, Joe Oppenheimer, and Oran Young observe, "A leader contemplating a program involving the supply of a collective good with a high initial cost who does not have a secure hold of his office on a long-term basis will consider such a venture very risky indeed."[33] Rather than pay any costs or take any risks, this leader—or principal participant, in my terms—is instead likely to defect for as long as she can, seizing whatever unilateral benefits are to be had and destroying any possibility of cooperation. In addition, once a principal participant is perceived as being short-lived, then its counterparts are also likely to begin to discount the value of protracted cooperation.[34] The game may still be structured under a long shadow, but to the principal participants, worried about their own reflections, it is only an ephemeral image.

[31] John E. Tilton, *The Future of Nonfuel Minerals* (Washington, D.C.: Brookings Institution, 1977), p. 87. For more on the effects of officials with short time horizons, see Raymond Vernon and Debora L. Spar, *Beyond Globalism: Remaking American Foreign Economic Policy* (New York: Free Press, 1989), pp. 22–24.

[32] Thus, as L. N. Rangarajan argues, the will of an actor to join cooperative agreements is not a fixed and invariant calculation; rather, it is directly related to the "ability to hold on." See Rangarajan, *Commodity Conflict*, p. 269.

[33] Norman Frohlich, Joe A. Oppenheimer, and Oran R. Young, *Political Leadership and Collective Goods* (Princeton: Princeton University Press, 1971), pp. 55–56.

[34] See Axelrod, "Emergence of Cooperation," p. 312.

The Pockets of the Competitor

In any cooperative agreement between competitors, restraint is important. The competitors must be able to resist the temptation to defect and forsake the easy gains of unilateral action even when times are bad. Maintaining cartels when supply is tight and prices are high is relatively easy; the real tests of cooperation come later, when the common rewards are more distant and the immediate costs of cooperation more apparent.[35]

In practical terms, restraint encompasses the firm that stockpiles its surplus and refrains from undercutting the competition, the union that accepts longer working weeks, and the nation that buys its allies' tanks instead of building its own. In all these cases, the competitor forswears short-term benefits in favor of the greater but less certain rewards of long-term cooperation. In most of these cases, the competitor's restraint imposes significant costs.

For a cooperative endeavor to succeed, therefore, competitors must be both willing and able to absorb the costs of restraint. Their pockets must be deep enough to permit them to absorb the losses and ride out the inevitable slumps. Once again, then, we see that the success of the overall arrangement depends to a great extent on the internal characteristics of the competitors themselves. Often an agreement will disintegrate not because the external situation has changed or because the competitors no longer recognize the benefits of cooperation, but simply because one or more of the competitors is unable to absorb the costs of participation.[36] Likewise, the pockets of

---

[35] For a theoretical model that suggests that oligopolists will revert to noncooperative behavior when demand is depressed, see E. Green and R. Porter, "Noncooperative Collusion under Imperfect Price Information," *Econometrica* 52 (January 1984): 87–100. More broadly, Valerie Suslow finds evidence that economic downturns tend to increase the risk of cartel breakdowns. See Suslow, "Cartel Contract Duration: Empirical Evidence from International Cartels," April 1991, forthcoming in *The RAND Journal of Economics*.

[36] As William Fellner notes, "The ability of the different parties to take losses obviously is one of the determinants of the struggle. This ability depends on wealth in general and on liquid wealth in particular; and it may depend importantly on the internal organization of the firm, that is, on the distribution of power within firms." See Fellner, *Competition among the Few* (New York: Alfred A. Knopf, 1949), p. 27. Similarly, Oliver E. Williamson notes that "adherence to a joint profit maximization agreement may be made difficult during times of adversity by current pressing de-

a competitor also appear to be very closely related to both its autonomy and its shadow. If the principal participant knows that its power or position make it immune to internal discontent, it can simply force its factions to accept whatever costs may be necessary. By the same token, if it knows its personal position is secure, it will be less sensitive to any pressures that might arise when the costs of cooperation fall unevenly on various internal groups.

The Capacity to Punish

Credibility is a central element of commitment and thus of cooperation. Credibility is also important to the flip side of commitment, that is, to threats and to punishment. Since cooperation is based, after all, on an underlying and ever present conflict between competitors, defection remains a constant possibility. Because the risks of unrequited cooperation are high, all competitors will be tempted from time to time to preempt the others' defection by defecting first. Even worse, each is aware that the others are similarly attracted. To decrease the likelihood of defection, both sides must be manipulated. The competitors must acknowledge not just the advantages of cooperation but the disadvantages of defection as well.

The most obvious way to raise the cost of defection, of course, is to threaten retaliation. Threats, as the game theorists make eminently clear, are the best means to signal both one's commitment and one's resolve.[37] To be credible, though, threats must be enunciated by a competitor with the demonstrated ability to carry through with the threat if need be.

Once again, then, the key factors that determine credibility appear to be vested not in the nature of the system or the structure of the game but in the competitors themselves. To threaten effectively, a competitor must also have the demonstrated ability to punish and to bear the costs of punishment.[38] In a cartel setting, punishment usu-

---

mands that cause short-run own-goals of one or more of the members to override collective considerations." Williamson, "Dynamic Theory of Interfirm Behavior," *Quarterly Journal of Economics* 79 (November 1965): 580.

[37] See, for instance, Schelling, *Strategy of Conflict*, pp. 35–43, 123–31.

[38] In addition, of course, the competitor must be able to detect the violation. For a classic discussion of how detection can be facilitated in an oligopolistic market, see

ally entails flooding the market and undercutting the defector, thereby rendering the defection useless. The problem is that this punishment is very costly; in the process of retaliation, the entire market is destabilized and prices plummet. In many instances, it would be easier and less costly if the violation went unpunished.[39]

Over the long term, however, even the smallest violation must be countered, or cheating will quickly become endemic. To preserve the sanctity of the cartel, therefore, someone within it must assume the responsibility and the costs of punishing defection. The institution can set rules and assign penalties, but ultimately it will fall to the competitors themselves to impose these penalties.[40] And the most likely candidates for this job are those competitors with sufficient resources to absorb the costs of punishment and sufficient autonomy to ensure that their retaliatory tactics are not blocked by any of their own internal factions.[41] Thus the same centralized control and immunity from internal discontent that allows them to deliver their commitments and absorb internal losses also enables them to threaten and to punish.[42] And once again, the picture of cooperation that

---

George J. Stigler, "A Theory of Oligopoly," *Journal of Political Economy* 72 (February 1964): 44–61.

[39] This is especially true if there are only a few competitors and a few possible new entrants. See Paul Milgrom and John Roberts, "Predation, Reputation, and Entry Deterrence," *Journal of Economic Theory* 27, 2 (1982): 280–312.

[40] For an elaborate treatment of the role played by leaders even within an institutional setting, see Oran R. Young, "Political Leadership and Regime Formation," *International Organization* 45 (Summer 1991): 281–308.

[41] For a related discussion of how domestic political consensus affects a state's ability to threaten countersanctions, see Lisa L. Martin, "Credibility, Costs, and Institutions: Cooperation on Economic Sanctions," *World Politics* 45 (April 1993): 406–32.

[42] Along similar lines, James D. Alt and his colleagues argue that Saudi Arabia was able to act as a hegemon among the oil-producing nations largely because its reserves gave it the capacity to bear the long-term costs of punishment and thus the ability to establish a credible reputation for toughness. See Alt, Randall L. Calvert, and Brian D. Humes, "Reputation and Hegemonic Stability: A Game-Theoretic Analysis," *American Political Science Review* 82 (June 1988): 445–66. The authors also demonstrate the means by which punishment, if applied strategically, can establish a reputation for the hegemon that serves to lower the overall costs of punishment or coercion. Likewise, the U.S. express cartel of the late nineteenth and early twentieth centuries was held together by the fact that several of its members had sufficient resources to punish severely all defectors and all possible new entrants. See Peter Z. Grossman, "The Dynamics of a Stable Cartel: The Express, 1851–1913," Paper presented at the Cliometric Sessions of the ASSA (Allied Social Science Associations) Meetings, January 3, 1992.

emerges from the cartel analogy is suspended somewhere between the hegemonic and the institutional explanations. It is cooperation that occurs within an institutional setting, yet it is very much dependent on the actions of at least one particularly strong competitor willing and able to bear the brunt of retaliation.[43]

Purposes and Preferences

One final point is in order. The central assumption of my internal approach is that different competitors will behave differently and that these differences can be explained in large part by how they are organized internally—the number of internal factions, the stability of these factions, and the relative power and resources that each possesses. As in most other models of cooperation and cartels, this approach still looks at structures and resources, but it focuses on the *internal* structures and resources of the relevant units rather than on those that define the overall system. Thus, although others have looked, for instance, at the power of a competitor vis-à-vis its rivals, the internal approach looks for the power, or autonomy, that a competitor can exert over its own *internal* factions.

At the same time, the internal approach also attempts to move away from a purely structural view of the cooperative process. I do not deny that structure is important. On the contrary, I start with the assumption that market structure is a critical precondition of cartels: quite simply, cartels will not form if there are too many producers or too many substitute goods. My argument, then, begins where the economists' structural observations leave off. The economists are interested primarily in explaining outcomes. They define cooperation in terms of economic effects such as prices and market share and seek to relate these effects to the structural variables outlined earlier. My intention, by contrast, is to focus on the process of cooperation and the behavior that facilitates it. I find cooperation

---

[43] This view of cooperation is well supported by Theodore H. Moran's description of the international oil industry. In OPEC, as well as in the prewar oil cartel, he finds that cartel leaders were willing to pay a high price in order to incorporate smaller members and were able to supply the public good of "deliberate cooption." See Moran, "Managing an Oligopoly of Would-Be Sovereigns," *International Organization* 41 (Autumn 1987): 605.

not in any specific market outcome but rather in the empirical evidence of ongoing collaboration between the producers.

Finally, the internal approach also assumes that although structures may be important, they do not determine either behavior or preferences. On the contrary, preferences exist independently of structure; and preferences and behavior are both liable to vary over time and among internal groups.

Whereas the neoclassical framework assumes goals from the outset[44]—firms will maximize profits, states will maximize power—I argue that goals are variable and must be examined empirically. Even in the same situation, different competitors may have different preferences: some, looking to the long term, may want cooperation at all costs; some, whose internal position is shakier, may favor the short-term benefits of cooperation. And some may reject an apparently optimal outcome if it would entail compromising an unrelated but deeply held belief.[45] There are competitors, as we shall see, that just don't like to cooperate. And the only way to discern these preferences and to distinguish them from apparent behavior is once again to look empirically at the internal characteristics that shape, define, and constrain each competitor.

Maintaining Cooperation: The Rules of the Game

Thus far, I have focused primarily on the conditions of cooperation, on the systemic and internal factors that must be in place before cooperation can occur. This analysis, though, still tells only part of the story. Cooperation is not a static or sudden phenomenon; it is instead a *process* that must not only be initiated but perpetuated as well. The pursuit of cooperation entails not just a single calculation

[44] In one of his earliest works, Williamson notes that within the neoclassical framework, all goals other than profit maximization are simply disallowed. See Williamson, *Corporate Control and Business Behavior*, p. 10.

[45] There is evidence, for instance, that U.S. Steel during its heyday did not operate to maximize either its market share or its long-term profits. Rather, its managers were largely concerned with maintaining stability in the market and avoiding prosecution for antitrust. See Thomas K. McCraw and Forest Reinhardt, "Losing to Win: U.S. Steel's Pricing, Investment Decisions, and Market Share, 1901–1938," *Journal of Economic History* 49 (September 1989): 593–619.

of costs and benefits but also an ongoing series of compromises and concessions that regulates the allocation of these costs and benefits. Thus, to understand cooperation, we must understand both the process by which it is forged and the means by which it is implemented and maintained.

In this context, it is useful to return to Schelling's conception of conflict as essentially a bargaining situation[46] and to view the maintenance of cooperation as a protracted series of successful bargains. When competitors cooperate they are trading the relative gains of unilateral and mutual action, and negotiating the price that each member must pay to ensure its place in the agreement. Sometimes the bargaining is explicit, and rewards and costs are laid out on the table and discussed. More often, "bargaining" occurs under the table and around the clock. It occurs whenever one competitor threatens, defects, or retaliates. It occurs each time a competitor departs even slightly from the agreement's terms or exceeds its mandate. In fact, implicit bargaining is so integral to cooperation among competing actors that cooperation can justifiably be described as a protracted bargaining session.

By using this description we get a concept of cooperation that captures the entire phenomenon rather than just a single static outcome. In addition, treating cooperation as a bargaining process affords us a better understanding of how various elements of the process can influence its success and how certain "rules of the game" permeate the cooperative bargain and help to perpetuate it. To a large extent, these rules vindicate the claims traditionally put forth by institutionalist scholars of cooperation. By establishing procedures and norms, they make the cooperative process more predictable and thus reduce the risk that uncertainty will prompt the competitors to defect. In this respect, the argument of the institutionalists seems valid in practice as well as in theory. In the cartel cases, at least, cooperation was indeed facilitated when all the competitors shared a common sense of the agreement, its goals, and the type of behavior that was permitted under its auspices.

By the same token, the cases that follow also suggest that some of the most successful rules, norms, and procedures are not necessarily

[46] Schelling, *Strategy of Conflict*, p. 5.

those that institutionalists would prescribe. On the contrary, three tactics that emerge as particularly useful in maintaining cooperation—secrecy, exclusivity, and informality—run directly against the institutionalists' suggestions.

Secrecy

In recent years, several prominent scholars of cooperation have emphasized the importance of transparency in the maintenance of cooperation. According to these scholars, governments that are closed to the outside world will have greater difficulties in convincing their would-be partners of their commitment to a proposed agreement. Because the other partners are left uncertain about the secretive actor's intentions and capabilities, they will be less willing to commit themselves to the partnership.[47]

My evidence suggests quite a different set of conclusions. What emerges as a central element of the cooperative process is not transparency but secrecy, not publicity but covert meetings and closed doors.[48] The importance of secrecy stems from the extent to which any cooperative bargain between competitors demands a certain amount of juggling, fine-tuning, and strategic retreats. By its nature, cooperation requires that the competitors make compromises and accept limits on their own flexibility and freedom of action. If this part of the bargaining process is conducted under the glare of public scrutiny, it becomes harder for competitors to make necessary concessions. If the negotiations are conducted out of the public realm, however, competitors can bargain more freely and make concessions without fear of losing face. When the negotiations occur in, or are reported to, the public realm, each competitor is accountable for every position it took, every deal it cut, and every advantage it traded away. By contrast, when the bargains occur behind closed

[47] See, for instance, Keohane, *After Hegemony*, p. 95. Schelling also argues that secrecy can be detrimental, as it eliminates the possibility of ensuring commitment by pledging one's reputation. See *Strategy of Conflict*, p. 29.

[48] In the related context of domestic coalition building, Paul J. Quirk also finds that "limited publicity," along with a simple and closed decision-making process, facilitates cooperation. See Quirk, "The Cooperative Resolution of Policy Conflict," *American Political Science Review* 83 (September 1989): 918.

doors, the negotiators can always report that they stood firm in the face of a powerful adversary and that the deal that was struck represents the best of all possible worlds.

In addition, the cloak of secrecy provides the principal participant with a cover under which to issue—and occasionally to implement— threats. Retaliation and threats are crucial to the maintenance of any cooperative agreement, yet many competitors are still uncomfortable with them. Behind closed doors, however, threats are easier. There are fewer people to hear them and less suspicion that they are being used as signals or reputation builders. Thus, secrecy may help to foster an environment in which tough bargaining is facilitated and cooperation encouraged.

In this context, secrecy is not necessarily at odds with transparency. Theoretically, meetings held behind closed doors can still be fully transparent to all the relevant participants. The important point is that transparency not extend beyond the inner circle of the negotiators and that the specifics of the agreement are shielded both from outsiders and from the greater glare of public opinion. To be sure, public opinion is already less of a factor for many successful cooperators. The more internal power and autonomy a competitor has, the less likely it is to be affected by adverse publicity. To that extent, the capacity for secrecy is already a function of the competitor itself. In addition, though, secrecy is also an instrument that any competitor can employ. And if it is employed successfully, it can do much to perpetuate cooperation.

Exclusivity

The second tactic that emerges from the case studies as being instrumental to the maintenance of cooperation is, like the first, largely a matter of closed doors. Just as cooperation is fostered and perpetuated by the competitors' ability to negotiate in private, so too is it facilitated by their ability to maintain their own narrow ranks and close the doors on others. Cooperation is a game that appears best played by small groups of like-minded players.

Once again we need to stress that cooperation is a constant process of compromises and concessions that becomes increasingly complex as the number of participants increases. The more participants in any given situation, the tougher it becomes to identify each one's interest and to transmit information about changes. Even with small groups of competitors, cooperative settlements are quite difficult to establish and maintain; as the number rises, so too does the complexity of interests and the likelihood that defection will appear attractive to at least some of the would-be participants.[49]

In addition, the cooperative process is likely to become more unruly as its membership is not only expanded but also diversified. Deals will tend to occur more frequently when negotiators are familiar with one another, when they know their partners' bargaining styles and limits, and when they have between them a history of promises made and concessions granted. In theoretical terms, exclusivity facilitates cooperation insofar as it fosters repeated interactions and helps solve the confidence problem. In practice, it means that every competitor will have had some experience in dealing with its partners and some faith in their ability to make commitments. Ideally, it will also mean a sense of camaraderie and personal accountability.[50]

Lack of Formal Rules

One of the key tenets of the institutional approach is that, to be successful, cooperation must be institutionalized and organized around an evolving system of formal rules and regulations. As Oye argues: "Explicit codification of norms can limit definitional ambiguity. The very act of clarifying standards of conduct, of defining cooperative and uncooperative behavior, can permit more effective resort to strategies of reciprocity."[51]

The evidence from my cartel cases, however, indicates that this

[49] The classic works on the "numbers problem" include Olson, *Logic of Collective Action*; and Hardin, *Collective Action*. For a discussion more directly related to international relations, see Oye, "Cooperation under Anarchy," pp. 18–22. For empirical evidence that cartels are more difficult to maintain as the number of firms increases, see Richard Posner, "A Statistical Study of Antitrust Enforcement," *Journal of Law and Economics* 13, 2 (1970): 365–419.

[50] This point is also made by Robert D. Putnam and Nicholas Bayne in describing the personal relationships between participants at the Western economic summits. See Putnam and Bayne, *Hanging Together: The Seven-Power Summits* (Cambridge: Harvard University Press, 1984), p. 197.

[51] Oye, "Cooperation under Anarchy," pp. 16–17.

relationship may not always apply. Instead, it appears that in some circumstances a distinct *lack* of formal rules and regulations may facilitate the initiation and, especially, the perpetuation of cooperation.[52]

The advantage of formal rules is that they set a common standard of conduct and define and delegitimize defection. The disadvantage, however, is that once rules are formalized, any breach—even a minor one—becomes an issue that must be addressed and rectified. If, on the other hand, rules are made less explicit, if they are allowed to remain somewhat vaguer and less clearly imprinted in the agreement, then minor breaches will not lead as inevitably to a confrontation and a questioning of the entire agreement.[53] This is not to argue, of course, that cooperation under anarchy can occur without a firm and mutual understanding of what the objectives of the agreement are and where the boundaries of acceptable behavior lie. It is merely to suggest that at a certain point, rule making sacrifices flexibility for an often false precision and that this may be too high a price to pay. Especially where competitors are engaged in a constant process of negotiation, cooperation will often depend on coming up with innovative solutions that move the negotiation frontier outward and expand the parameters of possible agreement.[54] Yet, this type of innovation or creativity will often depend on the ability to bend existing rules or to allow small violations in exchange for the promise of future modifications. If, as I have been arguing, cooperation is basically a perpetual process of bargaining, then the rules that govern

[52] The argument here pertains only to formal and specific rules; it does not extend to the broader categories of "norms," "procedures," and "principles." Indeed, I am not in any way arguing that a common agreement on how to conduct relations is detrimental to cooperation but only that a formal institutionalization of these common practices may reduce flexibility and thus the capacity to perpetuate cooperation.

[53] In this context, it is interesting to note that the Final Act of the Conference on Security and Cooperation in Europe (Helsinki) was *not* put into a legally binding agreement in order to avoid potential legal problems. See Louis Henkin, *How Nations Behave* (New York: Columbia University Press, 1979), p. 14. Similarly, economists have noted that explicit contracts tend to increase rigidity and thus create greater suspicion whenever alterations are needed. See Benjamin Klein, Robert G. Crawford, and Armen Alchian, "Vertical Integration, Appropriable Rents, and the Competitive Contracting Process," *Journal of Law and Economics* 31 (October 1988): 297–326.

[54] James K. Sebenius, for instance, discusses how the addition or subtraction of issues may help to enlarge the "zone of possible agreement." See Sebenius, *Negotiating the Law of the Sea* (Cambridge: Harvard University Press, 1984), pp. 182–217.

the overall agreement can not be so stringent that they impede the flexibility that is the key to bargaining.

Finally, formal rules may often hinder cooperation between competitors insofar as they require a formal bureaucracy to interpret the regulations and to judge violations. In practice, this means that another layer is added to the negotiations and that the negotiators must jostle with another set of officials. Although these additions do not necessarily condemn the cooperative arrangement to failure, they do complicate it and move it farther from the ideal of a small, self-contained, and powerful group of negotiators.

To be sure, cooperation can—and does—occur in the absence of the three tactics I describe. Indeed, there are quite a few examples of cooperative agreements that are transparent, inclusive, and highly institutionalized—the World Health Organization, for example, or the International Maritime Organization. My objective is not to deny that such agreements exist or to dispute the principles by which they are governed. It is, instead, to suggest that the toughest forms of cooperation—the cooperation between real adversaries, where defection is a constant possibility—demand harsher and more restrictive tactics. In particular, they require mechanisms that will shield the bargaining process from the public eye and thus afford competitors the opportunity to negotiate and threaten without worrying that news of their actions will frighten their allies abroad or anger their supporters at home.

Unfortunately, the ability to use these tactics is not generic, and some competitors will be much more capable and comfortable with them than will others. They are, after all, the tactics of authoritarianism, tactics that will not prove amenable to a competitor who is publicly accountable to a variety of constituencies or devoted to the liberal values of openness, equality, and justice. In fact, the competitors who are most likely to use these tactics comfortably and successfully are also those competitors who bear the internal attributes listed earlier. They are the competitors whose central authority and secure position give them the freedom to keep certain matters out of the public eye and to enforce international decisions at the domestic level. They are also likely to be competitors whose concern for their international reputation does not preclude them from extensive dealings behind closed doors.

These characteristics, of course, are an anathema to the modern liberal view of international relations and international cooperation. Instead of openness, they support secrecy; instead of inclusivity, exclusivity; and instead of legalism, ad hocism. They are the values against which the United States was founded and against which its entire domestic framework and international aspirations are structured. Unfortunately, though, they may also be the attributes that best enable competing states to cooperate. Insofar as cooperation remains a competitive rather than a harmonious process, it may require its followers to employ competitive tactics and engage in the type of diplomacy that existed when gentlemen did indeed read each other's mail.

Overall, then, this book suggests that cooperation is neither an easy goal to attain nor an unmitigated good. Insofar as it promises a cessation of conflict, cooperation will remain a paramount goal of the international system and of the competitors who drive and define this system. Yet insofar as cooperation is a game that must always be played on two levels, so too must these competitors acknowledge that peace does not come without a price. When cooperation is forged from anarchy, internal adjustments must be made, and any opposition to these adjustments must be modified, assuaged, or suppressed. At one level, then, cooperation occurs when competitors agree to shake hands and work toward their mutual self-interest. At another level, it can be perpetuated only by competitors with the power to make long-term commitments and the will to enforce them. As Cardinal Antonio Samore once wrote: "One speaks much of peace, and peace is the work of everyone, it is the fruit of a collaboration of the spirit in everyone. We must ask God our Father, prince of peace, and the Holy Virgin, queen of peace, but also, I would say, one must force it."

In the chapters that follow, I examine four commodity markets: diamonds, uranium, gold, and silver. To select the specific cases, I referred back to the structural theories outlined earlier. That is, because the dominant explanations of cartels still focus on structural determinants and because I was primarily interested in uncovering nonstructural determinants, I chose these cases to control for structural variation. Of course, because "structure" is such a vast concept, it is impossible to look only at markets with identical structures. What I did, therefore, was to compile a list of the commodity markets that, according to the five structural criteria outlined above, *should* be most conducive to the formation and perpetuation of either cartels or producers' agreements.[55] Admittedly, these markets are not identical. They are each marked by their own idiosyncrasies and by subtle variations in each of the structural criteria. Still, they are all very similar. All four markets have a high concentration of production, a small number of fringe producers, and high barriers to entry. All four commodities are nondifferentiated, nonsubstitutable, and have some additional speculative or strategic value that makes them exceptionally good candidates for cartelization. On the basis of structural criteria alone, they should all be similarly amenable to the creation of cartels.[56] The intent of my analysis was to determine the level of cooperation that did, in fact, prevail in each market and to explain any variation across the markets by reference to other, nonstructural factors.

But before examining the factors that separate success from failure, I needed to find some means of identifying this success—and the problem of identifying a successful cartel is more difficult than it appears. In the first place, most cartels, and especially most successful cartels, are not well publicized. In fact, one of the primary features of a cartel is the secrecy to which its members are bound. And even though explicit cartels such as OPEC have been formed, there is still no reason to suspect that any given cartel will announce itself to the public. To find a cartel one needs to look deeper.

At the same time, I wanted to avoid the classic mistake of identifying a cartel by its component parts. The fact that a market is highly concentrated or has high barriers to entry does not necessarily mean significant cooperation between the producers. Likewise, there is no way to deduce the presence of cooperation by relying on external economic data alone. Of course, certain economic circumstances are

[55] See the Appendix for a more detailed description of the codification and classification of these markets.

[56] There has long been a heated controversy among both economists and lawyers about whether structural indicators such as concentration ratios are sufficient evidence of cartel behavior. See, for instance, Harold Demsetz, "Two Systems of Belief about Monopoly," in H. J. Goldschmid, H. M. Mann, and J. F. Weston, eds., *Industrial Concentration: The New Learning* (Boston: Little, Brown, 1974), pp. 164–84.

likely to appear in conjunction with a successful cartel: prices will tend to be higher and more stable than in other markets, and producers may realize greater-than-usual profits. Unfortunately, though, these circumstances could occur for a variety of different reasons, making them unreliable as indicators of cartels. Even the most successful cartels may not exhibit all these economic characteristics all of the time. For instance, a cartel may forgo stability for a while to push prices even higher, or it might even force prices sharply downward to punish a recalcitrant member.

In an effort to get around these obstacles, some economists have attempted to rely on proxy variables. Joe Bain explores the use of profits as indications of monopoly power.[57] Fritz Machlup discusses an "index of depression sensitivity" based on the assumption that monopolies or cartels will be more able than openly competitive industries to maintain their price levels even during an economic depression.[58] And Abba Lerner suggests measuring the monopoly power of any industry by dividing the excess of the selling price over the marginal cost by the selling price.[59] For the most part, though, economists seem to have accepted some variation of the judge's assertion that he simply knew pornography "when he saw it."

For my purposes, however, the defining aspect of a cartel is the cooperative behavior that surrounds and sustains it. Unlike the economists, I am primarily concerned with the process of cooperation rather than with the effects it creates. Thus I argue that, insofar as a cartel is defined by cooperation among the producers, the only way to identify a successful cartel is to find evidence that the producers have, in fact, bound themselves to a cooperative agreement and that each has decided to maximize its profits by collaborating with its

[57] Joe S. Bain, "The Profit Rate as a Measure of Monopoly Power," *Quarterly Journal of Economics* 55 (February 1941): 271–93.

[58] See Fritz Machlup, "Measuring the Degree of Monopoly," in *The Political Economy of Monopoly: Business, Labor, and Government Policies*, ed. Machlup (Baltimore: Johns Hopkins University Press, 1952), pp. 469–528. This approach is also discussed in D. H. Wallace, "Monopoly Prices and Depression," in Edward S. Mason, ed., *Explorations in Economics* (New York: McGraw-Hill, 1936), p. 347.

[59] Abba P. Lerner, "The Concept of Monopoly and the Measurement of Monopoly Power," *Review of Economic Studies* 1 (June 1934): 157–75. For a discussion of ongoing measurement problems, see Richard Schmalensee, "Empirical Studies of Rivalrous Behavior," in Giacomo Bonanno and Dario Brandolini, eds., *Industrial Structure in the New Industrial Economics* (Oxford: Clarendon Press, 1990), pp. 146–49.

competitors. Formally, I borrow Ervin Paul Hexner's definition of a cartel as "a voluntary, potentially impermanent, business relationship among a number of independent, private entrepreneurs, which through co-ordinated marketing significantly affects the market of a commodity or service."[60] I also include Hexner's proviso that "cartel" need not refer only to legal contracts. Instead, "it includes all sorts of common understandings, whether enforceable, expressed or tacit, about future facts and performances or forbearances."[61] Specifically, my conception of a cartel includes four key components.

1. A cartel is a cooperative endeavor among producers in the same industry who would otherwise compete.
2. Cartels emerge from oligopolistic markets.
3. Cartels are not spontaneous or harmonious phenomena. Instead, they must be voluntarily and consciously maintained by those who participate in them; and those who participate must be willing to incur certain costs of cooperation in exchange for the expectation of future gain.[62]
4. Cartels seek, collectively, to limit the effect of market forces and instead to manage output and prices in order to maximize the individual profits of each of the producers.

In this manner, I use evidence of conscious collaboration among the producers to distinguish a cartel from price leadership or pure coincidence of behavior. And the only way to find this evidence is to examine each of the markets individually and in depth, searching for the ties that may bind the producers and looking for evidence of mutual accommodation and individual restraint.

[60] Ervin Paul Hexner, *International Cartels* (Chapel Hill: University of North Carolina Press, 1945), p. 24. For similar definitions of a cartel, see Eckbo, *Future of World Oil*, p. 47; and George W. Stocking and Myron W. Watkins, *Cartels or Competition?* (New York: Twentieth Century Fund, 1948), pp. 3–4.

[61] Hexner, *International Cartels*, p. 20n.

[62] This definition is in accord with the standard interpretation offered by U.S. courts that tacit collusion is not sufficient evidence of a cartel. Rather, as Moran notes, "the objective is to find concrete meetings, negotiations, and conspiracies where the participants explicitly agree to fix prices, divide markets, and place a ceiling on production." See "Managing an Oligopoly," p. 576. For the standard legal definition of cartels, see Standard Oil Company of New Jersey v. United States, 221 U.S. 1 (1911). For a dissenting view that tacit collusion is equivalent to an actual cartel, see Richard A. Posner, *Antitrust Law* (Chicago: University of Chicago Press, 1976), esp. chap. 4.

In the four case chapters that follow, I find a distinctly broad range of cooperative and noncooperative behavior. The diamond market is completely controlled by a formal and highly successful cartel. In gold, there is no formal cartel but a mutual agreement between two of the largest producers to exercise restraint and avoid competitive behavior. In silver, cooperative efforts have seldom even gotten off the ground, and in uranium, a brief attempt at cartelization ended in quick defection and disarray. The puzzle I set myself is to explain this checkered pattern of cooperation. In the final chapter I return to the broader questions with which I began: What are the conditions most likely to facilitate and sustain cooperation? What kinds of competitors will be best equipped to join in the cooperative game? And what can an internal approach contribute to our understanding of the cooperative dilemma?

CHAPTER TWO

The Power to Persuade and the Success
of the International Diamond Cartel

For centuries, diamonds have been regarded as one of the most valuable commodities in the world. They have been the stuff of legend and the privilege of royalty, the symbol of romance and of greed. They have been treasured for their beauty, their hardness, and their unique ability to hold and transform light. Most of all, however, diamonds have been treasured because they are rare.

Initially, scarcity defined the market for the stones. Known to exist only in the riverbeds of India and the jungles of Brazil, diamonds were considered the rarest of nature's creations, and the handful of stones that were unearthed each year were reserved for Indian rajas and European royalty. The most spectacular stones became jewels of various foreign crowns and some assumed mythical, nearly mystical, properties.[1] For the vast majority of people, diamonds were a sign of all that was romantic, regal, and entirely beyond their personal grasp.[2]

---

[1] For some of the stories of these stones, see C. W. King, *The Natural History of Precious Stones and of the Precious Metals* (London, 1870), pp. 76–83, 86–87; E. W. Streeter, *The Great Diamonds of the World* (London, 1882), pp. 63–78, 103–35; and Jean B. Tavernier, *Travels in India by Jean Baptiste Tavernier*, trans. V. Ball (London, 1889), II, app. 1, pp. 431–46.

[2] There is a considerable literature extolling the beauty and value of diamonds. See, for instance, A. C. Austin, *The Story of Diamonds* (Los Angeles: Gemological Institute of America, 1939); J. Willard Hershey, *The Book of Diamonds* (New York: Hearthside Press, 1940); and A. Monnickendam, *The Magic of Diamonds* (London: Hammond, Hammond, 1955).

By the end of the nineteenth century, however, the discovery of the South African diamond mines had brought an avalanche of stones into the market. Suddenly diamonds were transformed from a privilege reserved for the elite into a commodity for the mass market. Surprisingly, though, after an initial period of adjustment, the vast change in the supply of diamonds had little effect on their price, or the way in which the public perceived them. Indeed, even while tons of diamonds were being pulled from the "blue earth" of the Cape Colony, diamonds remained a treasured commodity, and diamond prices stayed high.[3] Moreover, the public still considered diamonds to be extremely rare, valuable, and worthy tokens of affection. The market for diamonds may have changed, but the allure that had surrounded them for centuries had not been tarnished at all.

Part of this allure was due, no doubt, to a deeply ingrained perception of scarcity that continued to linger even as diamonds were cascading into the markets of Europe. Most of it, though, was the result of a conscious effort by the new diamond producers to regulate the production of the stones so as to maximize the *illusion* of scarcity and thus to keep prices as high as possible. Realizing that South Africa's diamonds would be virtually worthless once they appeared commonplace, a young Englishman named Cecil Rhodes was working to consolidate the entire industry and keep the supply of gemstones sharply limited. Under his guidance, the international diamond cartel was born. Following his philosophy it became one of the world's most tenacious business organizations and one of the most successful cartels of all time.

Since then, the international diamond cartel has regulated the market for diamond gemstones and maintained the fragile illusion of their scarcity. The cartel's reach is legendary. It controls a significant number of the world's diamond mines; it handles all sorting and classifying of the stones; and through its Central Selling Organisation (CSO) in London, it determines who can buy which stones

---

[3] There is one exception. A depression in 1882 hit the diamond market particularly hard, throwing the industry into turmoil and leading to the creation of the diamond cartel. See William H. Worger, *South Africa's City of Diamonds: Mine Workers and Monopoly Capitalism in Kimberley, 1867–1895* (New Haven: Yale University Press, 1987), p. 191.

and how much each buyer must pay. Its tactics are varied and complex. Its strategy, though, is as simple now as it was in Rhodes's time: to restrict the number of diamonds released into the market in any given year and thus to perpetuate the illusion of diamonds as a scarce and valuable commodity.

This strategy is not unique. Indeed, it is the fundamental strategy of any cartel and the goal of any commodity producer. What makes the diamond cartel different is simply that it has been able to achieve these goals. Unlike most other would-be cartels, the diamond cartel has brought all the major producers into a tight cooperative arrangement and imposed on them the necessity of collective action. It has enforced a complex system of stockpiles, production quotas, and standards that are designed to keep prices and demand high even while overall diamond supplies are growing. In short, it has established a cooperative network that allows its members to reap the rewards traditionally befitting a monopolist.

To a certain extent, the success of the cartel is due to its unique business practices. As we shall see, the cartel has developed a series of brilliant tactics—advertising campaigns, official price lists, and a centralized distribution network, for instance—that boost profits for all its members and thus facilitate cooperation by increasing the rewards that it brings. More important, however, the diamond cartel has been able to use these tactics where no one else has. What makes them unique to this cartel is the members' singular ability to employ them.

Specifically, this ability is derived from the internal characteristics of the cartel's leading members: the DeBeers Corporation and, to a lesser extent, the former Soviet Union.[4] Before 1990 at least, both these producers were tightly controlled, highly centralized entities. They had no one to answer to but themselves and no internal factions to speak of. With complete and all-encompassing authority over their internal hierarchies, they could act autonomously in their external relations, confident that the deals they struck would never be compromised by internal dissent or domestic wrangling. This autonomy in turn enabled the Soviet diamond agencies and the

---

[4] Because most of the discussion here refers to events that occurred before 1990, I use the terms "Soviet Union" or "Soviet" in most cases.

DeBeers Corporation to bargain, threaten, and punish. In short, it permitted them to resist the temptations of defection in favor of co-operation's long-term rewards.

In the diamond cartel, moreover, the structures of cooperation have been vigorously upheld by DeBeers, its leading member. Contrary to popular belief, DeBeers is not the world's largest producer of diamonds. In fact, DeBeers's South African mines account for only about 8 percent of total gemstone production. Still, DeBeers controls the cartel. It establishes mechanisms for the "orderly marketing" of diamonds and enforces these mechanisms with a quick and occasionally ruthless hand. By the selective use of coercive tactics, DeBeers imposes cooperation on the rest of the cartel's members. In the end, all benefit: because the cartel can enforce compliance, it can stem excess supplies and maintain the critical perception of scarcity. And as long as this perception is maintained, diamonds will remain valuable.

To be sure, the diamond cartel has not been entirely free of tensions. On the contrary, as with any cooperative arrangement between competitors, it has been marked by a series of struggles, threats, and compromises. What makes this cartel so remarkable, though, is the success with which its two leading members have been able to resolve their conflicts without threatening the stability of the market or the sanctity of the cartel. For years, observers have predicted the imminent collapse of the cartel. Arguing that not even diamonds are forever, they have pointed to the inherent weaknesses of a cartel based on an illusion of scarcity and supported by a lone corporation from a pariah state. And for years, these observers have been proved wrong. The diamond cartel has survived depressions and defections and retaliation. It has fastened an economic partnership that denies political considerations and succeeds despite tremendous political obstacles. It is a cartel largely impervious to outside influences and external attacks.

Ultimately, what holds the cartel together is the tremendous internal strength of the DeBeers organization and the internal ability of the former Soviet Union—until recently at least—to play by the rules that DeBeers has established. And what could kill the cartel, therefore, is not recession or synthetic stones or a rash of new discoveries but simply the dissolution of control in what was once the

Soviet Union. If the republics dissolve into anarchy and the remnants of the Soviet diamond industry lose their authority, then they just may be capable of destroying what continues to be the world's most powerful cartel.

THE HISTORY OF DIAMONDS AND THE ILLUSION OF SCARCITY

Since its earliest days, the diamond trade has been haunted by the fear of oversupply. To be considered valuable, diamonds must be perceived as rare; and if this scarcity is to be credible, all excess diamonds must be kept off the market. Understandably, then, a common interest in restricting the entry of diamonds onto the market has persistently forced the members of the diamond trade to bind together to prevent diamonds from becoming "as common as flint."[5] The advantages of restricting supply, of course, are not unique to diamonds. Where diamonds are concerned, however, they appear to have been particularly irresistible, powerful enough to have compelled a history of cooperative behavior that culminated in the creation of the present-day diamond cartel.

Early Cooperation

In 1867 the accidental discovery of diamonds in South Africa changed the diamond industry forever. The first stone, picked up on the banks of the Vaal River by a thirteen-year-old boy, was generally dismissed as a geological fluke; the second find, though, a stone of 83 1/2 carats, was too tempting to ignore. By 1869, diamond fever had hit South Africa and some ten thousand diggers from around the world had rushed to the arid plains of the Transvaal to stake their claims and make their fortunes.

Trained in the goldfields of California and Australia, the early prospectors assumed that diamonds were carried by water, and thus they clung to the banks of the Vaal and its immediate vicinity. In

[5] The quote is from an early description of the diamond trade in eighteenth-century England that tells of merchants refusing to buy the newly discovered Brazilian diamonds. Cited in Godehard Lenzen, *The History of Diamond Production and the Diamond Trade*, trans. F. Bradley (London: Praeger, 1970), p. 125.

January 1870, however, a group of diggers unearthed diamonds away from the river at a spot known as Klipdrift. As word of their discovery spread, most of the diggers gave up their river, or "alluvial," claims and moved to the more profitable dry-land spots. By the end of 1872, five separate mines had been established in the Transvaal, producing an avalanche of gem-quality stones. For the first time, it seemed possible that diamonds might become a luxury that even the middle class could obtain.

Getting these diamonds out of the mines, though, was no easy task, especially for prospectors accustomed to panning for gold, a relatively painless job that an individual could easily manage alone. By contrast, the diamonds of the Transvaal were located deep in volcanic pipes, which forced the miners to engage in a considerably more treacherous task. It was a task, moreover, which demanded large-scale expenditures of energy and which depended on a certain amount of coordination among the thousands of miners engaged in it.

Diamonds exist primarily in "yellow dirt," a crumbling soil that lies below the first layer of topsoil. To reach the yellow dirt, the digger must first break through and dispose of the useless first layer. In some instances, the topsoil around the Vaal was thin, and the digger could be at work within days. In other cases, however, the two layers of dirt were separated by a substratum of rock and shale, thus forcing the digger to hack away for weeks just to reach the diamond-bearing, or "diamondiferous," ground.

Once in the yellow dirt, each digger had to go through the soil meticulously, washing each bit by hand and then poring over it to separate the tiny bits of diamond from all the other particles. Even in the richest soils of the region diamonds were rare, and even the most expert eye could not always spot a diamond in its rough state.

Within months, the difficulty of their task had forced the diamond miners of the Transvaal to cooperate to a rather remarkable degree. To begin with, even the earliest diggers had realized the utility of establishing some system of property rights; land was plentiful, there was no way of guessing by appearances which plots would prove more valuable, and no one wanted to waste precious time and energy fighting off squatters. Within a year after the rush had begun, various areas along the Vaal River had established Diggers Committees, which started by arbitrating disputes and quickly assumed the more central responsibility of issuing regulations and licenses. Customarily, each claim was limited to a thirty-one-foot-square plot of ground, and no digger was permitted to hold more than two claims simultaneously.[6]

Inevitably, the miners began to realize the benefits of cooperation. Because no one could ever tell whether his piece of ground would prove lucky or not, everyone stood to benefit by joining with his neighbor, thus allowing the two to pool their resources and double their chances. Over time, these partnerships grew larger and more complex, as the wealthier stakeholders gathered large conglomerations of plots amongst themselves and began to hire native diggers to work their holdings. Eventually these partnerships became so prevalent that the earlier restrictions on holdings became irrelevant. Thus, in 1876 the two-claim restriction was replaced with a ten-claim restriction, which was itself quickly abolished.[7]

The impetus to cooperate was hastened, moreover, by the geology of the land, a geology that had slowly revealed itself as the claims sank deeper and deeper into the soft yellow soil. As one correspondent who visited the region in 1879 noted: "As their depths increase, the difficulties of working them become greater. Crumbling reefs and the fast inflowing water are fast multiplying the expenses of working the claims."[8] To protect the ability of all prospectors to reach their claims, the diggers at the big open-pit mines had to band together and contribute to the building of pathways to span the surface of the mine. At the largest mine, the Kimberley Mine, roadways were cut straight across the mine's face, forty-seven feet apart and fifteen feet wide, forcing claim owners to forfeit seven and one-half feet of their land. Many complained about the rule, but unable to deny its necessity, none dared disobey it.[9]

---

[6] In 1870 the rules stated that no person was to have more than one claim, to be absent from his or her property for more than three working days, or to employ more than five black laborers. "Rules and Regulations for the Vaal-river Diamond-fields," 1870, South Africa Library, cited in Worger, *South Africa's City of Diamonds*, p. 11.

[7] See Brian Roberts, *The Diamond Magnates* (London: Hamish Hamilton, 1972), p. 103.

[8] *Jewelers' Circular* of 1879, cited in "DeBeers: 100 Years of Market Control," *Jewelers' Circular-Keystone*, March 1988, pp. 178–79.

[9] Emily Hahn, *Diamond*, 1st ed. (Garden City, N.Y.: Doubleday, 1956), p. 42. As an illustration, it is interesting to see how Cecil Rhodes described the situation in a letter to his mother: "There are constantly mules, carts, and all going head over heals [*sic*] into the mines below as there are no rails or anything on either side of the roads,

As they dug farther and farther into the yellow soil, the miners built pulley systems to haul the dirt up and then carted it off to washing tables set away from the mine. Before long, however, the pressure of so many carts and hauling networks proved too much for the crumbling soil to bear, and carts, mules, and drivers began to tumble into the maze of deep holes. By the end of 1872, not one of the roads across Kimberley Mine was traversable,[10] and many of the claim plots had started to crumble.[11]

Once again, the diggers were forced to resort to a cooperative solution. In 1873 the Kimberley miners dismantled their separate hauling apparatuses and erected massive platforms at the two edges of the pit. Miners then ran their individual cables from the platform (called a "staging") down into the depths of the mine.[12]

Still geology proved an obstacle. As the diggings sank deeper, they tapped into the underground water tables, flooding all the claims. Initially, miners fought back the water with small hand-held pumps, but these soon proved useless against the constant seepage. Again the common problem seemed to demand a communal solution. The miners were strong individualists by nature, people who thrived on

nothing but one great broad chasm below. Here and there where the roads have fallen in, bridges have been put, and they are now the safest part of the Kopje. The question now of course is, how are the roads to be worked[?] Every claim holder has an interest in them, as a portion of every man's claim is in the road, and one has no idea of leaving ground in every load of which stands fair chance of holding a diamond." Quoted in Robert I. Rotberg, *The Founder: Cecil Rhodes and the Pursuit of Power* (New York: Oxford University Press, 1988), pp. 61–62.

[10] Hahn, *Diamond*, p. 42.

[11] See, for instance, Frederick Boyle, *To the Cape for Diamonds: A Story of Digging Experiences in South Africa* (London, 1873), pp. 134–35.

[12] As one visitor described the Kimberley Mine at this time: "So thickly together were these lines set that the whole face of the vast pit seemed to be covered by a monstrous cobweb, shining in the moonlight as if every filament was a silver strand. Nor has any eye seen such a marvellous show of mining as was given in the grand amphitheatre, when the huge pit was sunk far below the surface level . . . when thousands of half-naked men, dwarfed to pigmy size, were scratching the face of the pit with their puny picks like burrowing gnomes . . . when hide buckets were flying like shuttles in a loom, up and down the vast warp of wires, twanging like dissonant harp-strings, with a deafening din of rattling wheels and falling ground; and where every beholder was wonder-struck at the thought that this weird creation in the heart of South Africa had been evolved by men for the sake of a few buckets of tiny white crystals to adorn the heads and hands of fanciful women." Quoted in Oswald Doughty, *Early Diamond Days* (London: Longmans, 1963), p. 83.

independence and shrank from contact with big business. But in the end, the hardships of the diamond mines forced even the most self-sufficient diggers toward conglomeration and cooperation.

Financially, cooperation was also becoming imperative. By the late 1870s, the vast increases in South African diamond production were dragging prices slowly downward and pushing the small miners out of business; by 1882, diamond prices had been cut in half, and one-third of Kimberley's diamond companies had been forced to shut.[13] Struggling to survive, the remaining companies consolidated their operations and cut their prices even further. The lower prices plunged, of course, the fiercer the competition became, which set off an insidious spiral that threatened to destroy forever the illusion of scarcity and thus the value of gem diamonds. The only way to stop the spiral was by stemming the flow of stones, and the only way to do that was to bring all the miners into a collective endeavor. As one local journalist reported, "The great bugbear of the digger is the word 'company', but even now small proprietorships are becoming merged with larger aggregations of claims, and the next phase must undoubtedly be that of several large and competing companies, or perhaps a single one controlling the whole mine."[14] And, indeed, this is precisely what happened.

Cecil Rhodes and the Creation of DeBeers

In 1874 a sickly English youth named Cecil Rhodes brought a steam-powered pump to the Kimberley Mine and began renting it out to the diggers. Within a year he had acquired enough pumps to take care of all the mines in the area.[15] With this new-found wealth, Rhodes and his partners then started to buy small claims in the newly formed DeBeers Mine. Over the next few years, they quietly annexed a series of other small holdings. In 1880, Rhodes formed the DeBeers Mining Company to control his growing stake in the mine, and by 1887 he had bought out all the other claim holders.[16]

[13] Worger, *South Africa's City of Diamonds*, p. 191.
[14] "DeBeers," p. 179.
[15] Hahn, *Diamond*, p. 44.
[16] Rhodes won his control through a combination of successful business schemes and tremendous personal ambition. For more details on this period, see ibid., pp. 82–

From the start, Rhodes realized that success in the diamond trade was contingent on the resolution of two serious problems. First, the very productivity of the South African diamond fields posed a threat to the long-term profitability of the diamond industry. If all new South African gems were suddenly to sweep into Europe, the market would be flooded and prices would plummet. Moreover, as Rhodes well understood, an oversupply could potentially depress prices forever, as the value of diamonds rests largely with the *perception* of their scarcity. Gem diamonds, after all, serve no real purpose. Their value is linked to the belief that they are rare, and therefore special, and a suitable token of sentiment.[17] Thus, to profit from his diamond investments, Rhodes had to find some way of selling diamonds to the masses without allowing them to be perceived as a mass-market item.[18]

Rhodes also had to find some means of tempering the industry's inherent conflict of interest between buyers and sellers. The sellers (the producers) have little control over the types and qualities of stones they produce; thus, they need to secure an indiscriminate buyer, one willing to purchase the smaller and uglier stones as well as the large and flawless ones. The buyer (or distributor), meanwhile, knows that profitability rests with the ability to obtain a constant stream of stones and to sell them at consistently high prices. The only relationship that serves both sides' interests is an ongoing arrangement between a single producer and a single distributor in which both benefit by keeping supplies low and prices high.

Realizing the extent to which prosperity in the diamond market thus rested with the dual ability to manipulate demand and coordinate it with supply, Rhodes was determined to wrest control of both

---

110; Roberts, *Diamond Magnates*, pp. 181–212; Worger, *South Africa's City of Diamonds*, pp. 191–236; Rotberg, *Founder*, pp. 180–214; and Geoffrey Wheatcroft, *The Randlords* (New York: Atheneum, 1986), pp. 92–110.

[17] As one of Rhodes's contemporaries explained it: "Diamonds are not a proper subject for exemplifying the theories of Political Economy. You cannot drown the market with an article only appertaining to the highest luxury . . . without swift and sudden catastrophe. These things require the most delicate manipulation." Frederick Boyle, quoted in Rotberg, *Founder*, p. 181.

[18] Rhodes was not the first to recognize the rewards of collaboration. He appears to have been, however, the only man with sufficient money, political connections, and personal ambition. See Worger, *South Africa's City of Diamonds*, pp. 202–3.

sides of the equation, regulating the entire industry so that the quantity of diamonds sold on the European market followed precisely the number of wedding engagements in any given year.[19] As Godehard Lenzen describes it:

> As early as 1873 the recorded pronouncements by Rhodes clearly indicate that his main aim is nothing less than the adaptation of the supply of rough diamonds to the market-dependent world by means of centralising the control of production. . . . As an inevitable result of future technological developments in diamond mining he saw the continually rising production reaching a market whose trend of demand, although likewise on the increase, appeared frequently to be rendered unstable by local as well as world-wide recessions. The quantity of rough diamonds produced was to be continually adjusted to the intensity of the demand.[20]

The solution Rhodes devised was ingenious. Having achieved full control over production at the DeBeers Mine, he then formed a coalition of merchants in Kimberley to whom he sold the full output of the mine. Under Rhodes's prompting, these merchants realized that they too stood to benefit from a system of coordinated selling and fixed prices. In 1873, the merchants' association was formalized as the "Diamond Syndicate," with all members pledged to buy diamonds from Rhodes's mines and to sell them in specific quantities and at set prices. By the end of the decade, Rhodes had completed his consolidation of the diamond industry by purchasing all the major South African mines.[21] And just as he had predicted, diamond

[19] Lenzen, *History of Diamond Production*, p. 155.

[20] Ibid.

[21] The one real threat Rhodes faced came from Barney Barnato, a former juggler and acrobat from London, who, like Rhodes himself, had dealt himself into full control of a South African mine—the "Big Hole" at Kimberley. By 1887, Rhodes and Barnato were the only major producers of diamonds in South Africa; but competition between them ran so high that neither could trust the other not to defect from their common position by underpricing their stones. "We had to choose between the ruin of the diamond industry and the control of the Kimberley Mine," Rhodes later said. "We saw this, that you could never deal with obstinate people until you got the whip hand of them and that the only thing we had to do to secure the success of our industry was to get the control of the Kimberley Mine." By 1888, Barnato had capitulated to Rhodes's persistence and to his greater financial resources. See Hahn, *Diamond*, p. 94.

prices rose, from eighteen shillings in 1889 to thirty-two shillings in 1890. The diamond cartel was in place. The only threats Rhodes faced were those which would haunt the market for decades to come: the threat of an outside producer competing for customers and destabilizing prices and the threat of a defection from his own tightly knit ranks.

Consolidation of the Cartel

After Rhodes's death in 1902, his vision of a diamond empire was taken up by Ernest Oppenheimer, a German who had come to South Africa to work as a diamond buyer and had quickly maneuvered himself into a position of power within the industry. Like Rhodes, Oppenheimer understood that the value of diamonds rested on their scarcity and that power in the market required full control over all aspects of the diamond industry. Even more than his predecessor, though, Oppenheimer realized that control of the diamond trade entailed a monopoly of distribution as well as of supply. Unlike many commodities, diamonds vary tremendously in quality. Only a tiny fraction of the stones are truly significant as gems; most are small, flawed, and not singularly attractive. Yet the diamond industry cannot survive on the top end of its market; it needs to sell the full range of stones, especially the lower-end goods that constitute the vast bulk of its production. Thus it needs to ensure that the diamond merchants will take the mediocre along with the spectacular and that all the links in the network commit themselves to selling the stones that together provide the mainstay of the industry.

Similarly, because diamond prices bear no relation to the cost of production, Oppenheimer understood the necessity of ensuring uniform prices across the industry and straight down to the retail level. In an industry where mass perceptions of value and scarcity are critical, any undercutting would be disastrous. To maintain full control of the market, the diamond cartel would have to control every link in the system and would have to provide every link with a vested interest in the well-being of the system as a whole.

With these concerns in mind, Oppenheimer worried that the Diamond Syndicate founded by Rhodes was too independent and that it might eventually be tempted to break away from the producers.

Thus he resolved to create a "new syndicate," intimately linked to his own diamond interests and designed to exert unbearable pressure on the existing group of distributors. His scheme worked, and in 1925, Oppenheimer bought out the old syndicate and replaced it with a new one joined by corporate links to his own company, Anglo American, and pledged to comply with the distribution levels desired by the diamond producers.[22]

In 1929, after a series of complicated financial maneuvers and stock buyouts, Oppenheimer was also named chairman of DeBeers. Nearly immediately, he presided over the formal incorporation of an enlarged syndicate, which was created to include the few outside distribution firms that still existed. In 1930 the Diamond Corporation was formed and empowered to deal with all outside stocks of diamonds. The members of the corporation agreed to relinquish the right to buy diamonds on their own account and promised to subject any contract with outside producers to a vote of unanimity. At this point, the link between DeBeers and the Diamond Corporation, between producers and distributors, had been permanently forged. Not surprisingly, within a matter of months Oppenheimer was presiding as chairman of both organizations, positions he held until his death in 1957.

THE STRUCTURES OF CONTROL: THE CARTEL AND THE INTERNATIONAL DIAMOND MARKET

During Ernest Oppenheimer's life, the strength of the cartel had rested largely with DeBeers's control over the South African mines. In recent years, however, the fulcrum has shifted. Although the Oppenheimer family still controls DeBeers and the corporation is still the dominant player in the international cartel, the source of DeBeers's strength no longer lies solely with the South African mines. Rather, it is the result of the vast cooperative arrangement over which DeBeers presides and the discipline that it has been able to impose on all its members. Today, the cartel is much more than a

---

[22] Sir Theodore Gregory, *Ernest Oppenheimer and the Economic Development of Southern Africa* (Capetown: Oxford University Press, 1962), pp. 109–57.

geographical monopoly. It is an intricate network of production quotas, quality controls, and stockpiles. It is a formidable system of fixed prices and controlled distribution. It is an incredible array of rules and regulations, rarely violated and meticulously enforced. Most of all, however, the diamond cartel is a staggering edifice of cooperation: it works because its members play by the rules of the game, resisting the temptations of defection and keeping their own sales within strictly defined limits.

Manipulating Supply

The unique price stability of the diamond market rests with the cartel's tremendous control over the supply of diamonds. Currently, between 80 and 85 percent of the world's rough (uncut and unpolished) diamonds are sold through one of the most effective distribution centers in the world, the Central Selling Organisation. Based in London, the CSO is at the core of a complex group of companies, all linked by interlocking directorates and stockholdings and all ultimately controlled by either DeBeers or its sister company, Anglo American.

DeBeers runs its entire operation in accordance with Rhodes's early insistence that the number of diamonds brought to market in any given year should be roughly equal to the number of wedding engagements occurring in that year. Toward that end, DeBeers has thrown all its vast corporate energies into ensuring that the supply of diamonds remains strictly limited and that no holes are created whereby "outside" diamonds would be able to slip into the market. To ensure such complete control over the supply of diamonds, DeBeers has been forced to erect a vast network of corporate entities that together form the diamond cartel.

In Rhodes's day, of course, the company could contain the supply of diamonds merely by regulating its own production; with the exception of several small outposts in Brazil, South Africa was the only source of diamonds in the world, and DeBeers controlled all the diamonds in South Africa. In the mid-1950s, though, the yield from the once miraculous pipes at Kimberley, Dutoitspan, and Bultfontein began to decline, while discoveries in Australia, Siberia, and other parts of Africa opened up rich new fields for exploration. De-

Beers was no longer alone in the market. By 1960, South African diamonds accounted for only 19 percent of total world gemstone production and by 1990, 9 percent.

To maintain its grip on the market, therefore, the DeBeers Corporation has been obliged to reach out to the other major producers of rough diamonds, urging them to participate in the cartel's activities and in the collaborative regulation of the international diamond market. To date, DeBeers's entreaties have been well received. Most diamond-producing states have signed long-term contracts with De-Beers,[23] agreeing to sell a fixed proportion of their rough stones solely to DeBeers and its agents.[24] The diamond cartel is, therefore, no longer solely the property of DeBeers. Rather, it exists as a series of intimate joint ventures between DeBeers and the other producers. Together, these ventures form a seamless web of collaboration, each strand linked to DeBeers at the center and then turning outward to form the larger network. Taken as a whole, the network exemplifies cooperation. The producers work together, following strict production and price controls and reaping the collective benefits of monopoly. The glue for the greater enterprise, however, remains the central power of DeBeers. Each producer is contractually bound, not to the cartel per se, but to the DeBeers Corporation; and each producer knows that any violation of its contractual obligations will subject it to retribution at the hands of DeBeers.

The precise nature of the diamond contracts is unknown because the parties involved have refused to release them. It is generally understood, however, that DeBeers insists on being both the sole purchaser and the price setter and that the CSO is the sole distributor. In addition, the company reserves the right to limit its purchases

---

[23] One exception to this pattern is Guinea, which sells its stones through an independent London-based distributor. Because the total Guinean production amounts to only 1.5 percent of the world total, DeBeers has decided to overlook this exception. In addition, though, the company that handles the Guinean stones had demonstrated that it has no desire to deviate from the pricing and sales pattern established by the cartel.

[24] In some cases the contracts allow for some independent sales of industrial stones. A huge new venture in Australia, for instance, has agreed to market only three-quarters of its industrial stones through the CSO. All its gem diamonds, though, will still be handled by the CSO. See "Diamonds Stockpile Shatters Illusions," Survey, *Financial Times*, May 25, 1982.

during years of slack demand, with the producer still agreeing not to seek other buyers.

In one contract that has been made public, an agreement signed in 1946 between DeBeers and a leading diamond producer in the Belgian Congo, these provisions were explicitly laid out. DeBeers reserved the right to set the minimum level of purchases from the producer, allowing the maximum to fluctuate in accordance with market conditions. If, for any period of the contract, the producer's output was higher than the amount DeBeers wanted to purchase, then the producer was obliged to stockpile the excess production at its own expense. DeBeers also reserved the right to set prices at whatever level it deemed appropriate and to change prices whenever it so desired. Finally, the producer also promised not to sell any rough diamonds "outside the agreed marketing channels."[25]

In return for complying with these rather rigid restrictions, the other producers reap the traditional returns of a cartel: stable prices, guaranteed purchases, and a buffer against the cold winds of competition. In particular, each producer knows that its own profits will never be compromised by a flood of outside diamonds. As long as all the major producers are tied to DeBeers, each one can be confident that the others will not defect and thus that their collective rewards are virtually ensured.

Regulating Sales

The power of the cartel does not, however, rest simply with its control of diamond supplies; rather, it extends throughout the length of the "diamond pipeline" and into the distribution and marketing of diamond gems. After DeBeers has obtained its diamonds—either from its own mines or purchased from outside sources—it then sends them to the London office of the Central Selling Organisation, known in the trade as the Syndicate. Here, under the watchful eye of DeBeers, over 80 percent of the world's diamonds trade hands in a bizarre, almost ritualistic, transaction.

DeBeers decides which of the world's diamond brokers will be permitted to attend the ten yearly sales, known as "sights." In the

---

[25] Lenzen, *History of Diamond Production*, pp. 189–90.

diamond world, being named a sightholder is the highest honor, and sightholders are held in the highest esteem. They are also in a position to reap significant financial rewards. About five weeks before each sight the sightholders inform the CSO of their preferences— how many stones, what quality, what colors, and so forth. The CSO then tries to match these preferences with its own needs and supplies, determining what stones will be offered to which sightholder and how much the entire package will cost. Next the gem stones are divided into individual parcels, placed in plain brown shoeboxes, and offered to the predetermined distributors. There is no bargaining. The buyers must either take the entire contents of their alloted parcel or turn all the stones back. Generally they take the parcel. "DeBeers," one dealer acknowledges, "is like the Mafia . . . but it is good for the trade."[26]

In this fashion, DeBeers and the Syndicate are able to shape the course of the international diamond market from year to year. If DeBeers sees an overabundance of large stones in its stockpiles, it will fill the packages with large stones. If it senses a recession, it will inflate the selling prices of the parcels so as to prevent diamonds from suffering a fall in real value.[27] And if it suspects that any of the brokers are undercutting prices or otherwise deviating from the established rules of the game, it will fill their parcels with inferior stones.[28]

Through mechanisms such as these the diamond cartel has been able to exert its legendary domination of the international diamond market. By regulating, down to the carat, how many and what types of stones are permitted to enter the market, the cartel can fine-tune both the supply and the price levels of diamonds. Moreover, even when external economic forces such as exchange rate changes and depressionary pressures threaten to cause fluctuations in the market, the cartel can take refuge in the fact that DeBeers will always act as buyer of first resort. Indeed, ever since the depression nearly closed the mines at Kimberley, DeBeers has used its significant financial resources to stockpile diamonds during economic downturns. Thus,

[26] Paul Gibson, "Can a Cartel Be Forever?" *Forbes*, May 28, 1979, p. 50.
[27] Eric Bruton, *Diamonds* (London: N.A.G. Press, 1978), p. 172.
[28] See, for instance, "The Cartel Lives to Face Another Threat," *Economist*, January 10, 1987, p. 59.

when the economy is weak and demand for luxury items low, both DeBeers and the CSO fill their stockpiles with excess diamonds; when demand improves, they sell from inventory. In the process, the cartel pays its dues to the producers, protecting them from the inevitable shifts in the market.

Acting as a buffer, however, can be extremely costly. In 1981, for instance, the CSO responded to rising interest rates and slumping commodity prices with its normal strategy of withholding stones from the market. By the end of the year, the CSO's sales had slipped to 46 percent below their 1980 level, which left DeBeers with a stockpile estimated to be equal to a normal year's worth of sales.[29] In the process, the company spent between $700 million and $1 billion of its own cash reserves to support diamond prices.[30] It also succeeded in protecting the diamond trade and preventing defection.

Still, not even the legendarily deep pockets of DeBeers are sufficient to protect the cartel forever. And even with its distribution network and its demand levels so tightly determined, the cartel is still haunted by supply-side fears. For despite its tremendous power in the market, DeBeers has not been able to eradicate its one great vulnerability: its profitability still depends completely on the public perception of diamonds as both scarce and special. If all the diamonds that exist in stockpiles were ever released onto the market, the illusion that surrounds diamonds would shatter and prices would plummet. Likewise, if diamonds were ever considered as investments, something to be bought and sold, traded and hoarded, their mystique would be undermined and their long-term value as jewelry decreased.

Thus, although the diamond cartel is extremely powerful, it is also more sensitive than are other cartels to even the smallest defection from its ranks. To maintain the value of diamonds, the mystique of scarcity must be perpetuated. And to ensure scarcity, the cartel must also ensure cooperation.

[29] "The Diamond Cartel Is Losing Its Edge," *Business Week*, March 22, 1982, p. 43.
[30] Peter W. Bernstein, "DeBeers and the Diamond Debacle," *Fortune*, September 6, 1982, p. 44.

COOPERATION AND COERCION

To a large extent, the cartel has been lucky. Because membership brings such privileges, the attractions of defection are easier to resist. In addition, though, the DeBeers Corporation has gone to great lengths to demonstrate the high costs of defection. Whenever a break in the ranks has appeared, DeBeers has responded quickly and forcefully, punishing the defector and creating a powerful example for those who might be tempted to follow suit. Eventually, the defectors come back after realizing that they cannot fight the concerted power of the cartel. Thus the cartel is perpetuated by a combination of cooperation and coercion, each of the members choosing to collaborate because the risks of defection are too high to bear.

Facing the Threats: Defection from Within

Ironically enough, it was the great prosperity enjoyed by the diamond cartel in the 1960s and 1970s that eventually created a series of challenges to the cartel's power. Thanks to a brilliant advertising campaign, diamond engagement rings had become nearly compulsory in the United States and Japan, and diamond sales had expanded consistently throughout the postwar years. Moreover, DeBeers and its advertisers had been remarkably successful in their efforts to convince consumers that "diamonds are forever" and therefore that a diamond, once bought and presented, should never be resold. As a result, no secondhand market for diamonds existed, and DeBeers and the CSO were able to take advantage of a very inelastic demand to set prices at whatever level they deemed most appropriate, constrained only, it seemed, by the number of engagements in any given year. During the 1970s, fourteen price increases were imposed, pushing the cost of a $1,000 diamond in 1970 to $3,690 by 1979 and resulting in a tenfold increase in DeBeers's profits.[31] Riding DeBeers's coattails, the other members of the cartel prospered as well; diamond producers received more from the CSO for their rough sales, and dealers who bought from the Syndicate could resell their purchases immediately for an instant profit of

---

[31] *Jewelers' Circular-Keystone*, March 1988, p. 191.

about 10 percent. Eventually business was so good that even industry insiders became greedy.

The real troubles began in Tel Aviv, a major diamond-cutting center and home to many of the world's largest diamond dealers. At the same time that the diamond industry was faring so well, Israel was suffering tremendous economic difficulties. With inflation hitting record levels and the shekel rapidly declining, many Israeli dealers began to turn to their own diamond stocks as a means of beating the country's rampant inflation and bolstering their own financial circumstances.

Before long, diamond hoarding had become commonplace among the Israeli dealers. Even the banks, many of which had a vested interest in the financial well-being of the Israeli diamond industry, helped out by providing the merchants with low-interest loans. In 1977, Israeli diamantaires could borrow money at a rate of 6 percent, about 25 percentage points below the prevailing market rate.[32] Flush with ready money and worried about the state of Israel's economy, the dealers rushed to convert all their personal wealth into diamonds.

The rest of the trade, of course, quickly realized what the Israelis were doing. Soon, despite pointed warnings from DeBeers about the evils of gambling in diamonds, dealers in other major centers joined the speculative fray. And the more diamonds they plucked from the pipeline, the tighter the consumer market became and the higher prices were pushed at the retail level. Even those dealers who did not hoard the stones fed the frenzy, often reselling their parcels from the CSO at a tremendous markup without even bothering to examine the contents.[33]

At this point, DeBeers was not threatened financially by the sideline dealings of its intermediaries; indeed, the rise in diamond prices meant that the company realized greater profits. But DeBeers also realized that in the long run the diamond cartel could not withstand such uncontrolled speculation or widespread disobedience in its ranks. Eventually the speculative bubble would burst and prices would collapse, leaving the cartel in disarray and the value of dia-

[32] Bernstein, "DeBeers and the Diamond Debacle," p. 44.
[33] Ibid.

monds uncertain. DeBeers was already having to fend off threats of defection from its own producers, who resented having to sell directly to the CSO when diamonds were fetching much higher prices on the open market. To prevent these defections and maintain stability in the market, the cartel had to restore order in its ranks.

DeBeers sprang into action. Early in 1977, Harry Oppenheimer sent his cousin Anthony on a mission to Tel Aviv. Oppenheimer informed the Israeli dealers in no uncertain terms that DeBeers was angry and that it intended to reduce by 20 percent the quantity of stones that the dealers in question would be permitted to purchase from the CSO. Given the mood of the moment, however, this message backfired. Faced with the prospect of fewer incoming stones, the Israelis became even more vigilant about holding on to those already in their possession. Moreover, the threat of a cutback prompted many Israeli dealers and manufacturers to pay huge premiums for diamonds sold to other CSO sightholders and even to purchase some diamonds illegally from small but flourishing black markets in Antwerp and Liberia.[34] Their purchases, of course, pushed prices even higher. And still, the banks complied; by 1978 the Israeli banks had extended $850 million in loans to diamond dealers, all of which was backed only by the diamonds lying in the dealers' vaults.[35] Most frightening for DeBeers, though, was the rapid increase in diamond stocks outside its control. By early 1978, prices had soared so high that CSO sightholders could turn around and resell their shoeboxes for 50 percent more that they had paid the Syndicate. Apparently, some dealers were doubling their money in one day.[36] Clearly the Oppenheimers had to find a new tactic and a more powerful way to force the liquidation of the Israeli stockpiles without further weakening the cartel.

Thus, in March 1978, DeBeers attacked the speculative bubble by levying an unprecedented 40 percent surcharge on all diamonds sold through the CSO. In effect, the surcharge was a temporary price increase that made speculation a far riskier business. With a 40 percent surcharge, a $100,000 lot of diamonds cost the dealer

---

[34] Edward Jay Epstein, "Have You Ever Tried to Sell a Diamond?" *Atlantic Monthly*, February 1982, p. 32.

[35] Ibid.

[36] Gibson, "Can a Cartel Be Forever?" p. 47.

$140,000; and because the surcharge could be withdrawn without warning at any time, the dealer's newly acquired lot would be worth only $100,000.

At the same time, DeBeers also began to exert more direct pressure on various members of the cartel. The most troublesome Israeli dealers were stripped of their valuable CSO sights, and even some merchants who had just done business with the Israelis were also summarily dismissed. One respected trade journal referred to De-Beers's action as a purge; industry rumors claimed that 125 out of 300 regular sightholders had been eliminated, including some of the best-known U.S. dealers.[37] Reportedly, DeBeers executives also paid a visit to several Israeli banks and urged them to raise the interest rates on all diamond loans.[38]

Together, the surcharge and the arm-twisting had an almost immediate effect on the market. By the summer of 1978, interest rates on diamond loans were back up to 50 percent, and diamond prices had cooled. Cut off from both diamonds and credit, the dealers in Tel Aviv began drawing down their stockpiles. Israeli diamonds then flooded the market, helping restore prices to normal levels and dampening the speculative fever. By July, DeBeers could safely reduce the surcharge to 10 percent, confident that the market was returning to normal.

In the process of readjustment, hundreds of dealers went bankrupt, and employment among Israeli diamond cutters dropped 25 percent, from twelve to nine thousand.[39] The cartel, though, had retained control.

Muddling through the Aftermath

Unfortunately, the full effects of the events of 1977 to 1979 could not be eliminated that quickly, and they continued to reverberate through the market, foiling DeBeers's efforts to restore full stability.

To a large extent, DeBeers itself was to blame. Uncomfortable

---

[37] Ibid., p. 46.

[38] See ibid., p. 44; and Ettagale Laure, "Report from Africa: The DeBeers Contingencies," *Jewelers' Circular-Keystone*, September 1987, p. 67.

[39] Patrick J. Regan, "The Shattering of the Diamond Market," *Financial Analysts' Journal* (July/August 1981): 15.

with the surcharge, the company removed it completely in August 1978 and went back to its traditional policy of simply dictating prices at the level befitting a monopolist. But because the market was still heated up, the price increases came in rapid succession—30 percent, 13 percent, and 12 percent, all in a matter of several months. By 1980, diamond prices had risen 140 percent above their 1975 level,[40] and thousands of investors had put their money in diamonds. Then, in 1981 the U.S. Federal Reserve Bank raised interest rates to unforeseen heights, and diamond prices, along with those of gold and silver, collapsed. All the dealers who had stockpiled diamonds at the elevated prices were now in serious financial straits, and the diamond pipeline was bursting with stones that nobody wanted to buy.

Once again, DeBeers responded quickly and definitively, asserting its control over the industry and restoring some measure of stability to the market. This time, though, the company paid a much higher price for leadership. Unwilling to allow the excess supply of diamonds to drive prices down any further, DeBeers began buying, using its own financial resources to stockpile all those diamonds that the market could not bear. Simultaneously, the CSO also cut back sharply on the quantities of diamonds it sold to its sightholders and added the rest to its own separate stockpile. By 1984, DeBeers alone had a stockpile estimated to be worth $1.95 billion.[41] But unlike OPEC or the International Tin Council, which never recovered from the commodity crash of 1981, the diamond cartel remained intact.

The Zairian Defection

The display of DeBeers's power and the fates that befell the Israeli dealers in 1979 were sufficient for a while to deter the cartel's intermediaries from defecting further. Indeed, as one broker described the general sentiment among the middle ranks of the trade, "They [DeBeers] sacrificed millions for themselves in order to prevent others from making money too; they want everybody to be slaves for DeBeers."[42] Added another: "The Syndicate knows when you sneeze

[40] Bernstein, "DeBeers and the Diamond Debacle," p. 45.
[41] Jewelers' *Circular-Keystone*, March 1988, p. 194.
[42] David E. Koskoff, *The Diamond World* (New York: Harper & Row, 1981), p. 147.

or take a leak. They have a spy system that would put the CIA to shame. They know everything there is to know about anyone of any significance in the diamond world."[43]

Nevertheless, in the early 1980s one of DeBeers's producers began to get restless and to pose a new threat of defection—this time from the supply side. In this case, the threat was straightforward: unless DeBeers paid the producer higher prices for its rough stones, the producer would strike out on its own, competing with the cartel and driving prices down.

In 1981, President Mobutu Sese Seko of Zaire announced that his country would no longer sell diamonds to the CSO. Instead, Zaire, the world's largest supplier of industrial diamonds, had negotiated separate marketing contracts with two Antwerp-based and one British diamond broker. Some financial analysts at the time claimed that Zaire was reacting against the financial terms of its contract with DeBeers; during the period from 1979 to 1981, the country claimed to have paid $40 million to DeBeers on sales of $200 million.[44] Other, more cynical observers suggested that "the Belgians and the Brits just offered Mobutu a bigger bribe than DeBeers would."[45]

Even if DeBeers had lost the bidding, however, it was still not willing to give up the game. As one observer noted, "For DeBeers the amount was small but the principle large: the confidence of producers is essential glue for the cartel."[46] Just two months after Zaire's diamonds entered the market independently, about one million carats of industrial diamonds from undisclosed sources suddenly flooded the market, causing the price of Zairian diamonds to drop from $3 per carat to less than $1.80. DeBeers executives solemnly denied that they had taken any specific actions to punish the Zairians for their defection. In public, the company defended any influx of industrial stones on purely commercial grounds. "There is a big difference between dumping and market support," asserted one company spokesperson. "Why should we, as a competitive company, support the price of boart [industrial diamond] when we have enough

[43] Ibid., p. 142.
[44] "All Eyes on Zaire's Game of Solitaire," *South*, October 1982, p. 59.
[45] Quoted in David E. Foltz, "The Cartel and the Congo," Unpublished paper, Princeton University, January 11, 1983, p. 22.
[46] Bernstein, "DeBeers and the Diamond Debacle," p. 48.

stockpiled? We are not a charitable institution."[47] Clearly, though, DeBeers had been at work. As a director of one of Zaire's major buyers described it: "After Zaire broke away from the CSO, we were offered a large quantity of boart by others presumably working for DeBeers. There were two elements involved. One was to preclude companies like ourselves from buying boart from Zaire. The other was to make the point that no matter what Zaire does, the CSO are still leaders in the market and can determine the price at will."[48]

By driving down the price of Zaire's diamonds, DeBeers was also driving down the price for its own industrial production. Moreover, it was accepting this financial burden to punish a supplier whose production had accounted for only about 3 percent of its total receipts.[49] For DeBeers, though, stable long-term profits were more important than short-term losses, and the principle of unity had to be maintained. The cartel would be preserved, and defectors would be punished.

Eventually, DeBeers made its point. Diamonds were Zaire's fourth largest earner of foreign exchange,[50] and facing a severe economic crisis due to lower commodity prices, a sharp drop in agricultural output, and a large budget deficit, Mobutu could no longer afford to hold out against DeBeers. Zaire simply realized that it did not have the financial resources to ride out a slump, especially not if the cartel continued to punish the country by depressing prices even further. In 1983, the government of Zaire met with representatives of De-Beers and requested a renewal of its old contract. DeBeers complied, but forced Zaire to accept terms that were much less favorable than those it had previously enjoyed. In the aftermath, one DeBeers executive quipped in a published interview, "Anyone want to follow Zaire?"[51]

---

[47] "All Eyes on Zaire's Game of Solitaire," p. 59.
[48] Pincas Rothem, quoted in *South*, October 1982, p. 59.
[49] Koskoff, *Diamond World*, p. 103.
[50] Zaire's other key exports were copper, cobalt, and coffee.
[51] Bernstein, "DeBeers and the Diamond Debacle," p. 48.

ACCOMPLICES IN CHAOS: THE SOVIET UNION AND THE DIAMOND CARTEL

In its relations with Zaire, as with most of the other diamond producers, DeBeers clearly retains the upper hand.[52] Because it speaks with the full power of the cartel behind it, the corporation can dictate its terms and demand retribution. The cooperation that ensues, therefore, is a coercive sort of cooperation, based not only on an understanding of joint gains but also on a very credible threat of retaliation.

There is, however, one significant exception to this general pattern, one case in which the potential power of its adversary is so great that even DeBeers has had to compromise rather than threaten and cooperate rather than compel.

Quite simply, the Russians have the potential ability to dethrone DeBeers and destroy the international diamond cartel. What was until recently the Soviet Union is still the world's second largest producer of gemstones and the third largest producer of industrials; by value, Siberia is the world's most important producer of newly mined gem diamonds.[53] If the Russians were ever to dump even a fraction of their stockpiled diamonds onto the market, diamond prices would plummet, and the diamond empire would crumble. Alternatively, the Russians could join with one of the other major producers—Namibia, Botswana, or Angola—and use their combined resources first to break the power of the South African–controlled cartel and then to replace it with a new network of their own.

---

[52] I have borrowed the phrase "accomplices in chaos" from Stanley Hoffmann, "International Systems and International Law," in Klauss Knorr and Sidney Verba, eds., *The International System* (Princeton: Princeton University Press, 1961).

[53] Although the figures for Soviet production are not wholly reliable, it is generally believed that the country has historically produced 10.5 to 11.0 million carats of diamonds a year, of which 20 to 25 percent are of gem or near-gem quality. In terms of value, Soviet diamond sales have been estimated at about $750 to $800 million a year; by contrast, diamond exports from Botswana and South Africa have been valued at only $550 and $650 million, respectively. See Peter Miller, "The Outlook for Diamonds," Mining Research Report (London: Messel, February 1987), p. 98. More recently the Economist Intelligence Unit estimated that the USSR/CIS produced 14 million carats of diamonds in 1991, and ranked their production first in the world in terms of total value. See *Diamonds: A Cartel and Its Future*, Special Report No. M702, Economist Intelligence Unit, August 1992, p. 5.

In its relations with the Russians, therefore, even DeBeers has had to tread lightly. Specifically, it has had to forgo coercion in favor of bargaining and collaboration. The affiliation between the Russian diamond agencies and the DeBeers Corporation is thus a striking example of competitive cooperation. Each one has the power to advance its own short-term interests by destroying the other; yet through a process of implicit bargaining and consultation, the two have managed to resist the temptation of unilateral defection and to join together in pursuit of mutual gains. In the process, cooperation has been forged and maintained. What remains to be seen, however, is how well this cooperation will survive the breakup of the Soviet Union and the collapse of its internal structures of control.

Forging the Link: DeBeers and the Soviets

Although it is not well recognized by the general public, the relationship between DeBeers and the former Soviet Union is a widely accepted "secret" within the diamond trade. Indeed, despite its potential ability to outproduce even the richest sources of diamonds and an ideological agenda that rails against both monopolies and South Africa, the Soviet Union was long a member of the diamond cartel, playing by its rules and abiding by its wishes.

As early as 1957, Harry Oppenheimer, the chairman of DeBeers, realized that the discovery of diamonds in Siberia gave the Soviet Union the latent ability to destroy the diamond cartel. Accordingly, rather than fighting the Soviets, Oppenheimer chose to employ the same tactics that his predecessors, Ernest Oppenheimer and Cecil Rhodes, had favored. Stressing that the profitability of the entire industry rested with the industry's ability to manage the number of diamonds on the market, Oppenheimer wooed the Soviets into the cartel, promising to buy up the entire Soviet production of gem diamonds for a price that would be renegotiated annually, and then to market the stones through the CSO in London.[54]

Apparently the Soviets consented to Oppenheimer's terms and signed the agreement, despite the fact that official relations between

[54] Kurt M. Campbell, *Soviet Policy towards South Africa* (New York: St. Martin's, 1986), p. 101.

the Soviet Union and South Africa had been terminated earlier that year. Because of the political delicacies involved, the full conditions of the contract were never revealed, and both parties repeatedly denied the existence of any agreement between them.[55] In 1963, Oppenheimer implicitly confirmed that a contract had been signed but asserted that it had been severed in response to growing political tensions between the Soviet Union and South Africa. In the DeBeers annual report for 1963, Oppenheimer stated that "on account of Russian support for the boycotting of trade with South Africa, our contract to buy diamonds has not been renewed."[56]

Still, all members of the diamond industry knew that the Soviets were still selling their rough diamonds through DeBeers and that the CSO still handled all distribution of Soviet rough stones. Although the details of the negotiation process were never described, it appears that executives from DeBeers met regularly with Soviet officials to fine-tune the specifics of purchases and price.[57] These meetings occurred secretly and were limited to the highest echelons of the diamond trade. When political tensions were at their peak, the meetings reportedly took place in such unlikely locations as foreign landing strips and the balcony of the Bolshoi Ballet.

During the course of these negotiations, the position of the two parties was consistently reinforced. DeBeers wanted to keep the Soviet diamonds off the market and ensure that the Soviets were never tempted to open an independent channel for diamond sales. The Soviets, meanwhile, wanted to use their vast diamond reserves to extract as much hard currency from DeBeers as they possibly could. They would comply with the cartel, it seems, but only if DeBeers would pay the price. And thus the stage was set for a continuous process of bargaining, compromise, and—ultimately—cooperation.

---

[55] See, for instance, "Russian Deals Denied," *Diamond Registry Bulletin*, August 15, 1981, p. 4; "DeBeers Denies Russian Deal," *Diamond Registry Bulletin*, January 31, 1985, p. 1; and "Soviet Sales to DeBeers—$700 Million Annually?" *Diamond World Review* 38 (Spring 1986): 54.

[56] Cited in Edward Jay Epstein, *The Rise and Fall of Diamonds*, (New York: Simon and Schuster, 1982), p. 116.

[57] Campbell, *Soviet Policy towards South Africa*, p. 103.

Shadowboxing

Despite its best efforts, DeBeers has never been able to control the full stock of Soviet diamonds. Rather, the Soviets have always kept a significant portion of their diamond production for their own domestic use and have marketed another portion through their own independent channels. For the most part, these independent sales have conformed to the general guidelines of the market and have done little to disturb the authority or stability of the diamond cartel. On several occasions, though, the Soviets have employed these channels more menacingly, using them to threaten DeBeers and wrest favorable concessions while still remaining within the confines of the cartel.

Before the breakup of the Soviet Union, all Russian diamonds that did not go to DeBeers were instead channeled to one of three uses. First, the Soviet state kept all its industrial production to serve its own domestic military and industrial needs. Second, the Soviet diamond agencies sold about 5 percent of their total rough production to the general public. And, third, a certain (and varying) percentage of the Soviet stones were cut, polished, marketed, and distributed by agencies of the Soviet state.

Several times a year, a select group of Western diamond dealers were invited to visit the Moscow offices of Russalmaz, the state agency that handled all Soviet exports of precious metals and jewelry. At these periodic "sights" or "tenders," the Soviets sold their rough gemstones directly to the diamond trade, thus avoiding the DeBeers intermediaries and occasionally shaving a few dollars off the going market price. Reportedly, the Soviet sights in Moscow mimicked the DeBeers sights precisely: the diamonds were sold only in prearranged parcels, no bargaining was permitted, and all deals were concluded with the traditional Yiddish blessing of "Mazel und brucha" (good luck and blessings).[58] Although figures are highly unreliable in this area, observers estimated that the Soviets regularly exported between twenty-six and thirty-seven thousand carats of rough diamonds a month and that their profits on these sales were at least 10 percent higher than what they received for their regular sales

[58] Epstein, *Rise and Fall of Diamonds,* pp. 195–96.

to the CSO.[59] In addition, the Soviets also regularly sold polished diamonds on the open market, a privilege that few other producers were allowed.[60] Through offices in Geneva, Antwerp, Frankfurt, and Toronto, Russalmaz's export subsidiary, Almazjuvelirexport, distributed small, extremely high-quality stones known in the trade as "silver bears." Although the figures are again somewhat unreliable, it has been estimated that these sorts of open-market sales regularly accounted for between 20 and 40 percent of the Soviets' total gemstone production.

Even more important than the amount of these sales, however, was the inherent power that they symbolized. Of all the producing members of the diamond cartel, only the Soviets had the capacity to produce and process their own fine-quality gemstones. To many industry watchers, therefore, the Soviet sales constituted a direct affront to DeBeers and a warning of the Soviets' potential to operate independently of the cartel.[61]

For the most part, these fears were unfounded. The Soviets generally conformed to the rules of the cartel, selling their diamonds at near-market rates and keeping their quantities within certain narrowly defined limits.[62] From time to time, however, the Soviets would explicitly break the rules. And when they did, their sales through Russalmaz assumed a new and rather threatening importance. Remember that every rough diamond that the Soviets did not sell to DeBeers was instead sold through Russalmaz. Thus, every diamond that Russalmaz sold represented a Soviet decision not to sell part of its production to the diamond cartel. Accordingly, sales through Russalmaz became the means by which the Soviet Union could tinker with the workings of the international diamond market and threaten the leadership of DeBeers.

Specifically, the Soviets were able to use their Russalmaz sales to

[59] "Signals to Russia," *Diamond Intelligence Briefs*, January 30, 1987, p. 1; and *Diamond World Review* 59 (July–August 1990): 54.

[60] Since the opening of the giant Argyle mine in Australia, the Australians have also been permitted by DeBeers to polish and market their own gemstones. Unlike those from Soviet production, however, most of the Australian stones are colored, or "fancies," and are not well received within the industry.

[61] See, for instance, "A Russian C.S.O.?" *Diamond Intelligence Briefs*, March 1, 1987, p. 1.

[62] See, for example, *Diamond World Review* 7 (Autumn 1982): 16.

flood the market with polished diamonds and exert tremendous pressure on DeBeers. Because the markets for polished and rough stones are so naturally and inevitably connected, any sudden outpouring of gemstones will cause drastic reverberations throughout the diamond industry. Not only will the traditional cutting centers find themselves competing against a new and unexpected source of finished gems, but the demand for rough diamonds is bound to suffer as well. When the new source of diamonds also offers them at prices much lower than those prevailing in the usual channels of supply, the effects are likely to be even more dramatic.

The first time that the Soviets apparently dumped diamonds occurred between 1970 and 1975, when millions of carats of Soviet diamonds were flowing annually into DeBeers's London office. As mentioned above, the original contract between DeBeers and Moscow had arranged for the company to buy all Russian rough production; but by the mid-1970s, not even DeBeers could keep up with the enormous number of diamonds flowing out of Siberia. Moreover, nearly all the Soviet stones were melees—medium-grade diamonds ranging from one-tenth to seven-tenths of a carat in weight. At first, DeBeers tried to deal with this oversupply by finding new uses for melees. With its advertising agency, the corporation quickly invented and promoted the "eternity ring," an anniversary band composed almost entirely of melees.

Even the eternity ring, however, could not absorb the surge in Soviet production. As Edward Jay Epstein notes: "By 1976, DeBeers was choking on the ceaseless flow of greenish diamonds that arrived each month in London on the Aeroflot jet from Moscow. DeBeers had little choice but to accept the Soviet consignments. Otherwise, the Soviets would almost certainly dump these diamonds, which now amounted to some 2 million carats a year of gems, on the world market, and cause a ruinous collapse in prices."[63]

[63] Epstein, *Rise and Fall of Diamonds*, p. 189. Here and elsewhere, Epstein argues that these diamonds were actually synthetic and that they came not from the mines at Mirny but were instead the result of Soviet advances in high-pressure physics. No one denies Epstein's contention that the technology to turn carbon into diamonds is available; indeed, Western scientists have been synthesizing diamonds since the mid-1960s. The problem that Western labs have always faced, however, and the problem that Epstein claims the Soviets have overcome, is to manufacture the synthetic stones at a cost low enough to make them competitive with naturally mined diamonds. As evi-

Simultaneously, the polished markets in Antwerp and Tel Aviv were reporting sudden large influxes of tiny, perfectly cut Soviet diamonds. Although Russalmaz offered no official statistics, dealers in Antwerp at the time estimated that in 1970 alone the Soviets had put half a million silver bears on the market.[64]

Publicly, DeBeers denied that the Soviets had either the capability or the desire to squeeze any sector of the diamond market. As it explained in the 1971 issue of the *International Diamond Annual*: "There has been no indication that the Soviet Russian authorities have the slightest intention of dumping their polished goods on Western markets. On the contrary, the Soviet authorities appear to accept that the industry they have been at great pains to develop and establish would founder if the market for diamonds in the Western world were undermined or were not held in strong hands."[65]

Privately, however, DeBeers could not afford to be so sanguine. And in 1973, the cartel began to move against the Soviets. Initially DeBeers contacted its largest buyer in Tel Aviv, Joseph Goldfinger, and asked him to go to Russalmaz's Moscow office and arrange to buy large quantities of the silver bears; the hope was that Gold-finger's preemptive buying would at least help to stem the tide of Soviet polished exports to Europe. When the Soviets' political leanings made them reluctant to deal openly with an Israeli, they agreed to sell approximately $2 million worth of silver bears each month to I. Hennig, a prominent London broker, with the understanding that it would then turn the stones over to Goldfinger.[66] Eventually, Gold-finger's purchases proved sufficient to absorb the glut. By 1976 the silver bear offensive had subsided.

In retrospect it seems that a deal of sorts had been made. The Soviets stopped flooding the market but, in return, extracted better terms from DeBeers—most probably, higher prices for their rough sales to the CSO. From the Soviet perspective, their threat had paid

---

dence of his claim, Epstein notes that the Soviet stones were all nearly identical in size and color, a phenomenon rarely found in naturally mined stones. No one else I spoke with, however, believed that the Soviet stones were synthetic.

[64] Ibid., p. 195.
[65] Ibid., p. 196.
[66] Ibid., pp. 197–98.

off. And from DeBeers's view, the cost of meeting the Soviets' demand was worth the market stability it ensured.[67]

In 1984, though, the Soviets began to flood the market again, concentrating on larger, more expensive stones. At the beginning of the year, Soviet exports of polished diamonds to Antwerp were approximately 20,000–30,000 carats a month, with an average price of $642 a carat.[68] In April, the Soviets suddenly lunged into the Antwerp market; exports rose to an average of 78,200 carats a month, while the average price per carat fell to little more than $500.[69] By October, they had delivered $242 million worth of diamonds, 98 percent more than they had delivered during the same ten-month period in the previous year—and they had delivered their parcels at prices 10 to 15 percent lower than the market rate.[70] Not surprisingly, the high quantities and low prices of the Soviet stones sent the market, built on a history of incremental price increases and stable sources of supply, into a frenzy. As one prominent dealer noted: "We were coming onto a good trend; the market was getting better. But then suddenly, the Russians started selling at cheaper prices and disrupted the market. . . . Customers became confused [because they didn't know where prices would go]. The Russians touched the market for only three or four months, but their presence has had lasting effects."[71] Added another: "It brought a break in the price structure from which we never recovered. . . . the lowest [priced] stone sets the price. . . . the Soviets' cheaper prices pushed a lot of people into the red."[72]

To ride out the onslaught, many dealers who typically purchased rough stones and then paid to have them cut and polished quickly switched their tactics. Instead, they bought the lower-priced Soviet finished goods; in the process, both DeBeers and the international cutting industry suffered tremendous losses. According to industry analysts, the Soviets' actions were directly responsible for cutting $75

---

[67] This account was confirmed to me in confidential interviews.

[68] "DeBeers: The Russians Won't Dump," *Jewelers' Circular-Keystone*, August 1985, p. 415.

[69] Ibid.

[70] "Diamond Dumping Aftermath Still Haunts Antwerp Market," *National Jeweler*, January 16, 1985, pp. 1, 114.

[71] Rafi Arslanian, quoted in *National Jeweler*, October 16, 1985, pp. 1, 114.

[72] Jules Polakiewicz, quoted in ibid., p. 114.

to $140 million from DeBeers's second-half profits.[73] And the diamond manufacturers, meeting at their biannual convention in July 1984, issued a rare petition to DeBeers, urging the company to take whatever measures were necessary to end the Soviets' discount sales.[74] Over the course of the next year, the Soviets and DeBeers played a cautious bargaining game. The Soviets wanted to push DeBeers as far as possible but not so far as to compromise the stability of the market and their own position within it. DeBeers, on the other hand, had to find some means of appeasing the Soviets without undermining its own reputation as a tough enforcer.

Indeed, one of DeBeers's primary concerns during the crisis period was to ensure the rest of the industry that the cartel was still in place and the market still solid. In a rare announcement from the Diamond Trading Company in London in the summer of 1985, DeBeers broke its customary silence concerning its relation with the Soviets and announced that it had been "authoritatively informed that the Soviet Union has no intention of increasing the supply of polished diamonds on the world market and that current price levels will be maintained."[75]

Meanwhile, the Soviets were bargaining. Although no one knows for certain whether any actual negotiating sessions occurred, it is clear that bargains were being struck between the major players in the diamond cartel. The Soviets demanded a greater share of the cartel's rewards and demonstrated their ability to punish those who refused their demands. DeBeers had no choice but to respond. And, thus, in the aftermath of the Soviets' "diamond dumping frenzy," DeBeers and the Soviets signed an unprecedented agreement in which DeBeers agreed to increase both the quantity of rough diamonds that it would buy each year from the Soviets and the prices that it would pay for them.[76] Early in 1985, DeBeers announced a 7.5 percent increase in rough diamond prices. Within months, Soviet

[73] Russell Shor, "Will Moscow Scuttle Diamond Market—Again?" *Jewelers' Circular-Keystone,* March 1985, p. 50.
[74] Ibid.
[75] Cited in "DeBeers: The Russians Won't Dump," p. 415.
[76] See, for instance, "Russia's Predicament and the World Diamond Market," *Diamond Intelligence Briefs,* April 30, 1986, p. 1.

polished exports to the West had subsided to more normal levels, decreasing by about one-third on the Antwerp market.[77]

For DeBeers, the price hike must have been an extraordinarily expensive measure. Not only was it forced to pay more for all the many diamonds that it bought, but because it was also buying more than it could possibly sell without allowing retail prices to fall, it had to increase its own extensive stockpiles. Thus, the result of DeBeers's new agreement with the Soviet Union was to force the company to pay higher prices for diamonds for which it had no possible use. In effect, DeBeers was paying a premium for the Soviet stones just to prevent them from entering the world market.

Seen from a more theoretical level, however, DeBeers was simply absorbing the costs of cooperation. Realizing the extent to which prosperity in the diamond industry depends on a tight network of collaboration between the producers, DeBeers decided long ago to take the burdens of cooperation upon itself and to do whatever may be necessary to prevent defection from its ranks. In the Soviet case, the higher stakes and greater leverage forced DeBeers to change its tactics. Retaliation and threats would not suffice for an adversary with the potential ability to destroy the existing cartel and establish an independent system. Instead, DeBeers had to bargain, cajole, and compromise. In the end, though, the result was the same: cooperation was restored, and the cartel remained intact.

THE STRENGTH OF THE CARTEL AND THE AUTONOMY OF THE PRODUCERS

As the following chapters make clear, the international diamond cartel is a rare, almost unique, phenomenon. It has maintained a level of cooperation that has not even been achieved in most commodity markets, and it has succeeded in keeping the supply of diamonds limited and their price high.

To a considerable extent, the success of the cartel can be attrib-

[77] "Diamonds: Review and Outlook," Confidential report, David Borkum Hare, November 1980, p. 3.

uted to the institutions it has built and especially to the remarkable distribution network created by Rhodes and refined by Oppenheimer. Without a doubt, this interlocked web of producers, distributors, and buyers has facilitated cooperation among the members and made it unlikely that any single strand will attempt to break from the whole and strike out on its own.

Still, the structure of the diamond cartel cannot be viewed separately from the competitors that preside over it. Indeed, it is the competitors who maintain the structure and allow it to function as efficiently as it does. Specifically, the success of the diamond cartel is inextricably linked to the internal workings of the DeBeers Corporation. If the cartel works, it is because DeBeers has the ability to lead it and to perpetuate the cooperation that sustains it. Initially, this leadership consisted primarily of coercion and retaliation, and DeBeers's success was due to its internal capacity to issue threats and to make good on them when necessary. More recently, however, the Soviets' growing role in the market forced DeBeers to seek cooperation through conciliatory means. Luckily for the cartel, though, the entry of the Soviet Union did not significantly affect the underlying pattern of cooperation. In the Soviet Union, DeBeers found a kindred spirit of sorts, a producer with the internal characteristics that enabled it to make credible commitments, to threaten and punish, and even to shoulder some of the responsibilities of leadership. All this could change, however, with the breakup of the Soviet Union. And as we shall see below, some of the changes may already be underway.

The Power of DeBeers

Structurally, the basis of DeBeers's power is its central position in the web that is the international diamond cartel. Because all the other members are linked to the cartel via DeBeers, there is little opportunity for them to break with DeBeers or to form third-party arrangements. Only DeBeers can guarantee the producers' cooperation to the distributors and the distributors' to the producers.

The reason that DeBeers is able to exercise its power, however, has less to do with its external position than with its internal characteristics. Simply put, DeBeers has the internal strength to exercise its external power. It can threaten, punish, and compromise largely because it speaks with the authority of a single voice. And because its voice is uncontested from within, it can make credible commitments in the outside world.

To a large extent, the modern DeBeers Corporation functions as it did in Cecil Rhodes's time. It is still very much a family company, run by the Oppenheimers, their relatives, and their long-time associates. Ernest Oppenheimer passed the mantle of leadership to his son Harry, and Harry in turn bestowed these same favors on his own son, Nicholas. For years the CSO was headed by Sir Philip Oppenheimer, Harry's cousin, and run by Monty Charles, a friend of the family since childhood. Gordon Waddell, an executive director of DeBeers's sister company, Anglo American, and the long-time chairman of Rustenberg Platinum, another related firm, was also Harry's son-in-law; a second son-in-law ran one of the company's major U.S. affiliates. In addition, nearly all the top management of DeBeers are members of a close inner circle, all carefully groomed and selected, and all personally accountable to Harry Oppenheimer.[78] The top managers are treated as part of the family and, reportedly, reward this treatment by staying loyal to the Oppenheimers and to DeBeers throughout their careers. As Nicky Oppenheimer describes DeBeers's diamond business: "It's a personal business. Face to face, the whole family is sitting there. In uranium, everybody brings their lawyers. In diamonds, there are no lawyers sitting around. It's a handshake business. It's a different world. A better world."[79]

[78] Describing the training process at Anglo American, DeBeers's sister company and another of the Oppenheimers' major concerns, the *Economist* notes: "The classic . . . career starts at Oxford. Then he (hardly ever a she) returns to Johannesburg as a trainee, where he can expect to work in a variety of departments and live a life of utter boredom enlivened by an occasional drink or lunch with the chairman. . . .

A trainee who catches the chairman's eye over his tomato juice can hope to become his personal assistant. The advantage of this is that, at the end of several years as a PA, the lucky youth will know the group's inner secrets. But, while learning them he is more likely to have acquired the habits of a diplomat than those of a businessman. Whoever survives this grueling process becomes, in effect, an honorary member of the family." See "The Oppenheimer Empire: South Africa's Family Affair," *Economist*, July 1, 1989, p. 60.

[79] Quoted in Ettagale Laure, "The Next Mr. Diamond?" *Jewelers' Circular-Keystone*, September 1978, p. 94. In this context, it is also interesting to note that some of the earliest advertisements run by DeBeers emphasized the link not only between diamonds and romance but also between diamonds and family. In 1940, for instance, a

These familiar relations also mark the overall corporate structure of DeBeers. Although the company is nominally independent, it is, in fact, intricately linked to a number of other firms that together compose the "Oppenheimer empire."[80] Indeed, the DeBeers Corporation is only one strand of an intricate corporate web. All companies in "the empire" are tightly interlocked with one another and tightly controlled by their own upper management, as well as by the guiding demands of the Oppenheimer family. In addition, through a complex series of linked directorates and stock ownerships, they are all largely owned by one another. Although the full picture of these corporate relationships remains murky, it is generally acknowledged that the Oppenheimers' reach extends to some six hundred corporations involved in everything from diamonds and gold to insurance and investment houses.[81] The details of cross-ownership have never been fully revealed, but evidence indicates that ultimate control over all the companies remains firmly in the hands of E. Oppenheimer & Sons, a privately held family concern. For all practical purposes, then, the entire conglomerate functions under the direction and at the will of the Oppenheimers.

In concrete terms, this corporate closeness has two effects: first, corporate policies tend to be centralized and consistent, and second, the company does not need to respond to any desires other than those of its own leaders. Unlike most modern corporations, DeBeers rarely faces the problems of complex organizations; because all policy emanates directly from the top, there are no competing divisions within the company and no divergent goals. Rather, all decisions are built on consensus, and all divisions are working for a common, well-defined goal. Every policy that is made, therefore, is implemented and carries the full weight of the corporation behind it. Moreover,

popular ad urged: "Diamonds have been the brilliant messengers of the unspoken secrets of the heart. In his gifts of them a man leaves earth's most brilliant record of his love, his pride of family."

[80] I am borrowing this term from the *Economist* ("Oppenheimer empire"). The conglomerate has also been less grandly dubbed "the Octopus." See Peter Schmeisser, "Harry Oppenheimer's Empire: Going for the Gold," *New York Times Magazine*, March 19, 1989, p. 36.

[81] See Schmeisser, "Harry Oppenheimer's Empire," p. 36. Some estimates are even higher. The *Economist*, for instance, speculates that Anglo American alone may control as many as thirteen hundred subsidiaries. See "Oppenheimer Empire," p. 60.

DeBeers's position within the larger conglomerate means that it faces virtually no chance of a hostile takeover and has no real need to respond to shareholder demands.[82] Instead, DeBeers can afford the luxury of a longer-term viewpoint and the broader sphere of action it entails.

DeBeers's options are also enhanced by its relationship with the South African government. Contrary to popular belief, DeBeers is not an arm of the South African government, nor does it operate in collaboration with it. In fact, Harry Oppenheimer has been a staunch opponent of apartheid and a persistent critic of many government policies.[83] Nevertheless, the sheer financial power of the DeBeers network puts the company in a rather special position. As of 1986, at least half of the South African stock market was composed of the stocks of DeBeers, its sister company, Anglo American, or one of the many other firms in the Oppenheimer empire. Moreover, these firms are not just producing ordinary commodities; they control all South Africa's strategic minerals and thus constitute South Africa's economic power base. For obvious reasons, then, the South African government has rarely found any reason to interfere with the internal workings of the DeBeers Corporation, or to impose any constraints on its overseas activities. Thus, although the corporation is in no way tied to the government, it operates as an officially sanctioned national monopoly, free from governmental restraints and bureaucratic interference.

Finally, DeBeers also derives internal strength from its legendarily deep pockets and from the enormous financial resources at its disposal.[84] These resources make it possible for DeBeers to "ride out the slumps"—to suffer through the inevitable market downturns without breaking the rules of the cartel and to stockpile its own pro-

---

[82] As one industry observer noted, "Were any of [DeBeers's] various entities U.S. corporations, the machinations of profit allocation would be subject to the scrutiny of potentially dissident minority stockholders, but that is not the case with . . . South African corporations, where minority stockholders must be content with what they get or get out." Koskoff, *Diamond World*, p. 127.

[83] See, for instance, "South Africa's Mineral King," *Time*, July 13, 1981, p. 50.

[84] In 1991, DeBeers reported a net income of $789 million and diamond stocks valued at over $3 billion. In addition, it reported investments and loans valued at approximately $4.1 billion and capital reserves of over $4 billion. DeBeers Provisional Annual Financial Statements and Dividend Notices, March 1992.

duction rather than allowing the excess stones to flood the market and push prices even lower. In the early 1980s, for instance, De-Beers was able to support its diamond purchases by leaning on the income it earned from its investments in other, nonrelated subsidiaries. As Nicky Oppenheimer put it: "DeBeers has not borrowed a lot of money relative to a number of companies around the world which are considered to be financially sound. DeBeers has tremendous assets outside the industry which were acquired in the past, just to make sure that it had the financial strength to see it through very bad times."[85] Together with its immunity from shareholder pressures, the financial resources of DeBeers thus give it the luxury of weathering the bad times without succumbing to the temptations of cheating or defecting. Even more important, perhaps, it also enables the company to bear the costs of retaliation; it can punish the Israelis or the Zairians, for instance, because it can afford the damage to its own short-term interests that occur as an inevitable result of the punishment.

Taken together, these various internal characteristics strengthen DeBeers's external position and enable the company to act with impunity in the international diamond market. Because DeBeers has no internal factions, it can make policy and implement it decisively without fearing that the effects of its decisions might stir internal discontent. Because it is relatively immune both to shareholder demands and to governmental interference, it can act without worrying about any hostile reactions its behavior might incur. And because its pockets are so deep, it can afford to pay the price for whatever actions it deems necessary. In the end, DeBeers can preside over the diamond cartel largely because it can control its own internal affairs with such autonomy.

The Power of the Russians

Currently, the Russians are the great question mark in the international diamond cartel. For decades, the Soviets cooperated with DeBeers, using their formidable production to extract as many bene-

---

[85] Quoted in Johnny Roux, "Cartels Come Cartels Go But Diamonds Are Still Forever," *Diamond World Review* 38 (Spring 1986): 49, 70.

fits as possible but still generally playing by the accepted rules of the game. Now, however, all is liable to change. The breakup of the Soviet Union has meant a dramatic restructuring of the Soviet diamond industry. In time, it may even threaten the cartel itself. For decades, the Soviets were able to maintain their cooperative relationship with the cartel because they had the internal capacity to do so. Specifically, like DeBeers, the Soviets could cooperate abroad because they had such tight control over their internal factions. Because their industry was centrally run and virtually autonomous, it could act strategically, flexibly, and with an eye to its long-term prospects. And because it faced no domestic opposition, it could act with surety abroad, knowing that it would always be able to deliver its threats and fulfill its promises. As this internal structure starts to change and the centralized control of the diamond industry begins to collapse, we should also expect to see the Russian producers falter in their cooperative efforts.

In the Soviet Union, diamonds were always an affair of the state. The Soviet diamond industry began in the wake of World War II, when the government decided that the strategic applications of diamonds meant that the state would have to secure its own independent sources.[86] Consequently, the Soviet government launched a vast effort to discover and develop diamond fields within the Soviet Union. After an initial survey revealed that the land of the Yakutia province most closely resembled the geological formation of South Africa, Soviet scientists were sent to explore the frozen tundra along the banks of the Vilyuy River. Although the initial forays were turned back by temperatures that dropped to minus seventy degrees Celsius and permafrost that extended five thousand feet, subsequent expeditions discovered Siberian pipes that would quickly become as instrumental for the development of the Soviet diamond industry as the Big Hole at Kimberley had been for South Africa.

By 1960, Soviet engineers had developed the techniques necessary for recovering diamonds under the severe climactic conditions of the

---

[86] Up until this point, the Soviets had been obtaining industrial-grade diamonds by smuggling them out of Africa. The stories of the various "rings" that were working for Moscow are fascinating, if somewhat apocryphal. See, for instance, J. H. duPlessis, *Diamonds Are Dangerous: Adventures of an Agent of the International Diamond Security Organization* (London: Cassell, 1960).

Arctic. Jet engines blasted through the permafrost and dynamite charges loosened the kimberlite ore. A diamond processing plant was built at Mirny, fourteen stories high, sheathed in aluminum, and operated around the clock by automated machinery.[87] An entirely new city was established four hundred kilometers to the north at Aikhal, built on ten-foot-high legs designed to prevent the city from sinking into the summer mud. Giant pumps were constructed to chill the air below the buildings so that their heat did not cause any further melting, and the whole complex was wrapped in sheets of translucent plastic.[88] All workers in the diamond areas were paid 250 percent more than their counterparts in other parts of the country, and additional bonuses were awarded according to geographical latitude: 40 percent extra north of latitude fifty-eight degrees; 50 percent for the Arctic Circle; and 70–100 percent for the high Arctic.[89] All this development, of course, occurred at the behest of the Soviet state, and all the proceeds were put at its disposal. At first, the mines at Mirny were used only to produce industrial-grade diamonds, which were then distributed by the central authorities to defense and manufacturing concerns. It soon became evident, however, that the Siberian diamonds were too valuable to be used only as drill bits; indeed, they were among the highest-quality gemstones ever discovered. It was at this point that the Soviet state entered the international diamond market; soon afterward it also became a silent member of the diamond cartel. By 1968, diamonds had become the Soviet Union's leading cash export to the West, prompting Victor I. Tikhonov, head of the Mirny Diamond Administration to boast, "We call ourselves the country's foreign exchange department."[90]

During this period, all aspects of the Soviet diamond industry were state-owned and tightly controlled. Through a small but powerful web of agencies, the government regulated the production, processing, and sales of all stones that flowed through its domestic pipeline. All mining operations fell under the auspices of Yakutal-

[87] R. V. Huddlestone, "Siberian Diamonds," *Journal of Gemmology* (October 1984), reprinted in *Diamant*, June–July 1985, p. 13. See also N. V. Sobolev, "Siberian Diamonds—Minerals from the Earth's Mantle," *Indiaqua* 26, no. 3 (1980): 9–15.

[88] Epstein, *Rise and Fall of Diamonds*, p. 186.

[89] Huddlestone, "Siberian Diamonds," p. 14.

[90] Epstein, *Rise and Fall of Diamonds*, p. 186.

maz, an agency that was in turn subordinate to the Soviet Ministry of Nonferrous Metallurgy. Yakutalmaz handled all production of the stones and then distributed them, according to state plans, to the appropriate military and industrial consumers. Stones that remained were transferred to Russalmaz, a branch of the Ministry of Foreign Economic Relations. From that point on, Russalmaz (and its export division, Almazjuvelirexport) were the only agencies concerned with diamonds. There were no independent consumers, suppliers, or distributors—only Almazjuvelirexport, which had complete authority to decide when, how, and to whom to sell the Soviet diamonds.

In practice, then, Almazjuvelirexport could act autonomously in the market. Because its authority was unlikely to be compromised by any competing internal factions and because the longevity of its offices was well recognized, it was not under any pressure to produce short-term results; it could make its decisions without any outside counsel and implement them without any fear that they would be checked, blocked, or vetoed by any other domestic institution. Likewise, because its existence did not depend on its ability to turn a profit in any given year, it could afford to absorb occasional losses that seemed likely to yield longer-term rewards. In depressed markets, therefore, it could still stockpile its surplus stones because, for all practical purposes, the costs of the cutback were minimal.

Admittedly, cutting back meant that the country lost a portion of its foreign exchange and perhaps even an opportunity to increase its market share at the expense of the other producers. Still, under the centralized economy of the former Soviet Union, this loss could usually be covered by gains in other sectors, as the leadership had a fair amount of leeway in reallocating resources and adjusting expenditures. Even more important, though, any economic or financial loss that did occur was unlikely to have long-term adverse consequences for Almazjuvelirexport itself. There were no private industries to protest an enforced drop in their productivity and no independent dealers to protest cuts in their supply. There were, in short, no groups that would suffer disproportionately as a result of the government's restraint in the market. And even if a particular group did see its interests as having been unjustly slighted, it was unlikely to seek redress through political channels. As a result, Almazjuvelirexport was able to act independently, authoritatively, and strategically. It could operate free from the demands of short-term profits, away from the glare of public scrutiny, and with the authority to implement its decisions.

Ultimately, of course, the agency was still bound by the demands of the state. When the state was desperate for hard currency, it would tighten its own controls over Almazjuvelirexport's activities and may at times have forced it to maximize its short-term revenues. In 1984, for instance, it is generally believed that Soviet diamonds flooded the market at least in part because the Soviet government needed hard currency to cover a deficit caused by lower oil prices.[91] The situation of 1984, however, seems to have been the exception rather than the rule; for the most part, it appears that Almazjuvelirexport acted autonomously, handling all aspects of the Soviet diamond trade by itself and obliged only to tend to the Soviets' long-term interest in the international diamond market.

THE POWER TO PERSUADE AND THE POTENTIAL FOR CHANGE

In the former Soviet Union, autonomy was thus derived from the economic organization of the state; in DeBeers, it is the product of a particular corporate structure. In both cases, though, the end result was the same: DeBeers and the Soviet diamond agencies could choose their own course in the market, free from short-term profit constraints and without fear of any domestic opposition to their external affairs. This freedom, in turn, gave them the ability to act strategically. Because they were not compelled solely by short-term profits, they could afford to absorb occasional losses and stockpile the surpluses that threaten the market from time to time. Because authority was tightly controlled and highly centralized, the leaders could make policy as they chose and change it as they saw fit. Because they could discipline all factions within their own ranks, they could bargain more freely at the international level, making compromises without worrying about their international ramifications.

Ultimately, then, the Soviets and the South Africans were able to

---

[91] See, for instance, "Russia's Predicament and the World Diamond Market," p. 1.

cooperate with each other because they could each command such authority at home. With few obstacles on the domestic level, both sides could engage in the bargaining that is so vital to any cooperative endeavor. They could negotiate and compromise and threaten, knowing that they could implement whatever it was they decided. And because their partners knew that they could implement these policies, the policies became more credible. The Soviets' promises were credible, for instance, because they demonstrated the ability to abide by them and to accept whatever internal costs they might require. Similarly, DeBeers's threats are credible because the cartel members know that DeBeers is willing and able to punish defectors. Cooperation is thus facilitated by the capacity of the cartel's leaders to make commitments and stick by them.

In addition, both the Soviets and DeBeers were able for decades to take advantage of certain distinct internal conditions. Both were able to rely on extraordinarily docile labor pools and thus never had to consider the effect of their international commitments on their internal work force. Similarly, and perhaps even more important, both managed to conduct their affairs out of the public eye. Occasionally, of course, the secrecy that cloaked their relationship would draw attention to itself. But for the most part it allowed the Soviets and DeBeers to work out their deals in private, without the added pressures of public declarations and the obstacles to compromise that they inevitably create.

Recently, though, the entire edifice of cooperation has been called into question. If the success of the cartel has been due largely to the internal autonomy of the Soviets and DeBeers, then a disintegration of this autonomy cannot bode well for the long-term viability of the cartel. At the time of this writing, it is too early to tell precisely what the breakup of the Soviet Union will do to the international diamond cartel. But already there are signs of trouble.

The troubles began in 1988, when Mikhail Gorbachev created a new agency, Glavalmazzoloto (Directorate of Precious Metals and Diamonds) to serve as an umbrella organization for all branches of the diamond industry.[92] Ostensibly, the move was part of Gorbachev's overall campaign to give individual enterprises greater control over

[92] *Diamond World Review* 59 (July–August 1990): 40.

their own operations. In practice, however, the creation of Glavalmazzoloto as a superministry meant that the diamond industry was
now under greater central control than it had been previously. Presumably, this deviation from Gorbachev's stated policy reflected the
economic importance of the diamond industry and the government's
determination to retain its own autonomy in such a key sector.

Very quickly, though, the waves of perestroika began to manifest
themselves in demands for local autonomy. In September, officials
in Yakutia were publicly decrying the Soviet Union's control over
"their" natural resources.[93] They were joined by local leaders in
Archangelsk, who condemned their position as "an insignificant unit
begging for alms" and proclaimed their intent to develop their own
diamonds "in the name of the people."[94]

Realizing the potential impact of these claims, DeBeers sprang
into action in the summer of 1990, going to unprecedented lengths
to ensure that the Soviet diamonds did not fall into unfriendly or
disorganized hands. On July 25, a newly established subsidiary of
DeBeers signed an exclusive agreement with Glavalmazzoloto. In return for a $1 billion hard currency loan, DeBeers Centenary re-
tained the right to purchase for export all the Soviet Union's diamond production for the next five years. The total value of the deal
was estimated at approximately $5 billion. As collateral for the loan,
Glavalmazzoloto agreed to transfer a sizeable portion of its stockpile
of uncut diamonds to the CSO offices in London.[95] With one deal,
DeBeers did more than any country to help the Soviet Union solve
its hard currency shortage.[96] DeBeers, however, was by no means
acting out of charity. Instead, it had simply paid to get the Soviet
stockpile out of the country and encourage other members of the

---

[93] See, for instance, Speech by Comrade O. M. Zakharova, operator at Concentration Factory No. 12 of the Yakutalmaz Research-and-Production Association, *Current
Digest of the Soviet Press*, September 14, 1988; and Speech by Comrade Yu. N. Pro-
kopyev, first secretary of the Yakut Province Party Committee, *Current Digest of the
Soviet Press*, May 14, 1986.

[94] "Diamonds for Local Soviets: Prosperity or Misfortune?" *Izvestia*, September 25,
1990, p. 2. Translation by author.

[95] Diana B. Henriques, "Soviets to Sell Diamond Stockpile through a Subsidiary of
DeBeers," *New York Times*, July 26, 1990, pp. A1, D5; and Neil Behrman, "Soviets to
Sell Diamonds to DeBeers's Swiss Arm," *Wall Street Journal*, July 26, 1990, p. A12.

[96] See Kenneth Gooding, "Soviet Union Takes 'Rightful Place' in Diamond Cartel,"
Financial Times, July 26, 1990, p. 28.

cartel to toe the line. With the Soviet stones added to its own already voluminous stocks, DeBeers had so many diamonds that any other producer would quickly realize the futility of trying to strike a tough deal for its own production. Reportedly, producers who were negotiating with DeBeers at this time were taken down to the CSO vaults to see the Soviet stones laid out on dozens and dozens of tables. After their "tour," they generally agreed to the terms DeBeers had suggested.[97]

Initially it seemed as if the deal would be sufficient to protect DeBeers and the cartel against the turmoil in the Soviet Union. DeBeers had most of the existing Soviet diamonds, after all, as well as the exclusive right to market any new production. Within weeks, however, the deal had incited storms of protest in Russia's diamond-producing regions. The Russian republic, in its first significant claim to independence, declared the Soviet deal with DeBeers invalid.[98] Then the Autonomous Republic of Yakutia, a region within Russia, declared that all the Soviet diamonds were in fact the sovereign property of Yakutia. In response, Soviet officials stressed the importance of maintaining centralized control in the diamond industry. As the general director of Glavalmazzoloto argued: "Decentralization in our business is so far impossible. We can compete only to the detriment of our country."[99]

Still, the progressive deterioration of Soviet power that occurred after 1990 in effect completed the process of decentralization set off by Gorbachev in 1988. In October 1991 Glavalmazzoloto was disbanded and replaced by republic-level diamond organizations. Two months later, Russian president Boris Yeltsin announced that Yakutia would be permitted to market 10 percent of its diamond production

[97] This information was revealed to me in confidential interviews. See also Sven Lunsche, "DeBeers Tightens Its Grip through Soviet Deal," *Johannesburg Star*, August 1, 1990, p. 16; and "DeBeers, Soviets in $5 Billion Diamond Deal," *Jewelers' Circular-Keystone*, September 1990, p. 15.

[98] "These business arrangements," claimed one member of the Russian Council of Ministers, "violate the sovereignty of Russia. We take the view that there is no property of the Soviet Union, only the property of the different republics." Quoted in Celestine Bohlen, "Soviet Zone Strives for Sovereignty and Diamonds," *New York Times*, August 15, 1990, p. A3.

[99] Quoted in "An Expensive Scandal," *Moscow News Weekly*, September 2–9, 1990, p. 4.

independently. From this point on, the key question in the diamond industry was whether these local organizations would be able to establish their own structures of autonomy or whether control in the industry would disintegrate entirely. Clearly DeBeers was doing all it could to encourage the first outcome. As early as 1990, it recognized the inherent power of the Yakutians and attempted to bolster and contain this power by dealing directly with Yakutian officials.[100] Simultaneously, it continued to negotiate with Russian officials and joined forces with Yeltsin in supporting a plan to create a new company, Diamonds of Russia, that would include among its founding members the Russians, the Yakuts, the remnants of Russalmaz—and DeBeers.[101] As usual, it seems, DeBeers did not care with whom it negotiated as long as it could ensure that its partner had sufficient control to deliver its promises. As a DeBeers spokesperson explained, "I think that as long as a rational political authority is in final ultimate control over the diamond industry as it exists today in Russia, I have absolutely no problem, no doubt but that the political authority would be persuaded by the experts . . . that they should continue, whatever the political authority, the partnership they have formed with DeBeers."[102]

It remained to be seen, however, whether any such "rational political authority" did indeed exist in the former Soviet Union. During the summer of 1992, visible cracks began to appear in the Russian diamond industry and potentially even within the cartel itself. Diamonds from Yakutia were popping up in world markets, leaking through the channels that DeBeers had tried so hard to block. One Japanese company had reportedly agreed to purchase fifty to one hundred thousand carats a year from the Yakutians, thus avoiding completely the CSO pipeline. Another association of Japanese firms was negotiating a joint venture to develop new Yakutian diamond fields.[103] Meanwhile, rumors of Yakutian diamonds were racing

[100] See Mikhail Nikolaev, "Yakutiya: A Taste of Freedom," *Delovie Lyudi,* July–August 1992, p. 48.

[101] Yulia Pospelova, "Diamond Wars: Parliament Leaders Blast Yakut Diamond Deal," *Kommersant* 28 (1992): 1.

[102] Gary Ralfe, DeBeers press conference, Moscow, December 18, 1991.

[103] Sergei Agafonov, "Cheap Diamonds from Yakutia," *Izvestia,* July 29, 1992, p. 5; and Vladimir Kruchko, "Diamond Rush," *Delovoi Mir,* May 23, 1992, p. 4.

through the international diamond industry.[104] In August 1992, in a virtually unprecedented move, the DeBeers Corporation announced that its final dividend would be reduced and imposed a 25 percent reduction in all diamonds purchased through the CSO.

Officially, the cuts came as a response to the general sluggishness of the world economy and a sudden increase in diamonds smuggled out of Angola, another member of the cartel whose tightly controlled diamond industry had just been splintered by the turmoil of domestic politics.[105] Unofficially, though, many suspected that the real source of the problem lay deep within Siberia.

In the end, the fate of the international diamond cartel may very well rest with the political restructuring of what was once the Soviet Union. If new structures of control emerge within Yakutia, then it is entirely likely that these new authorities will remain within the confines of the existing cartel. If, however, the entire industry is thrown open to competing claims, if all decisions are, as some hope, left to the whims of the market and individual entrepreneurs, then the autonomy of the Russian diamond industry will be shattered for good. For now, it remains within the power of the Russians to destroy the international diamond cartel.

Finally, though, the extraordinary success of the diamond cartel emphasizes both the necessity of leadership and the coercive measures that the leader may have to employ. Ultimately, the story of the diamond cartel is the story of DeBeers and of the skill with which it has forged an orderly market out of the usual chaos of the competitive marketplace. To be sure, the corporation may rule the market with an iron fist and may act ruthlessly against all defectors from its ranks. In the end, though, it has managed to survive where so many others have failed and to craft upon a fragile illusion one of the world's most enduring cartels.

[104] See Kenneth Gooding, "Oppenheimer to Visit Moscow as Diamond Shakeup Looms," *Financial Times,* August 28, 1992, p. 24; and "Is It a Crack or a Scratch?" *Economist,* September 12, 1992, p. 76.
[105] Bill Keller, "DeBeers May Be Losing Grip on Diamond Market," *New York Times,* September 3, 1992, pp. A1, D12.

CHAPTER THREE

Yellowcake: The Rise and Decline of the International Uranium Cartel

Sometime in the summer of 1976, a robbery occurred at the of-fices of Mary Kathleen Uranium Ltd., an Australian mining com-pany that was then the country's only uranium producer. The rob-bery itself was never reported, nor the thief revealed. The theft, however, made big news some time later, when the stolen property turned up at the Melbourne headquarters of Friends of the Earth (FOE), an international environmental organization that was em-broiled in a domestic debate over the future of the uranium industry in Australia.

According to FOE, the package from Mary Kathleen Uranium (MKU) had been sent anonymously and contained hundreds of pages of documents detailing the company's participation in an in-ternational uranium cartel involving governments and mining com-panies in Canada, Australia, France, and South Africa. Immediately after seeing the evidence contained in the Mary Kathleen papers, FOE staffers began duplicating them as fast as possible, hoping to present them the following day to a national commission that was just completing public hearings on the desirability of an increased role for Australia in the international uranium market. FOE, which opposed uranium mining on both ecological and political grounds, felt sure that the revelation of the Mary Kathleen documents would help their cause by exposing the political intrigue and collusion that was occurring in the uranium industry. The commission, however, was not so impressed. Ruling that the documents were "not relevant" because they were concerned primarily with pricing, the commission refused to include the MKU papers in their deliberations and instead turned the documents over to the police.[1] Thus, contrary to the FOE's hopes and expectations, the stolen documents created hardly a stir in one of Australia's hottest political debates. Two weeks later, though, the papers surfaced again, this time with an explosive and far-reaching impact.

In late August, an FOE employee en route to Britain from Australia left a package of papers covered in a plain brown wrapper on the doorstep of James Harding, a former Friend who was then working as an assistant to the California Energy Commission in Sacramento. As soon as Harding realized the implications of the documents, he turned them over to the United States Department of Justice and then called a news conference to publicly announce the contents of the Mary Kathleen papers. On August 29, 1976, Harding, along with two other state energy officials, reported to the press that "there is a single uranium market worldwide and the existence of a cartel and its success suggests that we are at least at the financial mercy of another foreign cartel like OPEC."[2] In a subsequent letter to the U.S. attorney general, Edward Levi, the officials also stressed the collusion that was revealed by the MKU papers and the dangers it posed to the U.S. nuclear industry:

> It is impossible to tell from these documents whether the cartel was responsible for the seven-fold increase in world prices, but it is apparent that the U.S. domestic price of uranium has moved upward in parallel with world prices, and that an effective world-wide cartel would cost American consumers billions of dollars. . . . If the foreign cartel continues and America's nuclear commitment increases as planned, we will be at the mercy of a uranium OPEC.[3]

In retrospect, Harding's insistence was hardly necessary. Instead, the implications of the papers were eagerly seized by several offices

---

[1] Earle Gray, *The Great Uranium Cartel* (London: McClelland and Stewart, 1982), p. 11. The best summaries of the Mary Kathleen affair are in Gray and in June Taylor and Michael D. Yokell, *Yellowcake: The International Uranium Cartel* (New York: Pergamon, 1979).

[2] Bill Richards, "Uranium Cost Deal Alleged," *Washington Post*, August 30, 1976, p. 1.

[3] Cited in Gray, *Great Uranium Cartel*, p. 12.

of the federal government, and within months the documents were at the center of a heated political, economic, and legal battle. In the most visible political arena, the House Subcommittee on Oversight and Investigations of the Interstate and Foreign Commerce Committee launched a massive investigation to determine whether a foreign producers' cartel had influenced the price of uranium in the United States.[4] Simultaneously, nineteen foreign and domestic utility companies brought lawsuits against the Westinghouse Corporation, demanding that the company repay them for uranium it had failed to deliver; Westinghouse in turn brought suit against the Gulf Corporation and several other uranium companies, charging that it was their participation in an international uranium cartel that had forced prices to a point where Westinghouse could no longer afford to deliver on its contracts. In all the cases the central issues were the same: was there an international uranium cartel, and had it succeeded in pushing uranium far beyond its free-market price?

Certainly all external evidence indicated that a cartel was in place and that it had achieved spectacular results. Since 1972, periodic rumors of secret "producers' meetings" had appeared in the trade journals and even in the popular press. In fact, as early as 1972, the *Wall Street Journal* had reported: "French, Canadian, Australian and South African government experts completed a round of backstage talks aimed at putting some order into the international uranium market. . . . This suggested moves to coordinate uranium production and marketing policies."[5] Within the industry, the cartel was a generally acknowledged "secret"; although few utility executives or uranium marketers knew any of the details of the cartel, they were all vaguely aware that a "club" existed and that it concerned itself with stabilizing the traditionally volatile uranium market.[6]

---

[4] See "International Uranium Cartel," Hearings before the Subcommittee on Oversight and Investigations of the Committee on Interstate and Foreign Commerce, 95th Cong., 1st sess., May 2, June 10, 16, and 17, and August 15, 1977, ser. no. 95-39, p. 22 (hereinafter cited as *Hearings*).

[5] "Uranium Market Discussed by Four Producer Nations," *Wall Street Journal*, February 8, 1972, p. 8. Other early articles included John Picton, "Canada Taking Part in Secret Uranium Talks," *Toronto Globe and Mail*, February 4, 1972, p. B1; and "Uranium Producers' Talks," *Mining Journal*, February 11, 1972, p. 120.

[6] For example, the president of the Nuclear Exchange Corporation later noted that "we do not think it came as a surprise to anyone in the industry to have the Canadian Government's confirmation that it [the cartel] existed." See "International Uranium

The allegations of collusion in the uranium market were further strengthened by the tremendous changes that had occurred in the early 1970s. In 1971, the U.S. Atomic Industrial Forum had reported that the U.S. industry "was plagued with over-capacity," while overseas, "most mills were operating at less than capacity or are simply adding to inventory."[7] Uranium was selling for as low as $3.55 a pound, and the entire industry was haunted by the discovery of tremendous ore deposits in Australia that threatened to push prices even lower. In 1972 and 1973, however, the market suddenly began to turn around, and prices inched slowly upward. Then they began to skyrocket. Between October 1973 and August 1975, the spot price of uranium quadrupled, from $6.50 per pound to $26 per pound. By 1976, *Business Week* was reporting prices of $55 a pound for uranium to be delivered in 1980.[8] As many observers hastened to point out, the uranium industry had witnessed one of the most spectacular turnarounds of all time and had achieved price increases that made OPEC, by comparison, seem unsuccessful. Together with the open secret of a uranium "club" and the revelations of the Mary Kathleen papers, the price increases of the 1970s painted a picture of a tight, invincible, and potentially dangerous uranium cartel.

Within just a few years, however, the market had begun to slide downward again, and the uranium cartel, by all indications, had disintegrated. In 1980, uranium prices stood at $30 per pound; by 1989, they had fallen to approximately $11 per pound. Inventories were once again overflowing, and new exploration had ceased. The Westinghouse cases were settled out of court, and uranium dropped out of the spotlight. The great uranium cartel was gone.

In part, the demise of the cartel could be attributed to the publicity it received after the Mary Kathleen affair and to the legal pressures brought to bear by the U.S. government. But this is by no means the whole story. Instead, a closer look at the internal work-

---

Supply and Demand," Hearings before the Subcommittee on Oversight and Investigations of the Committee on Interstate and Foreign Commerce, 94th Cong., 2d sess., November 4, 1976, p. 4. Also cited in Larry R. Stewart, "Canada's Role in the International Uranium Cartel," *International Organization* 35 (Autumn 1981): 675.

[7] Quoted in Gray, *Great Uranium Cartel*, p. 95.

[8] See "The Uranium Dilemma: Why Prices Mushroomed," *Business Week*, November 1, 1976, p. 92.

ings of the cartel reveals that it never really functioned effectively. Its members cheated persistently, neglected to punish violations, and broke the rules of secrecy to which they had pledged themselves. Even during its heyday the uranium cartel failed to induce anything but the most superficial cooperation among the producers. The members of the cartel agreed to the rules of market coordination but still proved unable to abide by them. In particular, the Canadians, who had initially assumed the lead position, quickly proved incapable of sustained cooperation. They were so constrained by domestic political forces and so besieged by their own internal factions that they could never maintain the discipline demanded by the cartel.

In structural terms, establishing a cartel in the international uranium market should have been a relatively easy task. There were only a handful of producers, high barriers to entry, and very little fringe production. Uranium is also nonsubstitutable, nondifferentiable, and vitally important to the governments and utilities that purchase it. Still, the uranium cartel faltered. Despite the conduciveness of the market, the uranium producers could not cooperate. They were overwhelmed instead by dissent within their own ranks, a loss of internal control, and the shortsightedness of their members. In the end, the story of the uranium cartel is largely a story of failure. It reveals the extent to which any cartel is vulnerable to both pressures from without and dissension from within. It illustrates the ways in which the internal characteristics of the producers influence their ability to maintain cooperation. Finally, and perhaps unfortunately, it underscores the special difficulties that plague a state that tries to combine secret cooperation abroad with open democracy at home.

THE INTERNATIONAL URANIUM MARKET

The Strategic Value of Uranium

Before 1939, uranium ore, or "yellowcake," was generally considered a useless by-product of copper, vanadium, or radium mining. Although uranium's radioactive properties had been realized since 1896, no one knew how to harness the potential power of the ore, and so it was routinely discarded or sold in minuscule amounts as a coloring agent for paints, ceramics, and glass.[9]

In 1939, however, the Danish physicist Niels Bohr announced a discovery that was to change the uranium market forever. At an international conference on theoretical physics, Bohr reported that scientists in Berlin and Copenhagen had achieved nuclear fission, creating a self-sustaining, energy-producing reaction from the splitting of uranium atoms. To the scientists who had been wrestling with the problems of nuclear fission, Bohr's announcement had drastic implications: on the one hand, it meant one of the most exciting areas of theoretical research could now be subjected to laboratory tests; on the other, it meant that scientists now had the power to create weapons more deadly than anything man had ever known. In the United States, a group of emigré scientists realized at once that the government would have to be alerted and that the development of nuclear fission should be placed under governmental control. In a letter sent to President Roosevelt, Albert Einstein and Leo Szilard informed the president: "Early this year it became known that the element uranium can be split by neutron bombardment. . . . There is some reason to believe that if fast neutrons could be used, it would be easy to construct extremely dangerous bombs. The destructive power of these bombs can only be roughly estimated, but there is no doubt that it would go far beyond all military conceptions."[10] Within a year, the U.S. government was intimately involved in the business of nuclear fission, and yellowcake had been transformed from the stuff of wastepiles into one of the most precious, most carefully guarded commodities on earth. As a necessary consequence, the uranium market was also changed forever. From here on, the market would be largely devoted to and regulated by governments, and the twin security interests of procurement and nonproliferation would be the forces driving the supply and demand of yellowcake.

Since 1939 the supply of uranium has thus been affected by national programs designed to procure uranium at any price, and demand has been influenced by international efforts to limit the

---

[9] Taylor and Yokell, *Yellowcake*, p. 23.
[10] Quoted in Gray, *Great Uranium Cartel*, p. 21.

proliferation of nuclear weapons by controlling access to enriched uranium. Despite these interferences, however, the international uranium market has basically performed like any other, and prices have shifted according to changes in supply and demand. Governments have been actively concerned with the market, but they have done little to alter its basic structure. And aside from a brief flurry of activity in the mid-1970s, they have been wholly unable to cooperate in the regulation of what remains one of the world's most strategic and sensitive markets.

The Supply Side: Boom and Bust

Unlike most "strategic" minerals, uranium is fairly common. In fact, in geological terms, uranium is actually quite plentiful. It occurs naturally a thousand times as frequently as gold and nearly as frequently as tin, nickel, and zinc.[11] Yet, for practical purposes, uranium is still relatively hard to come by, and the uranium market is far more susceptible to supply-side squeezes than its geological frequency would indicate. First, the uranium atom is arranged in such a way that makes uranium particularly likely to form compounds; thus, most uranium occurs *not* in its pure form but in any one of a number of various compounds. As a result, as L. C. Jacobsen has noted, finding uranium is made considerably more difficult: "In theory, it can occur almost anywhere. . . . The great variety of uranium occurrences enormously complicates exploration; few areas can be rejected out of hand."[12] Complicating matters even further is that uranium's propensity to form compounds means that extracting the uranium can be a difficult, costly, and time-consuming process, especially since even "significant" concentrations of uranium ore often contain less than 1 percent pure uranium.[13] Third, uranium is made rarer due to its geological—and thus economic and political—concentration. Currently, over three-fourths of the world's Reasonably Assured Resources (RAR) exist in only five countries—Australia,

[11] Norman Moss, *The Politics of Uranium* (London: Andre Deutsch, 1981), p. 2.
[12] L. C. Jacobsen, "U.S. Uranium Price and Supply," *Materials and Society* 3, 2 (1979): 136.
[13] Anthony David Owen, *The Economics of Uranium* (New York: Praeger Special Studies, 1985), p. 26.

Canada, South Africa, Sweden, and the United States[14]—and an additional three-fourths of the world's Estimated Additional Resources (EAR) are thought to exist in Canada and the United States.[15] This concentration is even greater than it would initially appear, given that three of the second-tier producers—Gabon, Niger, and Namibia—sell mostly through the state agencies of France (Gabon and Niger) and South Africa (Namibia). As a result, international sales of uranium are realistically under the control of just five countries: Canada, France, South Africa, Australia, and the United States.[16] Thus, although uranium may be plentiful in geological terms, in terms of practical economics and politics, its supply is restricted insofar as it remains in the hands of a few key players.

Traditionally, such a high concentration ratio would imply that the suppliers had a considerable bargaining advantage over the consumers. In uranium, moreover, the advantage should logically be enhanced by the unique nature of the commodity and its uses. Uranium, after all, is only purchased for one of two purposes: to make bombs and to fuel nuclear reactors. In both these uses, price is a relatively minor consideration. For a nation that feels its national security would be enhanced by the possession of a nuclear weapon, virtually no price is too high to pay for the necessary uranium. Similarly, because nuclear reactors entail such tremendous lead times and construction costs, changes in uranium prices have only a minimal effect on the overall financial calculations of a reactor.[17] As Mar-

[14] See O. J. C. Runnalls, "Ontario's Uranium Mining Industry—Past, Present, and Future," Report prepared for the Ontario Ministry of Natural Resources, Ontario Mineral Policy Background Paper no. 13 (Ottawa: Ministry of Natural Resources, 1981), p. 21.

[15] The Joint OECD/IAEA (International Atomic Energy Agency) Report defines "Reasonably Assured Resources" as uranium that occurs in known mineral deposits of such size, grade, and configuration that it could be recovered within the given production cost ranges with currently proved mining and processing technology. "Estimated additional resources" refers to uranium in addition to RAR that is expected to occur mostly on the basis of direct geological evidence, but where specific data and measurements of the deposits and knowledge of the deposits' characteristics are considered to be inadequate to classify the resource as RAR. See "Uranium Resources, Production, and Demand," Joint OECD/IAEA Report (Paris, 1983), pp. 9–13.

[16] For more data on concentration within the uranium industry, see Taylor and Yokell, *Yellowcake*, pp. 44–51, 68–76.

[17] It has been estimated that an increase in uranium prices leads to an increase in electricity costs that is only one-twentieth as great. See ibid., p. 68.

ian Radetzki writes: "Uranium constitutes a small fraction of the overall costs of nuclear electricity generation, while most of these costs are accounted for by capital investments. Since there are no substitutes for uranium in nuclear power generation, once the investment funds have been committed, uranium will be bought at any price within a very wide range."[18]

Finally, the supply side would appear largely invulnerable to market downturns because of the strategic and nonsubstitutable nature of uranium. Although there obviously are energy sources aside from nuclear reactors and weapons aside from nuclear bombs, there is nothing but uranium that can be used to fuel existing nuclear reactors and supply the raw material for nuclear bombs. Once a nation has decided to take the nuclear route to either energy or national security, it is completely dependent on uranium. There simply are no substitutes in either the short or the medium term. Taken together, then, the combination of high concentration, price inelasticity of demand, and nonsubstitutability in the uranium market would seem to make the suppliers of this strategic commodity virtually invincible. By all external criteria, uranium should be a sellers' market, one rife with opportunities for producer collaboration.

Optimism and Anarchy

In practice, the supply side has not had it so easy. In fact, the market since 1939 has been notably volatile, marked by a series of dramatic price falls that have often forced the closings of once-booming mines and have transformed mining communities, particularly in Canada, into ghost towns.

At first, the market for uranium was entirely a sellers' market. Governments—especially the U.S. government—were desperate to get uranium and willing to pay virtually any price for it. Very quickly, though, the critical shortages of the wartime years gave way to an oversupply of uranium as new producers hastened to fill the needs of their government. Existing mines were expanded throughout the 1940s and 1950s, and hundreds of prospectors attempted to

[18] Marian Radetzki, *Uranium: A Strategic Source of Energy* (London: Croom Helm, 1981), pp. 112–13.

join what appeared to be an infinitely profitable market. By the mid-1950s, the industry was already experiencing overcapacity.[19] The demand side, meanwhile, was not only flat but also rigid. Because uranium was still used primarily as a fuel for nuclear weapons, the customer base was small and unchanging. Governments purchased nearly all uranium sold, and govermental agencies, particularly the U.S. Atomic Energy Commission (AEC), were increasingly dictating the terms of trade with their (largely Canadian) suppliers. And although the producers grumbled about the dismal state of the market and the heavy hand of official purchasers, they had nowhere else to go.

In the late 1960s, however, the rapid commercialization of nuclear reactor technology seemed certain to transform the entire situation. Indeed, the 1960s were a time full of promise for the uranium industry. The international spread of atomic energy meant a potentially enormous increase in the total world demand for uranium and a radical change in the type of potential uranium consumers. With the advent of atomic power, uranium would at last become a commercial commodity, freed at least in part from the constraints imposed by national security and sought after by a much broader group of customers. Coupled with the decline in production that had followed the demand cutbacks of the late 1950s, the development of nuclear energy promised an unfettered international demand for uranium, higher prices, and a booming market.

By the early 1970s, the market seemed even more auspicious, as enthusiasm for nuclear energy increased and supplies began to level off. Nuclear energy generating capacity was growing worldwide, and even countries that were committed to self-reliance had conceded that they would probably have to look to foreign sources by the 1980s. Official forecasts from 1970 indicated a 20 percent growth in nuclear generating capacity between 1970 and 1980 and 17 percent growth from 1970 to 1985. Although existing world supply in 1970

---

[19] As a result of an ambitious program of exploration, domestic production in the United States had grown from 1,200 short tons in 1952 to 4,100 short tons in 1955, and reserves had risen from nearly nothing in 1952 to more than 100,000 short tons by 1956. See Radetzki, *Uranium*, p. 39; and "Uranium Price Formation," Electric Power Research Institute (EPRI), October 1977, prepared by Charles River Associates, Cambridge, Mass.

was sufficient to meet demands for several years, new capacity would be needed by the mid-1970s,[20] and nuclear experts were beginning to express concern over the industry's ability to satisfy the projected demand for uranium.[21] In addition, the first signs of OPEC's growing restlessness were making energy planners wary of rising oil prices and more concerned about ensuring stable supplies of uranium ore.

More than ever before, the market was ripe for cartelization. Demand was spreading, but supply remained tightly in the hands of just a few producers. These producers, moreover, also had the structural advantage of longer lead times. Because the start-up time for a nuclear reactor was about ten to twelve years, firms and countries looking to begin operations in the early 1980s needed to contract for their uranium supplies in the early 1970s. Had the producers presented any sort of a united front, they could have negotiated long-term contracts at fairly high prices given the relatively small role that uranium prices play in the overall cost-benefit calculations of nuclear energy.

As it was, however, there were no attempts at even minimal coordination. Instead, the producers continued on their separate paths, eagerly chasing after all new contracts and driving prices down. The Canadian government was still sitting on a uranium stockpile of nearly ten thousand tons, uranium towns were calling themselves "modern ghost towns," and the president of France's uranium export agency was complaining publicly that "uranium is one of the least profitable investments you can find these days."[22] The conditions for collaboration were in place, but no one within the industry seemed anxious to take the initiative.

Then suddenly the combination of a new face in Ottawa and new ideas in Europe at last proved sufficient to break the camel's back and propel uranium producers toward cooperation.[23]

[20] Radetzki, *Uranium*, p. 53.

[21] See, for instance, John F. Hogerton, "Remarks before the Atomic Industrial Forum Conference on Energy Alternatives," Washington, D.C., February 19, 1975, cited in Mason Willrich and Philip M. Marston, "Prospects for a Uranium Cartel," *Orbis* 19 (Spring 1975): 168.

[22] *Business Week*, April 11, 1970, p. 40. See also D. J. LeCraw, "The Uranium Cartel: An Interim Report," *Business Quarterly*, Winter 1977, p. 77.

[23] One other factor that *may* have helped the cartel form when it did was a change in the United States's "tails" policy. At this time, all uranium in the Western world was

THE CARTEL IS BORN

No one knows exactly when the seeds of the uranium cartel were first planted. The most logical story, however, and one that is particularly relevant in light of the preceding chapter, traces the roots of the uranium cartel back to a multinational mining company called Rio Tinto Zinc and a Canadian policy entrepreneur named Jack Austin. The mining company, it seems, had been harboring ideas of international cooperation for some time but had lacked the political and institutional means to implement any official arrangements. Once Jack Austin came on board, though, he was able to bring the entire Canadian government along with him and to use the powers of the government to set the cartel in motion.

As outlined above, the economic conditions of the uranium market had been ripe for cartelization since the early 1960s, with the commercialization of nuclear power and the international spread of nuclear reactors. Demand was growing and projected to grow even more, while supplies were tight and still highly concentrated in the hands of four major producers. Even the international dependence on U.S. enrichment capacities should have worked as a spur to cooperation as the United States had basically severed itself entirely from the international market, thus inciting a certain mutual outrage among all the other producers. What was still needed but had heretofore been absent, however, was a spark of initiative and one player who was willing to take the lead. As it turned out, Rio Tinto Zinc

---

enriched at one of the AEC's facilities in the United States. During the enrichment process, the percentage of U-235 isotopes is increased from about 0.7 to about 3.0. The amount of uranium oxide necessary to obtain a desired amount of U-235 depends on the amount of U-235 discarded in the leftovers, or "tails." If a greater percentage of U-235 is left in the tails, the process of enrichment is easier and cheaper, but more natural uranium is needed. In 1971, the AEC decided that the enrichment of foreign uranium for domestic reactors should be deferred indefinitely. In 1973 it increased the amount of U-235 in the tails, which meant that more natural uranium would be needed to produce the enriched uranium that the customers had paid for. This additional uranium came directly from the AEC's own stockpiles. In effect, then, the United States was able to force its foreign partners to buy American uranium at prices considerably above the prevailing market rate. See Radetzki, *Uranium*, p. 49; and Thomas L. Neff and Henry D. Jacobs, "World Uranium: Softening Markets and Rising Security," *Technology Review* 83, 3 (January 1981): 24. Needless to say, this change in U.S. policy caused considerable outrage abroad, but because the AEC had a fairly distinguished record of outrageous policies by this time, it is unclear whether this "change in the tails" prompted uranium producers toward a cartel.

(RTZ) eventually planted the idea,[24] and Jack Austin brought it to fruition.

Conceptualization: The Global Ambitions of RTZ

The suggestion that the cartel was actually the brainchild of RTZ is especially plausible once one understands what RTZ is and to whom it is connected. Ostensibly, Rio Tinto Zinc is a British-based multinational corporation whose primary interests lie in copper, iron ore, and zinc, as well as in uranium. RTZ, however, is more than a successful British mining company. It is also a major international player in both financial and economic circles, with links extending into the British government, the French nobility, and the Anglo American/DeBeers conglomeration. By nearly all the criteria established in previous chapters, RTZ is a natural candidate for cartel leadership.

Through its network of affiliates and subsidiaries, it actually controls mining interests throughout the world, including some of the world's largest and most profitable concerns. No one knows exactly how much of the world's mining industry RTZ controls through interlocking directorates and the like, but there is within the company a book called "the Bible" that lists the other companies that RTZ either owns directly or has a majority interest in: the book is four inches thick.[25] Moreover, it has also been widely alleged that RTZ is under the control of the powerful Rothschild family and that it therefore has powerful connections to the French government.[26] At the same time, the company's historic ties to Britain have been strengthened by the fact that some of the country's most notable diplomats—including Anthony Eden and Lord Peter Carrington—

[24] The RTZ link has never been proved. It is, however, alluded to in most of the major works on the cartel. See for instance, LeCraw, "Uranium Cartel," p. 77; Moss, *Politics of Uranium*, p. 108; Gray, *Great Uranium Cartel*, pp. 107–16, and Confidential report to Irwin J. Landes, chairman, Corporations, Authorities, and Commissions Committee, from William F. Haddad, director, Office of Legislative Oversight and Analysis, May 20, 1977, in *Hearings*, p. 649.

[25] Taylor and Yokell, *Yellowcake*, p. 72.

[26] See, for instance, Stephen Probyn and Michael Anthony, "The Cartel That Ottawa Built," *Canadian Business*, November 1977, p. 36ff. See also Gray, *Great Uranium Cartel*, p. 111; and Taylor and Yokell, *Yellowcake*, p. 75.

have also been actively involved with RTZ and that Queen Elizabeth is believed to be a major shareholder in the company. Indeed, in referring to his company's close relations with the British government, one RTZ executive recently asserted that "it's one of the great assets of the country."[27] Likewise, an article in the *Times* of London argued that it was "almost patriotic" to own shares in RTZ, whose "own particular brand of colonialism secures for Britain the raw materials it must have to remain one of the world's leading trading and industrialized nations."[28] Moreover, in light of the previous chapter, it is interesting to note that RTZ also appears to be linked to Harry Oppenheimer's vast financial empire. The main corporate connection here runs through Charter Consolidated, another London mining house in which Anglo American owns a significant interest. RTZ's board of directors is also composed of many of the same people who run various other parts of Harry Oppenheimer's empire. Therefore, one might expect the highest levels of RTZ to be well versed already in the intricacies of cartel management and aware of the benefits that producer cooperation could bring. Indeed, as Stephen Probyn and Michael Anthony note, "RTZ's economists undoubtedly noted [that] the uranium business seemed almost perfectly designed for cartelization."[29] And although RTZ never had the market share in the uranium market that Anglo American or De-Beers enjoyed in their respective spheres, it did have a similar sense of silent power and a faith in the possibilities offered by quiet collaboration among like-minded businesspeople.

Allegedly, RTZ had presided over an informal "club" of European and African producers since at least the early 1960s.[30] Certainly, an "inner club" of this sort seems logical, especially since both the other major producers concerned were, like RTZ, highly centralized and tied into the same business circles. All French uranium, for instance, came from two producers, both of which were partially owned by

---

[27] See Taylor and Yokell, *Yellowcake*, pp. 72–73.

[28] Cited in Jane Margolies, "R.T.Z.'s Wonderful Multinational Money Machine," *Nation*, October 18, 1980, p. 374.

[29] Probyn and Anthony "Cartel That Ottawa Built," p. 37.

[30] The existence of an "inner club" or "secret club" was mentioned to me repeatedly in confidential interviews, May 10–12, 1989, Toronto and Ottawa. It is also mentioned in ibid., p. 36; Gray, *Great Uranium Cartel*, pp. 107–9; and *Hearings*, p. 242.

the French government and one of which was reportedly controlled by the Rothschild family and linked to the Oppenheimers and Anglo American by stock ownership and interlocking directorates.[31] This uranium was then marketed through a single governmental entity called Uranex. Similarly, most of the uranium produced in South Africa was a by-product of gold mines owned by DeBeers's sister company, Anglo American. The uranium was marketed through a private company called Nuclear Fuels Corporation (Nufcor), which had close ties to the South African government. In fact, according to one lawyer familiar with the market, "Nufcor is really an alter ego for the government of South Africa."[32] Finally, many of the ostensibly independent companies such as Rio Algom of Canada, Rossing of Namibia, and Mary Kathleen of Australia also fell under the corporate auspices of RTZ.

The purposes of this "club" were likely quite limited: for producers to keep one another informed of their activities in the market, to limit unnecessary competition among themselves; and, whenever possible, to keep the "colonial upstarts"—Canada and Australia—from gaining too much headway in the European market.[33] By the late 1960s, though, this casual coordination was probably not enough, especially because prices were so low and the market so ripe for cartelization. Forming a cartel, however, was not something that RTZ or even the entire club could do on its own. The Canadians were still the largest producers of uranium in the world, and the Australians were finding vast reserves of their own. For any serious collaboration to work, the Canadians and Australians had to be brought on board and convinced to play by the rules of the game.

Quietly, then, and working primarily through representatives of its own Canadian subsidiary, Rio Algom, RTZ began to discuss the possibility of an "orderly marketing arrangement" with a variety of high-ranking officials in the Canadian government and the uranium industry.[34] Initially, RTZ's suggestions fell on deaf ears. Although

[31] At the time of the cartel, for instance, the board of Imetal, the French uranium company, included Baron Guy de Rothschild, Harry Oppenheimer of Anglo American, and Sir Val Duncan, chairman of RTZ.

[32] Quoted in Taylor and Yokell, *Yellowcake*, p. 70.

[33] This speculation is made explicit in a memorandum from L. T. Gregg to H. E. Hoffman, February 17, 1972, reprinted in *Hearings*, p. 466.

[34] It is unclear who was acting as RTZ's main representative in Canada at this time or how the initial contacts were made. One story suggests that RTZ actually worked

both the firms and the government officials wanted to do something to ease the plight of Canada's uranium industry, the officials had no institutional position from which to launch such an unprecedented project, and the firms were too worried about possible violations of Canadian antitrust law.

The obvious agency to take the lead was the Ministry of Energy, Mines, and Resources (EMR), the arm of the government officially charged with formulating and implementing Canada's energy policy. Initially, though, no one in the agency wanted to get involved. Most of the officials were physicists and geologists by training and had little interest in making policy, much less in setting up a highly controversial, potentially illegal cartel. But then, early in 1970, Pierre Trudeau named Jack Austin, a lawyer from Vancouver, to be the new deputy minister.

Implementation: The Canadians Take the Lead

By all accounts, Austin became the catalyst for Canada's participation in an "orderly marketing arrangement" and thus for the entire uranium cartel that eventually emerged. Austin had come to EMR with no specific direction from Trudeau but endless amounts of energy and ambition. While he was there, EMR was transformed from a relatively obscure bureaucracy into one of the most active and influential bodies in the Canadian government. As Peter Foster describes Jack Austin's tenure at EMR: "External developments combined with forceful intellects and egos to create an enormously powerful internal momentum. . . . [A] fast-developing external crisis created the need for new and complex domestic policies, and a brilliant team of young bureaucrats gathered around an equally brilliant catalyst."[35] Austin was also already ideologically predisposed to commodity arrangements, having written a doctoral dissertation on the

---

through the French government, which then made official contact with the Canadians (cited in Stewart, "Canada's Role in the International Uranium Cartel," p. 663). See also Peter Cook, "How the Uranium Cartel Was Formed," *Financial Times* (Canada), September 20, 1976, p. 36.

[35] Peter Foster, *The Sorcerer's Apprentices: Canada's Super Bureaucrats and the Energy Mess* (Toronto: Collins, 1982), pp. 56–57. Foster is actually writing in reference to Austin's other great achievement, the creation of PetroCan, Canada's national oil company. As both the uranium cartel and PetroCan were built about the same time, however, his description still applies.

subject at Berkeley. Moreover, like many Canadians, he was deeply concerned over the depressed state of the Canadian uranium industry and resentful of the United States's efforts to bend the rules of the market to fit its own immediate needs. Finally, Austin also believed that uranium would become an exceedingly important energy source by the end of the century. Thus, when he got wind of RTZ's suggestion, he was more than willing to adopt it as his own and put the full force of the ministry behind it. Initially, Austin suggested the establishment of a formal uranium marketing board, even though the producers whom he contacted had all been vehemently opposed to any such rigid controls.[36] When the minister of finance also expressed outrage at this idea during a cabinet meeting, Austin backed down and began to scratch out the details of a more informal, more secretive arrangement that would still enable the producers to regulate their own production and coordinate their activities with their counterparts around the world.

Considering that the French and South African producers had already (allegedly) been involved in some form of market coordination, getting them to agree to join in preliminary discussions regarding the current state of the uranium market was fairly simple. Far more difficult was to convince all the independent Canadian producers to agree to follow the dictates of a common policy and to find some means of accommodating this policy under existing Canadian law. None of the cartel's other potential members faced such serious difficulties. In France and South Africa, production was already so centralized that there were no legal obstacles to further regulation and little practical difficulty in setting prices or allocating market shares. In Australia, the uranium industry was so new that the companies had no set operating procedures, and the government could start with a clean slate.

In Canada, by contrast, the problems were more daunting. In the first place, even though some of the largest producers were national companies, most others were private concerns, unaccustomed to any sort of formal governmental regulation. Second, the Canadian government was not altogether comfortable with the authority it would have to take upon itself to oversee national participation in an or-

[36] Personal interview, Toronto, May 10, 1989.

derly marketing arrangement, especially as the government had a long history of nonintervention and the entire uranium operation was being run by a handful of people on the outskirts of power.[37]

Eventually, though, Jack Austin pushed through a series of ingenious measures that made participation in the cartel both mandatory and legal. Basically, EMR asked for and received a blank check from the Canadian cabinet. Although the cabinet, for obvious political and electoral reasons, did not want to involve itself in the creation of any formal mechanism, it did agree in principle to Canadian participation in international discussions on the subject of export markets and floor prices.[38] Then, as these discussions got further underway, it also passed a number of facilitating and supporting measures. In July 1972 it issued a regulation that authorized the Atomic Energy Control Board (AECB) to deny export permits if the prices and quantities of uranium did not comply with levels that were to be "specified in the public interest" by the minister of EMR.[39] Several weeks later, the minister informed the AECB of the specific market quotas and floor prices that it was to follow in issuing its export licenses. These numbers, not coincidentally, were identical to those that had been agreed on by this time within the cartel.[40] In effect, these regulations forced all Canadian producers to accede to the cartel's rules. Simultaneously, because they placed export sales under governmental regulation, they shielded the companies from prosecution under Canada's antitrust law, the Combines Investigation Act.[41]

One company that was particularly nervous about participating in any marketing arrangement was Gulf Minerals Canada Limited (GMCL), a Canadian subsidiary of the U.S.-based Gulf Oil Corporation. Aware of the vigor with which the United States had prosecuted antitrust cases in the past, Gulf worried that it would be liable

---

[37] Canada's participation in the cartel was largely supervised by just four men: Donald S. Macdonald, minister, Jack Austin, deputy minister, and Gordon MacNabb, assistant deputy minister of EMR; and Dr. O. J. C. Runnalls, a leading uranium expert.

[38] See Stewart, "Canada's Role in the International Uranium Cartel," p. 664.

[39] Runnalls, "Ontario's Uranium Mining Industry," p. 7.

[40] Memorandum from Donald S. Macdonald, minister, EMR, to Dr. D. G. Hurst, president, AECB, Ottawa, August 17, 1972.

[41] Note that the amendment to the Atomic Energy Control Regulation had been passed, not by an act of Parliament, as is customary, but by an order-in-council.

under U.S. law for any collusive activity that it committed in Canada. And thus Gulf initially balked at the Canadians' suggestion, arguing that participation in a formal arrangement was not necessarily in Gulf's best interest and repeating its counsel's advice that any action undertaken by GMCL had to be in compliance with U.S. antitrust laws.[42] In the end, however, Jack Austin and the Canadians prevailed.

Early in the spring of 1972, Minister of Energy, Mines, and Resources Donald Macdonald officially informed Gulf's top management that a coordinated marketing arrangement would be in Canada's interest and that he "urgently hoped" Gulf would participate.[43] Moreover, Macdonald apparently implied "that if the Canadian producers could not unanimously arrive at a position regarded as acceptable by the government, the government was prepared to enforce agreement by creating a uranium marketing board or in some other formal compulsory fashion."[44] This implicit threat was made even clearer when Gulf officials were shown a draft copy of a proposed Uranium Mining Control Act, which would have limited foreign ownership of uranium-producing companies to 33 percent.[45] Finally, government officials allegedly threatened Gulf directly, arguing that unless Gulf agreed to participate in the cartel, it would be forbidden to export Canadian uranium.[46] Throughout, Gulf maintained that any compliance on its part would put the company at risk of prosecution under U.S. antitrust laws.[47]

In the end, the Canadian officials won Gulf's participation by building a legal trail that would demonstrate that Gulf had been forced by Canadian law to join with the other uranium producers. A formal letter was drafted on government stationary, directing the company to join the mutual efforts underway, and on May 9, 1972, Gulf joined with the other Canadian officials and signed an aide-

[42] *Hearings*, p. 135. See also Gulf's File Note on the April 19, 1972, Paris Meeting of Canadian Producers, *Hearings*, pp. 484–87.

[43] See Earle Gray, "Shotgun Wedding," *Canadian Business*, March 1982, p. 97.

[44] Ibid.

[45] Testimony of L. T. Gregg, *Hearings*, pp. 261–62; and Probyn and Anthony, "Cartel That Ottawa Built," p. 78.

[46] Testimony of L. T. Gregg, *Hearings*, pp. 268–69; and Memorandum from L. T. Gregg to H. E. Hoffman, February 17, 1972, in *Hearings*, p. 462.

[47] See note on April 19, 1972 meetings, *Hearings*, p. 485.

memoire agreeing on the desirability of a formal marketing arrangement designed "to stabilize the present chaotic market situation and
to avoid a further acceleration of the present price war."[48] In retrospect, it appears that Gulf's change of heart was due both to the
economic pressure being exerted by the Canadians as well as to its
own internal determination that its participation would not constitute a violation of U.S. antitrust laws insofar as the cartel would have
no economic impact on the United States and insofar as the company's involvement was being compelled by the Canadian government.[49]

And thus, reluctantly, Gulf agreed to join the rest of the Canadian
producers and to participate in the orderly marketing of all uranium
sold outside the United States. This was a decision that was to haunt
them—and the entire uranium cartel—for years to come.

With Gulf securely on board, the Ministry of Energy, Mines, and
Resources was able to work out a coherent national strategy with the
participation of Canada's uranium producers and to go to the international negotiations with a united front. The possibility of defection
on a national level had been largely precluded by a combination of
official arm-twisting and the establishment of formal procedures
that engendered an atmosphere of trust and made cheating nearly
impossible. It remained to be seen, however, how well these procedures could be re-created on an international level and how well
the Canadians would be able to stick by their own rules.

The Cartel in Operation

The first secret meeting of the international uranium cartel took
place in Paris, early in February 1972. Official representatives of
Canada, France, Australia, and South Africa were present, along
with representatives of the twenty-three major companies from
those countries, plus RTZ.[50] The meetings were held in tandem, one

---

[48] Aide-Memoire Accepted by the Undersigned Canadian Uranium Producers on
May 9, 1972, in *Hearings*, p. 528.
[49] Memorandum from Roy D. Jackson to I. W. Coleman, April 28, 1972, in *Hearings*, p. 488.
[50] Throughout the life of the cartel, RTZ was basically treated as a separate country.

series open only to government officials and the other for corporate representatives.

According to most reports, no concrete arrangements were established in Paris. Instead, as one company representative recalled, "We just came together and cried on each other's shoulders."[51] Still, the basic outline of the cartel emerged. The producers agreed that cooperation would be necessary to regulate and stabilize the market and that they would meet in the near future to divide up the non-U.S. market for uranium and create the formal mechanisms of a uranium cartel. Most important, the members also all explicitly realized that they were in the same desperate straits. As D. J. LeCraw notes: "The cartel was held together by the members' past 'painful experience,' a combined available supply more than four times the projected demand over the period 1972–1977, the belief that the competitive market would lead to a 'dreaded' price war and continued $4/pound uranium, the threat of entry of low-cost Australian uranium in large volumes, and a veiled threat by the French to dump their 10,000 ton stockpile on the world market at less than $3/pound."[52] Facing such severe threats on all fronts, the uranium producers had at last acknowledged that cooperation offered the only means of escape.

At this initial meeting, the producers laid out the various issues that would need to be resolved before cooperation could ensue. First and most important, they accepted the idea of country and firm allocations that would divide the world uranium market among the four major suppliers and, hopefully, forestall any further devastating price competition. Second, the members agreed that current prices of $4.50 per pound or less were too low and that a concerted effort would be necessary to maintain price levels at which the producers could afford to keep producing. Interestingly, though, the members never discussed the possibility of pushing prices very much higher than was necessary to cover their costs. Instead, their purpose legitimately seems to have been to keep prices just high enough for the mines to remain open.[53] The producers also gave some consid-

---

[51] Moss, *Politics of Uranium*, p. 109.

[52] LeCraw, "Uranium Cartel," p. 78. He bases this statement on a memorandum sent by Dr. John Runnalls to Jack Austin on May 1, 1972.

[53] For instance, an internal Gulf memorandum written at this time suggested that a price of $6.25 per pound would "cover operating costs plus capital recovery at a

eration in Paris to the prospect of bringing the utilities into their discussions "since both producers and consumers had an interest in assuring that needs for uranium be met after 1980 and this would only be the case if uranium could be marketed at an adequate price in the first half of the decade."[54] Finally, the members discussed and agreed on the need to maintain an "extreme secrecy" with regard to their common venture and suggested expulsion from the cartel as a suitable punishment for leaking information about it.[55]

The hazy agreements scratched out in Paris were soon formalized and expanded in subsequent meetings in Johannesburg, London, and the Canary Islands. At each of these meetings, the cartel became more structured, and a growing body of rules emerged to govern its various functions. The most crucial and controversial arrangement concerned the system of allocation. Although the producers naturally realized the importance of limiting competition between themselves, each also wanted to ensure that it got as large a share of the total world market as possible. In addition, several more specific problems presented themselves. For instance, the Australians wanted their share to be based on uranium that was known to exist but had not yet been produced, and both Canada and France had tremendous stockpiles that they threatened to dump on the market if their own demands were not met.[56] At the initial meeting, the French had proposed that all new orders would be divided among the members on the basis of their current production, so that the South Africans would receive approximately 20–25 percent of new orders; France, 20 percent; RTZ, 20–25 percent; Canada, 25 percent; and Australia, 8 percent.[57] By the second meeting, however, each of the national groups had had time to calculate allocation to its own various companies, and each thus returned with a revised estimate of its needs.

---

reasonable rate of interest, together with an additional amount which would provide an incentive for high risk exploration." Memorandum from L. T. Gregg to H. E. Hoffman, February 17, 1972, in *Hearings*, p. 462. This point was also stressed to me repeatedly in interviews with both corporate and government officials.

[54] MKU Document no. 2, att. II, p. 7.

[55] Ibid. As Taylor and Yokell note, however, the threat of expulsion is not particularly credible, as the expelled member would retain the ability to expose or undercut the entire scheme. See *Yellowcake*, p. 77.

[56] See Moss, *Politics of Uranium*, p. 110.

[57] Taylor and Yokell, *Yellowcake*, p. 77.

The Australians, especially, insisted that their share be significantly enlarged, based on the vast reserves known to exist in the country. The other producers, understandably, were reluctant to reduce their own shares, especially because Australia was considered such an upstart and it had not suffered the doldrums of the 1960s along with the older producers.[58] At the same time, though, the older producers still realized that Australia's huge low-cost reserves would give it the power to kill the cartel before it was even born. Somehow the Australian demands would have to be met.

Eventually, the dilemma was resolved by establishing two different quota systems, one to cover the period 1972–77 and the other to extend from 1978–80. Some time later, a third period, from 1981 to 1983, was also calculated.[59] The Australians thus succeeded in boosting their share over the longer term and in forcing the other producers to compromise their own demands. The South Africans, French, and RTZ all settled for considerably less than the 25 percent they had initially expected, and the Canadians had to trade one-third of the market in the first period for slightly over one-fifth in the second. It was a classic cooperative move. To ensure the prosperity of the common venture, the players had to accept less than they individually would have liked and less than they unilaterally might have been able to attain.

What the producers hoped to get in return, of course, were higher prices. To achieve the desired price level, all the firms pledged themselves to honor a fixed price below which uranium would not be sold. Initially this price was set at $5.40 per pound for immediate delivery and $7.50 per pound for uranium due to be delivered in six years.[60] These prices were to be ensured by a complicated system of noncompetitive bidding in which the cartel would determine beforehand which firm would "win" the bid. This "lead bidder" would then

[58] See ibid., p. 79. A participant in these meetings also hinted that there was a fair amount of Commonwealth jealousy within the cartel and a resentment by the British and Canadians of the Australian "newcomers." Personal interview, Toronto, May 10, 1989. Regarding the troubles caused by the Australians' demands, see Memorandum from John Runnalls to Jack Austin, "Meeting of International Uranium Producers in Paris, April 20–21, 1972," May 1, 1972, in *Hearings*, pp. 493–524.

[59] See MKU Document no. 8, p. 5, and Gulf Document no. 72.24, "Clean Draft," p. 2, reprinted in Taylor and Yokell, *Yellowcake*, p. 81.

[60] Moss, *Politics of Uranium*, p. 111.

offer a contract price already agreed on by the members. A designated "runner-up" would offer at least eight cents more, and all other bidders would add fifteen cents or more to the "winning" bid.[61] For instance, in response to an open bid by a Yugoslavian utility, the cartel decided "that Uranex would open at $6.55, compared with a club price of $6.45, that Nufcor would open 3 to 5 cents higher, and that all others should offer at least 15 cents higher."[62] In addition, the posted prices for uranium delivered to Japan, Taiwan, and Korea were to be twenty to twenty-five cents higher than those used elsewhere. The rationale here was simple: all three countries had committed themselves to the long-term development of nuclear energy, and all three had very limited energy resources.[63] If all cartel members charged the East Asians more, they would still pay.

This complex system of allocation and pricing was quickly ensconced in a formal secretariat, housed in the Commissariat à l'Energie Atomique (CEA) building in Paris and run under the direction of André Petit, a CEA official and French representative to Euratom. All contracts, inquiries, and other documents relating to the actual or proposed sale of uranium were supposed to be sent directly to Petit. Working under the guidance of the cartel, he was to determine which company was to win each contract and ensure that no cheating occurred.[64]

Over its short lifetime, the cartel became increasingly institutionalized. Price increases were determined by the cartel's leaders and implemented by participating countries via the rigged bidding process. The cartel publicly organized an international research group called the Uranium Marketing Research Organization (UMRO) and created an operating committee composed of two representatives from each of the four countries plus RTZ. An administrative budget was calculated and contributions arranged according to each member's average market allocation.[65] By early 1974, the cartel was formulating plans for a related uranium institute in which utilities would be eligible for associate membership, and it had formed a

[61] See the testimony of L. T. Gregg, *Hearings*, p. 257.
[62] Cited in the *Wall Street Journal*, April 25, 1977, p. 19.
[63] See Stewart, "Canada's Role in the International Uranium Cartel," p. 671.
[64] See Taylor and Yokell, *Yellowcake*, p. 90; and Moss, *Politics of Uranium*, p. 110.
[65] Testimony of L. T. Gregg, *Hearings*, p. 257.

subcommittee to collect the cartel's internal documents and rules into a "clean draft" to be entitled "Rules for Orderly Marketing."[66]

Thus, in just two years the chaotic uranium industry had not only managed to pull itself into a cooperative endeavor but had also created the formal structures by which cooperation could proceed and be maintained. As Congressman Moss noted during the hearings: "The cartel was a sophisticated operation. It had a paid secretariat, a policy committee, an operating committee, a formal document governing its actions, and a system of sanctions for those who would interfere with their view of an orderly market for uranium."[67] Add Stephen Probyn and Michael Anthony, "Within the constraints of secrecy that bound its members [the cartel was] a highly-structured, formalized operation."[68]

To a large extent, however, the external organization of the cartel was only masking the vast internal problems that still raged within it. Although rules and procedures had officially been agreed on and put into place, they were often blatantly disregarded as the members continued to pursue their individual interests and undercut the common policy of the cartel. In particular, the cartel was perpetually wracked by two problems: a lack of secrecy and cheating.

From the start, the members of the cartel were aware that their agreements would have to be secret. This belief rested not only on the common assumption that covert cooperation was most effective but also on the very real fear of some members that participation in any sort of cartel would not be greeted favorably by their own voters and stockholders. Thus, the members took special pains to keep their arrangements quiet, and to use the terms "marketing arrangement" or "research institute" rather than "cartel." As an early letter from RTZ's representative to the general manager of Mary Kathleen Uranium urges: "In your letter you mention a word which we would not even like to mention, as some members of the club are rather worried about informal price agreements. I would like to stress very strongly that under all circumstances there can be only an official

[66] Testimony of L. T. Gregg, *Hearings*, pp. 255, 283–84. For a copy of the complete rules, see "Rules for Orderly Marketing," Clean Draft, Doc. 74.24, in *Hearings*, pp. 628–40.

[67] *Hearings*, p. 130.

[68] Probyn and Anthony, "Cartel That Ottawa Built," p. 38.

agreement and whatever agreement is struck it should be done on a *strictly confidential basis.*"[69]

The cartel's inner documents and memoranda were treated by both the companies and the governments as "especially confidential," and circulation of the documents—and thus knowledge of the cartel—was restricted to a small circle of top-ranking officials. For instance, not even the board of directors of one of the major Canadian participants was informed of its company's involvement with the international group.[70] Throughout its life the cartel took careful steps to disguise its very existence. The secretariat, for instance, was purposely "buried" in the French headquarters of the CEA because the members thought that the French would be best equipped to provide the necessary "security."[71] Similarly, the elaborate scheme of bid rigging was really just an effort to make market allocation look like competition. Unlike OPEC, which was gathering steam at about the same time, the uranium cartel was clearly designed to remain as secretive as possible.

In practice, however, it was never very good at keeping secrets. In fact, from its very first meeting in Paris, the cartel became something of an open secret, acknowledged by the industry and basically just ignored by the public at large. In February 1972, the *Toronto Globe and Mail* reported that the Canadian government had participated in "secret uranium talks" that might be the first steps in "an international agreement governing the marketing of uranium."[72] These revelations (and others appearing elsewhere) might have been taken as the work of overly ambitious investigative reporting were it not for the fact that the Canadian government was itself responsible for most of the early leaks that occurred. Indeed, again in February

[69] Letter from L. C. Mazel to H. F. Melouney dated May 2, 1972. Quoted in U.S. Congress, "International Uranium Supply and Demand," Hearing before the House Subcommittee on Oversight and Investigations of the Committee on Interstate and Foreign Commerce, 94th Cong., 2d sess., November 4, 1976.

[70] Confidential interview, Toronto, May 10, 1989.

[71] See John Picton, "Suggestions of Cheating Almost Spark Fist Fight at Cartel Meeting," *Toronto Globe and Mail*, November 12, 1977, p. 2. This point was also confirmed to me in many interviews.

[72] John Picton, "Canada Taking Part in Secret Uranium Talks," *Toronto Globe and Mail*, February 4, 1972, p. B1; and Leo Ryan, "Meeting Viewed as Possible Step to International Uranium Pact," *Toronto Globe and Mail*, February 8, 1982, p. B1.

1972, the Canadian commercial counsellor in Washington wrote to one of the directors of the U.S. Atomic Energy Commission and informed him that "Canada took the initiative in calling a meeting on February 2 in Paris of goverment officials from Australia, France, South Africa and Canada, to explore all facets of present uranium marketing problems. . . . It was understood that at the . . . meeting such matters as floor prices and market allocation would be reviewed."[73] Canadian officials also took considerable pains to ensure that their own cabinet was kept completely up to date on the cartel's activities.

To the Canadians involved, this concern was a natural outgrowth of their own belief that the cartel was a good thing for both producers and consumers. In their eyes, an orderly marketing arrangement offered the only means of saving the uranium industry. At the same time, though, their eagerness to inform all relevant parties in both the United States and Canada reflected a lingering uneasiness with the cartel itself and a certain wariness about the possible legal ramifications. In any case, their openness meant that the cartel was never really a secret and that its elaborate schemes proved, in effect, quite transparent. As one broker delicately phrased it, "I *infer* they are setting prices because their asking prices always seem to come out the same, if you know what I mean."[74] Even the U.S. Atomic Energy Commission was well aware, albeit somewhat reluctantly, of the cartel's activities. As one official explained: "They are a little sensitive about being called a cartel. . . . One can only look at the evidence, that after they started meeting, the uranium market started getting . . . let's say, less cut-throatedly competitive."[75] Despite all its disguises, therefore, and its own good intentions, the uranium cartel was never more than an open secret at best.

The cartel was also less than successful in its attempts to prevent its members from breaking with the agreement and signing their own contracts instead. As with any cartel, the uranium cartel needed to prevent all such defections if it was to create a united front to

[73] Letter of February 14, 1972, from the commercial counsellor of the Canadian Embassy, Washington, to the acting director of the Division of International Programs of the U.S. Atomic Energy Commission.
[74] "It Worked for the Arabs," *Forbes*, January 15, 1975, p. 20.
[75] Ibid.

regulate competition and keep prices at a reasonable level. Like most cartels, however, it failed to establish the mechanism that would have made defection either impossible or unattractive.

Most important, the cartel failed to establish any sanction that was severe enough to stop its members from acting unilaterally whenever the opportunity presented itself. For instance, when the cartel discovered that RTZ had attempted to sell two hundred tons of ore to a Japanese utility without going through the official bidding process, it punished RTZ by deducting ten tons from its annual quota—hardly a steep price for a two-hundred–ton sale.[76] Likewise, when Denison, a Canadian firm, signed a contract that diverged significantly from the cartel's agreed procedures, it was merely reprimanded;[77] and when RTZ's representative, Louis Mazel, relied on a family tie to secure a covert contract with a Spanish utility, he personally was censored, but RTZ was not.[78] Reportedly, some penalties were levied by the cartel and enforced successfully.[79] But for the most part, infractions either went unnoticed or unpunished. Moreover, in a particularly odd twist, much of the cheating that occurred took the form of over-, not underpricing. For instance, many of the larger and more diversified firms such as RTZ and Gulf were able to use their business clout and corporate connections to win higher-priced contracts with certain "preferred customers." These types of deals had clearly been going on before the cartel was formed, but once it was in place, the companies concerned could play off what they knew to be the floor price, confident that their higher-priced deal would not be subject to competitive offers from other producers.[80]

[76] Gulf Memorandum, September 21, 1972, "Minutes of Canadian Uranium Producers' Meeting," in *Hearings*, p. 594.

[77] Taylor and Yokell, *Yellowcake*, p. 91.

[78] The Mazel story is one of the more interesting anecdotes to come out of the cartel. Apparently he had arranged the sale by working through the brother of someone who worked for the utility. When the other members discovered what he had done, the meeting got so acrimonious that it almost came to blows. Louis Mazel was soon transferred by RTZ to one of its Brazilian offices. See the testimony of L. T. Gregg, *Hearings*, p. 290; and Picton, "Suggestions of Cheating," p. 2.

[79] Testimony of L. T. Gregg, *Hearings*, p. 290. See also LeCraw, "Uranium Cartel," p. 79.

[80] This practice was described to me in confidential interviews with corporate managers.

As these defections were revealed, they quickly undermined whatever trust the members had originally vested in one another. Because commitments to the cartel were distinctly not credible, the producers had no incentive to forfeit their individual gains for the sake of the collective good. This general lack of faith in the cartel was revealed, among other places, in the congressional testimony of L. T. Gregg, marketing manager of Gulf Minerals Canada Limited:

> *Mr. Haddad*: Tell me a little bit about how the members of the cartel felt about each other. Did they trust each other?
> Candidly. You can characterize it.
> Were they friends? Were they suspicious of each other?
> *Mr. Gregg*: Some trusted one another more than others. Some were friends; others were not. It varied all over the map, Mr. Haddad.
> *Mr. Haddad*: But there was not a great sense of mutual camaraderie; was there? Everybody was protecting their own interests?
> *Mr. Gregg*: That is my feeling. Yes.[81]

Likewise, as Larry Stewart notes, although the participants were politically and culturally homogenous, "there was no overwhelming sense of camaraderie. Rather, an apparent lack of trust existed among the members."[82]

Nearly from its inception, therefore, the cartel was hobbled by its members' inability to keep secrets and play by the rules. Still, to an outsider looking at the cartel from 1972 to 1975, it *seemed* to be effective. After hovering in the doldrums since the late 1950s, prices were at last turning around. In June 1972, the cartel set floor prices at $5.40 for immediate delivery and $7.50 for six-year contracts. In March 1974, prices were $8 and $12, respectively.[83] The spot price, meanwhile, was moving even faster, rising from $5.95 per pound in July 1972 to $6.50 per pound in October 1973 and then to $26 per pound in August 1975.[84] Moreover, uranium output, which had

---

[81] Testimony of L. T. Gregg, *Hearings*, pp. 289–90.

[82] Stewart, "Canada's Role in the International Uranium Cartel," p. 672.

[83] See letters from Donald S. Macdonald, minister, EMR, to Dr. D. G. Hurst, president, AECB, Ottawa, Canada, dated August 17, 1972 and March 6, 1974.

[84] Owen, *Economics of Uranium*, p. 49; and Radetzki, *Uranium*, p. 25. All spot prices for uranium are calculated and reported by NUEXCO, formerly known as the Nuclear Exchange Corporation, a leading uranium broker.

been rising since 1966, began to slow down in 1973 and then to fall in 1974 and 1975. For the first time ever, producers were withdrawing from the market rather than entering into new long-term contracts.[85] By 1975, uranium supplies had become significantly tighter, and analysts were beginning to worry that existing production would be unable to meet the demands of the nuclear industry.[86]

Prices were high, supplies were down, and demand was rising. The uranium industry was experiencing its first significant boom since the late 1940s, and the uranium cartel seemed to be an unqualified success. As it turned out, however, this success was as short-lived as it was illusory.

DISMANTLING THE CARTEL

In nearly all accounts of the uranium cartel, the climax of the story occurs in 1976–77, when the Westinghouse Corporation charged most of the world's uranium producers with price fixing and illegal collusion. According to these accounts, the revelations contained in the documents stolen from Mary Kathleen Uranium gave Westinghouse an airtight case: there *had* been a cartel, prices had risen phenomenally, and the world uranium market had undergone significant changes. The denouement, then, is the flurry of litigation that ensued, the humiliation of the foreign (and especially the Canadian) producers, and the eventual dismantling of the great uranium cartel.

This section will argue, however, that the story did not occur quite that way. First, the charges brought by Westinghouse were inaccurate, as the cartel never even achieved most of the things that have since been attributed to it. Second, and more important, the Westinghouse affair did not *cause* the cartel to dissolve; rather, the cartel dissolved because it was wracked with internal problems and because its members saw no need to continue their cooperation once the market had improved. The Westinghouse affair certainly played a considerable role, especially insofar as the legal pressures it created

[85] See NUEXCO Reports no. 62 (September 20, 1973), no. 63 (October 22, 1973), and no. 67 (February 19, 1974). See also Radetzki, *Uranium*, p. 120.
[86] See "Uranium Backfires on Westinghouse," *Business Week*, August 18, 1975, pp. 29–30.

underscored the problems that some of the cartel's members—particularly the Canadians—were having with the cartel and with their own role in it. Ultimately, though, it was these internal problems, not the shock of Westinghouse, that caused the cartel to crumble.

The Westinghouse Affair

During 1973 and 1974, the Westinghouse Corporation came up with an innovative marketing strategy to sell its popular light-water nuclear reactors. In an attempt to undercut its competitors and realize the greatest benefit from the OPEC-induced spurt in reactor sales, Westinghouse promised to provide all purchasers of its reactors with all the uranium they would need to operate the reactors, at a fixed price of about $10 per pound.[87] In effect, the company offered itself as an intermediary, freeing the utilities from having to negotiate their own uranium purchases and protecting them against market fluctuations. By 1975, the strategy had significantly boosted Westinghouse's sales.[88] It had signed contracts with nineteen utilities and had committed itself to providing them with about seventy-two million pounds of uranium.[89]

What slowly became apparent, though, was that Westinghouse had nowhere near the uranium it needed to cover these commitments. The company had simply planned to buy the uranium as it needed it from the open market, assuming—rather naively in retrospect—that prices would remain at the depressed levels of the early 1970s.[90] In-

[87] The actual price varied with the time each contract was signed. Ten dollars is the average price.

[88] See Michael D. Yokell and Christy A. DeSalvo, "The Uranium Default: Westinghouse and the Utilities," *Public Utilities Fortnightly*, February 7, 1985, p. 21. Mr. DeSalvo, who now works as an independent consultant in uranium marketing and purchasing, was apparently the architect of Westinghouse's scheme.

[89] See "Westinghouse's Kirby Leads the Defense," *Business Week*, July 10, 1978, p. 24.

[90] A more sinister version of this story suggests that Westinghouse knew exactly what it was doing and that it calculated that even if it had to renege on its contracts and pay the ensuing legal costs, it would still realize a tremendous net profit on its reactor sales. And in fact, Westinghouse reaped considerable profits from its "disaster." Not only did it receive out-of-court settlements in its own lawsuits, but it also settled the suits against it partly by paying the utilities "in kind," that is, with Westinghouse components that, happily enough, ensured that the utilities would still have to rely on Westinghouse to provide parts and servicing. This side of the Westinghouse affair was related to me by a former official of the U.S. AEC and confirmed in subsequent interviews.

stead, spot prices started to rise, doubling from about $7 per pound in December 1973 to $15 per pound in December 1974. For Westinghouse, stuck with insufficient reserves and no uranium mines of its own, each dollar increase above its contract price meant a $65 million loss.[91] By September 1975, with prices pushing $26 per pound, Westinghouse could not fulfill its commitments. On September 9, 1975, it announced that it would be forced to renege on its contractual obligations to the utilities, claiming protection under the doctrine of "commercial impracticality."[92] At this time, the company was short about 32,500 tons of uranium, or about two and a half times total U.S. uranium production in 1975.[93]

Within months, the Westinghouse affair had turned into a huge legal battle, as the affected utilities rushed to sue the company for breach of contract and compensation.[94] By 1977, the estimated cost to Westinghouse of these suits was over $3 billion.[95]

Fallout from MKU

At first it seemed that the Westinghouse suits would remain a relatively self-contained affair. Although the corporation—like everyone else in the nuclear industry—*knew* of the "producers' meetings" that had taken place since 1972, it does not appear that they planned to use the cartel as a central part of their defense.[96] But then the MKU documents appeared on the scene, demonstrating unequivocally

---

[91] Yokell and DeSalvo, "Uranium Default," p. 21.

[92] "Westinghouse: A Blow in the Uranium Wars," *Business Week*, November 13, 1978.

[93] Owen, *Economics of Uranium*, p. 52.

[94] Eventually, three separate suits were filed and tried in Pittsburgh, three in Sweden, and the rest, filed in courts throughout the United States, were bundled together and transferred to a U.S. district court in Richmond, Virginia. See Taylor and Yokell, *Yellowcake*, p. 123.

[95] "Westinghouse Says Suit Could Cost $3 Billion," *San Francisco Chronicle*, November 30, 1977, p. 28.

[96] In an analysis commissioned by Westinghouse early in 1975, two outside economists had argued that a series of external events—including the OPEC oil embargo and the AEC's tails policy—had contributed to the rise in uranium prices. Although this analysis also mentioned the "foreign marketing arrangement," it did not describe it as a significant factor in accounting for the price increases. See James H. Lorie and Celia S. Gody, "Economic Analysis of Uranium Prices," Report prepared for Westinghouse Corporation, July 9, 1975. Summarized in Taylor and Yokell, *Yellowcake*, p. 122.

that the major uranium producers had been engaged in secret arrangements designed to reduce competition in the market and raise uranium prices. To Westinghouse, these documents were a godsend. If the company could show that a cartel had been operating during the time of the price increase, then, given the powerful antitrust sentiment in the United States, it could blame the cartel for its own inability to fulfill its contractual obligations.

And thus the MKU papers became the backbone of Westinghouse's defense and the subject of subsequent congressional inquiry and federal litigation in the United States. Congressman John E. Moss launched a massive congressional investigation of the uranium cartel. In its attempt to discern whether a foreign cartel had been responsible for the sevenfold increase in domestic uranium prices,[97] the Moss subcommittee heard testimony from a dozen high-ranking officials in the U.S. nuclear and uranium industries and subpoenaed all Gulf's internal documents related to the cartel.[98] Simultaneously, the Westinghouse Corporation brought suit against both U.S. and foreign producers, claiming that they had conspired to raise uranium prices and preclude Westinghouse from purchasing uranium on the open market.[99] In 1978, the Tennessee Valley Authority also joined the fray, suing uranium producers around the world for violation of U.S. antitrust law. Eventually, the Westinghouse and TVA suits were brought together into a single case before a Chicago court. Throughout these various proceedings, the Canadians and other producers who refused (quite understandably) to be tried in the United States on the basis of U.S. law for actions committed abroad were declared in contempt of court, and their assets in the United States were frozen.[100]

In response to what was widely perceived as a U.S. intrusion into their legal and economic sovereignty, most of the producing governments soon passed their own legislation forbidding their national

---

[97] *Hearings*, p. 23.

[98] The committee also tried, unsuccessfully, to subpoena officials from all the foreign companies and countries and to gain access to their records. In response, the foreign governments concerned passed their own legislation forbidding the release of these documents.

[99] Runnalls, "Ontario's Uranium Mining Industry," p. 65.

[100] Ibid.

companies from appearing before the U.S. courts on the matter of uranium.[101] In Canada, the country most severely affected by U.S. antitrust actions, the government went so far as to draft the Uranium Information Security Regulations, which made it illegal for any Canadian citizen to release to any foreign government "any note, document or other written or printed material in any way related to conversations, discussions or meetings that took place between January 1, 1972 and December 31, 1975 involving that person or any other person in relation to the exporting from Canada or marketing for use outside Canada of uranium."[102] In effect, the "Gag Order," as it was quickly dubbed by the press, made Canada's participation in the uranium cartel an official secret. And although the order caused tremendous opposition in Canada,[103] it remained on the books, and Canadian officials stayed out of U.S. courts.

Eventually, all lawsuits were settled out of court or allowed to fade away. Westinghouse received a reported $400 million settlement from the domestic defendant producers,[104] and it reached an out-of-court agreement with the Canadian companies "without any admission of wrongdoing." In turn, Westinghouse also compensated the plaintiff utilities with various combinations of cash, uranium, equipment, and services as well as a share of its own proceeds from the antitrust litigation.[105] In the end, the only ones who won were the lawyers. Indeed, the entire uranium industry had become, as one official put it, a "Lawyers' Heritage Fund."[106] Remarked another, "The cartel produced more paper than uranium and enriched more lawyers."[107]

By the time the proceedings at last drew to a close, the uranium cartel was a distant memory and the industry once more in a sham-

---

[101] Ibid., p. 66.

[102] Press release by the Honourable Alastair Gillespie, EMR, Ottawa, October 14, 1977.

[103] See, for instance, Stewart, "Canada's Role in the International Uranium Cartel," pp. 673–80.

[104] Westinghouse's suit in these cases alleged, first, that U.S. firms had benefited from and taken advantage of the foreign cartel and, second, that U.S. parent corporations (such as Gulf) were responsible for the actions of their foreign subsidiaries.

[105] See Yokell and DeSalvo, "Uranium Default," p. 22.

[106] Quoted in Runnalls, "Ontario's Uranium Mining Industry," p. 66.

[107] Personal interview, Toronto, May 10, 1989.

bles. By 1982, prices had fallen to about $20 per pound. By 1988, uranium was selling for approximately $11 per pound. In Canada, Eldorado Mines had purchased Uranium Canada's assets and was then itself shut down and consolidated into the smaller CAMECO. Together with Rio Algom and Denison, the three Canadian firms were competing vociferously even with one another, thus driving prices lower and lower. In 1992, despite prospects of tightening supplies and rising demand in the 1990s, the uranium industry was still showing no signs of a comeback.

By all economic criteria, at least, this need not be the case. The uranium market is still very highly concentrated, especially as the troubles of the 1970s caused several firms to close their mines for good. Also, since 1977 the U.S. AEC has modified its policies to allow for the import of uranium, vastly increasing the number of potential buyers of foreign uranium. And, finally, most analysts are now predicting a significant shortfall in supply by 1995.[108] In fact, the only economic explanation for the depressed market is the existence of substantial stockpiles of uranium in the hands of the producers and utilities. Still, were the producers to take a page from DeBeers's book, they could no doubt manage their stockpiles strategically and keep any excess supply off the market. Moreover, it has even been suggested that the three Canadian producers—who control a very large portion of the world's lowest-cost reserves—could, by working together, manage to set the international price for uranium at a substantially higher level.[109] By all indications, however, even this moderate and national form of cooperation will never again occur in the uranium industry. In fact, according to industry insiders in Canada, there is no possible way that Canadian producers could ever be compelled to do *anything* on a collaborative basis.[110]

To understand why future cooperation in the uranium market appears so unlikely despite the presence of a number of conducive structural factors, it is necessary to examine more closely the underlying internal story of the international uranium cartel and to under-

[108] See, for instance, Neil Behrmann, "Uranium Prices Could Gradually Head Higher on Possibility of 1990's Shortage, Specialists Say," *Wall Street Journal*, November 14, 1988, p. C14.

[109] Personal interview, Ottawa, May 11, 1989.

[110] This was confirmed to me repeatedly in interviews.

stand why it was created, why it disintegrated, and why it may never be repeated.

THE INTERNAL FACTORS

On the surface, the rise and decline of the international uranium cartel can be explained by simple legal and economic criteria: the cartel arose when economic circumstances permitted it, and it fell away under the tremendous legal pressure brought to bear by the U.S. government. Implicit in this reasoning is the assumption that there was, in fact, a uranium cartel, that is, that the members of the group were able to resist the temptations of defection and collaborate instead on a common project of equitable distribution, higher prices, and decreased production.

A deeper view of the uranium cartel, however, reveals considerably more ambiguity on these points. First, although the structural economic conditions were undeniably in place at the time the cartel was formed, the same conditions have existed at other times and are widely thought to characterize the basic state of the market. Yet at these other times, cooperation did not occur. Second, the cartel fell apart *before* the full implications of the Westinghouse affair were known. It disintegrated not because of any external pressures but because its own members repeatedly refused to play by the rules and because its internal structure was incapable of compelling them to do so. Third, the story of the cartel and its aftermath reveals the extent to which one of its central players—the Canadians—were shackled by domestic constraints and deep-seated values that ultimately prohibited them from any cooperative action. In fact, a more in-depth view of the cartel reveals that it was never very effective at all. If anything, it was lucky.

Economic Causes and Effects

As with most cartels, there are basically two economic questions that surround the uranium cartel: did it arise under the structural economic conditions generally deemed most favorable for a cartel, and was it successful in attaining the goals of higher prices and greater profitability usually associated with a successful cartel?

On the first issue, the judgment is mixed. Cooperation in the uranium industry definitely occurred when the right economic conditions—a high concentration, nonsubstitutability, a low fringe, and high barriers to entry—were in place. Yet, these conditions had been operating since the commercial nuclear market first emerged in the mid-1960s and remain in place today. Clearly, some other factors must have intervened for the cartel to have been forged, and the dissipation of these factors must explain why the cartel disintegrated and never reappeared. As was the case with diamonds, economic factors alone do not tell the whole story of the uranium cartel.

The second question, whether the uranium cartel actually affected the world market for uranium, has been the subject of a heated and prolonged debate. On one side, both Westinghouse and the U.S. congressional subcommittee went to great lengths to demonstrate that the tremendous price increases of the 1970s coincided almost identically with the formation of the producers' group in Paris and therefore that the cartel was directly responsible for the increase and guilty of international collusion. As one study concludes, "It is our determined opinion that the uranium cartel, whether formal or informal, was highly successful in its actions to keep back supply and to force prices to rise far higher than they would have risen if competition had prevailed among producers."[111] The study then goes on to argue that the cartel also succeeded in suppressing excess production and pushing uranium prices to a preselected target of $40 per pound.[112] Likewise, during the congressional hearings, Congressman Gore repeatedly argued that "domestic utilities which purchased uranium from cartel members paid higher prices because of price fixing."[113]

The problem with these allegations, logical though they may seem, is that they pay too much attention to the fairly meager efforts of the

---

[111] Radetzki, *Uranium*, p. 118. As critics of Radetzki's analysis have pointed out, however, even he acknowledges that his interest in uranium was "aroused through an assignment by the Westinghouse Corporation" (*Uranium*, acknowledgments). It is therefore somewhat difficult to believe that he writes as a wholly impartial observer.

[112] Ibid., pp. 118–20.

[113] *Hearings*, p. 338.

cartel and too little to a host of outside factors. For instance, the initial rise in prices between 1972 and 1974 also coincided with three serious external shocks: the oil crisis of 1973, which sent all energy prices soaring; the decision by the newly elected Labour government in Australia to halt all uranium export licenses pending a decision on the morality of nuclear power; and a long-awaited announcement by the U.S. AEC that it would gradually phase out its embargo of uranium imports.[114] Any one of these events would have been enough to push uranium prices beyond their 1972 level of $5 to $6 per pound; taken together, they are probably sufficient to explain a spot price of about $14 per pound by the end of 1974. Moreover, all inside reports indicate that the 1974 price was, in fact, much higher than anything the producers had even anticipated. Indeed, it appears in retrospect that the market by this time was leading the producers, instead of vice versa. As a report by NUEXCO, a leading independent uranium broker, concludes, "The prices reportedly established by the 'cartel' at its periodic gatherings were, by the time such prices were implemented, below those then prevailing in the domestic market place, as opposed to leading it."[115]

Likewise, Stewart notes that in late 1973 and early 1974, "world prices for uranium were rising so fast that the cartel could not meet frequently enough to keep its floor price ahead of them."[116] In effect, by 1974 the cartel was actually implementing prices that had already been reached—and occasionally even exceeded—on the open market. Thus, even the U.S. Justice Department was eventually forced to concede that although there had been "an attempt at price fixing in Canada, France, and apparently in a couple of other countries . . . the attempt failed. Ironically, the price the cartel was trying to set was too low. Other forces actually carried it higher than the members expected."[117]

The second aspect that the Moss subcommittee and the Westing-

[114] See Moss, *Politics of Uranium*, p. 111.

[115] Exchange Corporation, "Significant Events in the Uranium Market, 1969–1976," October 15, 1976. Reprinted in *Hearings*, p. 145.

[116] Stewart, "Canada's Role in the International Uranium Cartel," p. 669.

[117] Cited in "The Uranium Dilemma: Why Prices Mushroomed," p. 92. A similar view is also expressed in the congressional testimony of Jerry McAfee, chief executive officer of Gulf. See *Hearings*, pp. 136–39.

house Corporation both chose to overlook was that of timing. The cartel, as will be discussed in greater detail below, was effectively terminated by early 1974. Yet the real price increases did not come until late 1975 and 1976, in the wake of Westinghouse's admission that it would be unable to supply all the uranium for which it had contracted. Arguably, it was the revelation of this tremendous shortfall, plus the subsequent entry of all the affected utilities onto the spot market, that sent uranium prices soaring to over forty dollars per pound by the end of 1976. Ironically, then, the true villain of the price increases may have been Westinghouse and not the producers.[118] Indeed, the producers had agreed early on that uranium prices should not be allowed to rise too high lest they tempt new exploration and a flood of supplies. The price rises of the 1970s, therefore, are evidence not only of the cartel's inability to keep ahead of open-market price pushes but also of its inability to squelch these pushes when they threatened to move prices too high.[119]

Overall, it appears that the uranium cartel had little, if any, effect on prices and even less success in bringing some measure of stability to the market. Although prices did undeniably begin to creep upward only after the cartel was formed, the biggest increases came after it was already gone, and even the initial push can easily be attributed to a number of outside factors. There is, it seems, a great deal of truth in a Gulf official's description of the cartel as "the most ineffective organization known to man. By the time it got going they didn't need it anymore."[120]

Disintegration from Within

A second characteristic of the uranium cartel that was overlooked in much of the ensuing litigation was the degree to which it was

[118] This argument is put forward, for example, in Paul L. Joskow, "Commercial Impossibility, the Uranium Market, and the Westinghouse Case," Working Paper no. 186, Massachusetts Institute of Economics, September 1976, esp. pp. 62–63.

[119] It is interesting to compare the inability of the uranium cartel to keep prices from going too high with DeBeers's extremely successful efforts to stem speculation in the diamond market. See Chap. 2.

[120] Quoted in Ian Anderson, "With a Little Help among Friends," Maclean's, June 8, 1981, p. 23.

completely wracked by internal problems, institutional deficiencies, and defection from its own ranks.

Contrary to popular belief, for instance, the cartel did not disintegrate in the wake of the Westinghouse suits and federal litigation. Rather, the cartel consciously decided to break up early in 1974, when its members (and in particular the Canadians) decided that the upturn in the uranium market made their arrangements obsolete and unnecessary. The only thing holding the participants together was their common interest in keeping prices above the disastrous levels of the late 1960s and early 1970s. Once OPEC and an increase in worldwide demand for uranium had pushed prices back to competitive levels, no one within the cartel saw any compelling reason to continue cooperation.[121] As Jerry McAfee, chief executive officer of Gulf, stated in congressional testimony, the termination of the cartel was brought about by "the fact that the world price so completely and utterly outstripped the ideas then existing as to what the world price should be."[122] The market had changed for the better, prices were up and consumers were anxious to buy. In the eyes of the members, this meant that competition would still allow them all to make a profit and thus that coordination was no longer necessary.

This decision was made easier by the fact that cooperation in the cartel had never been particularly successful. As described earlier, cheating in the cartel had been persistent and widespread. From the start, it had been evident that at least some of the producers were consistently eager to break the rules of the cartel and perpetually unable to resist the temptations of unilateral defection. This proclivity was enhanced, no doubt, by the lack of any type of serious enforcement mechanisms. When the cartel did assign penalties, they

[121] According to a number of participants, the cartel was effectively terminated at its last formal meeting in Johannesburg, when the members decided that any further cooperation was simply not worth the acrimony and effort involved. Personal interviews, Ottawa and Toronto, May 10–12, 1989; see also the testimony of Jerry McAfee, *Hearings*, p. 208. Unfortunately for some of the companies and countries involved, however, the members did not *formalize* the termination of their agreement until October 1975, when the Westinghouse affair began to raise questions about possible prosecution. Thus, although the cartel officially ended after a meeting in Toronto at which representatives from Rio Tinto Zinc and Rio Algom read identical statements declaring that they would no longer participate in any cooperative endeavors, the cartel had actually ceased its operations a full year and a half earlier.

[122] *Hearings*, p. 208.

amounted to little more than timid slaps on the wrist and could simply be absorbed as an operating expense by the offending parties. Thus, although the uranium producers had established all the formal mechanisms of a cartel, the institutions they created never helped them to attain what they needed most—a sense of trust, camaraderie, and commitment. Throughout the life of the cartel, RTZ was still secretly collaborating with the French and the South Africans, the French and the South Africans worried about Canada's ability to sustain its commitment, and everybody resented the Australians. Formal institutions could help paper over these differences by establishing a system in which the rules were clearly laid out and costs and benefits allocated to each, but in the uranium cartel, at least, the institutions were insufficient to create the trust that is central to any cartel's success.

Finally, and most important, the cartel collapsed because its two largest players—the Canadians and the Australians—were, in the end, constrained by domestic politics to such an extent that their continued participation in the cartel became increasingly uneasy and ultimately impossible. Economically, they wanted to cooperate. Politically, they were utterly incapable of doing so.

THE DOMESTIC POLITICS OF URANIUM

The uranium cartel is a story of many things: it is a story of the promises and threats of nuclear power, of corporate treachery, and of the ambitious reach of American antitrust law. Most of all, however, it is a story of how internal characteristics can impede a cooperative international arrangement that, by all external criteria, would result in mutual gains for all participants. Indeed, the uranium cartel is a prime example of the extent to which the structure of a market is insufficient to establish cooperation between the producers and the extent to which it is factors internal to the producers themselves that determine when cooperation will occur and whether it will be successful.

Moreover, the uranium market is particularly interesting insofar as it has always been mainly controlled by governmental actors and mainly driven by the dual national security interests of weapons and energy. Accordingly, it would seem to fit most of the internal criteria for successful cartelization outlined in previous chapters. For instance, all the major producers have always kept their domestic uranium industries under tight national controls and have regulated production, prices, and sales with a degree of centralized authority that is otherwise unheard of in these capitalist democracies.[123] Likewise, the major producing nations have also broken with domestic precedent in most instances by shrouding the entire nuclear industry in a veil of security-inspired secrecy. Although this secrecy is quite out of the ordinary for most of these governments, it is understandable given uranium's extremely strategic nature, and thus any attempt by these governments to coordinate their activities could, theoretically at least, have been covered by this veil. In addition, exclusivity could also have been easily established in the uranium industry. Not only were there just a handful of major producers, but they could also have legitimized any exclusive dealings amongst themselves by citing the needs of nonproliferation. That is, by emphasizing the international caretaker role that they had already adopted by virtue of their regulations concerning the export of enriched uranium,[124] the five major producers could have created their own club that, more likely than not, would have been immune even from international reproach.

Thus, the unique penetration of the uranium markets by governments and govermental actors created many of the conditions that should be conducive to the formation and perpetuation of a cartel,

---

[123] For instance, the authors of the Atomic Energy Act, the legislation that created the U.S. Atomic Energy Commission, admitted that "the Act creates a government monopoly of the sources of atomic energy and buttresses this position with a variety of broad governmental powers and prohibitions on private activity. The field of atomic energy is made an island of socialism in the midst of a free economy." Quoted in Gray, *Great Uranium Cartel*, p. 39.

[124] In this context, it is interesting to note that several of the uranium-producing states—the United States, Canada, the former Soviet Union, and Australia—are also signatories of the Nuclear Non-Proliferation Treaty and have pledged themselves not to export nuclear materials without international safeguards. Insofar as these states are determined to prevent the spread of nuclear weapons outside their own ranks, they can be considered members of one of the world's most exclusive "clubs." See, for instance, Joseph S. Nye, "Maintaining the Non-Proliferation Regime," *International Organization* 35 (Winter 1981): 15–38; and Roger K. Smith, "Explaining the Non-Proliferation Regime: Anomalies for Contemporary International Relations Theory," *International Organization* 41 (Spring 1987): 253–81.

or at least to a degree of market coordination among the producers. What we find instead is a record of defection and demise that can be attributed only to the internal characteristics of several leading producers. As a 1976 report by NUEXCO concluded:

Following the 1972 election of the Labour Government in Australia, uranium sales activity essentially ceased in that country. Similarly, the Atomic Energy Control Board of Canada was directed by the Canadian government to deny export licenses for uranium sales when the prices were below certain established levels. Thus, the ability of the "cartel" to affect the course of prices was sharply circumscribed by political considerations within the countries of its reported members.[125]

To be certain, not all the cartel's members were hamstrung by their internal values and institutions. On the contrary, three of the major producers in the cartel—France, South Africa, and Rio Tinto Zinc—faced little or no internal opposition to their participation in the cartel. This is not to argue, of course, that the three are authoritarian or totalitarian institutions. It does seem however, that they all enjoy a greater degree of centralized control and isolation from internal factions than do Australia and Canada. In France, for instance, there is a much greater tradition of business-government cooperation and a much closer intermingling between the various actors in the uranium market. Similarly, South Africa's Nufcor appears to be a perfect mixture of government and industry interests and is not likely to run into domestic opposition from either the business community or the population at large. And, finally, although RTZ is a publicly held British corporation, it is also a fairly secretive organization and a company whose discreet links to the Anglo American empire and the Rothschild family probably make it an unlikely candidate for either a corporate take-over or a stockholder rebellion.[126] Thus, the allegation that France, South Africa, and Rio

[125] NUEXCO, "Significant Events in the Uranium Market, 1969–1976," in *Hearings*, p. 145.
[126] A slightly different interpretation of Rio Tinto's role in the cartel would suggest that, in fact, the company was susceptible to international pressures because of its closeness with the British government and its leading role in a number of other metals markets. By this interpretation, RTZ was instrumental in dismantling the cartel once it felt that litigation in the United States would be too hot to handle politically. In either case, though, the basic argument of this section would remain unchanged.

Tinto Zinc have been cooperating in their own "inner club" makes a great deal of sense in light of the arguments advanced thus far. The problem, however, was that these three actors were not alone in the uranium market. Rather, to affect the international market, any cooperative endeavor needed to include the largest producers—the Americans, the Australians, and the Canadians. And these countries, for better or worse, were characterized by a variety of internal political factors that limited their ability to participate in any cooperative regulation of the international market.

To begin with, the United States provides the greatest example of the impediments that can be created by domestic politics. Even though the United States is one of the largest producers of uranium in the world and its own domestic needs and international position should have offered it both the desire and the possibility to regulate the long-term security of the uranium market, it has been completely unable to participate in even the mildest form of market coordination.[127] Instead, the various agencies that have controlled the nuclear industry in the United States[128] have been constantly barraged by competing constituents and bureaucratic claims. For instance, wartime cooperation between the United States, Great Britain, and Canada broke down, *despite* the vehement protests of the scientific community, because probusiness interests in the United States had begun to see the cooperative program as a relative boost for the Canadians and the British and therefore as a threat to postwar industrial competition. Likewise, although the U.S. Atomic Energy Commission initially invested millions of dollars to ensure a viable Canadian uranium industry, the agency abruptly cut off the Canadian contracts in 1959 in response to growing political pressures from U.S. producers. In imposing this virtual embargo, the United States was not only incurring the outrage of one of its foremost allies and trading partners but was also acting in gross violation of its obligations under the General Agreement on Tariffs and

[127] Admittedly, the United States has been an active participant in international efforts at nonproliferation. These efforts, however, are directed primarily at the export of enriched uranium and are therefore several steps removed from the uranium market with which we are mainly concerned here.

[128] The AEC was succeeded by the Energy Research and Development Administration (ERDA) in 1974. In 1977, responsibility for uranium matters was transferred to the Department of Energy.

Trade (GATT). Nevertheless, domestic pressures had become so intense and so geographically diverse that ultimately the AEC had no choice. Ever since that time, moreover, the policies of the United States concerning uranium production, trade, and enrichment have vacillated widely. The mandates given to the various regulatory agencies have evolved in response to changing administrations and political priorities and the entire program has been buffeted by the conflicting pressures exerted by producers, utilities, and the antinuclear movement. As a result, the United States has been forced to isolate itself from any international attempt at collaboration and has acted as a unitary actor in the international uranium market.

A similar pattern, though with somewhat different overtones, has emerged in Australia, where the development of a vocal and powerful antinuclear movement has made uranium production a national issue and precluded the country from participating in any international arrangements in the uranium market. When Australia joined the cartel, it was not yet an active force on the world market. Most of its existing mines had either been depleted in the 1960s or had simply closed as the market stagnated and prices fell. By the early 1970s, however, the expected boom in nuclear energy had rekindled the interest of many Australian mining companies, and by the end of 1972, more than eighty companies were engaged in uranium exploration.[129] Just as quickly as the boom had begun, though, it was subjected to a passionate debate concerning the rights of the Aborigines, the morality of any Australian involvement in the nuclear industry, and the environmental detriments of strip-mining. Thus, even while Australia was using its vast prospective production as a means of achieving leverage within the cartel, its own domestic politics were making that production increasingly more difficult to achieve. In 1973, in response to domestic pressure, the Australian government announced that all future export contracts would be stalled pending the development of policies for environmental protection, Aboriginal land rights, and safeguards. In 1974, work on the uranium deposits of the northern territories was delayed even further by extensive negotiations with the Aborigines and by the need to comply with increasingly severe environmental regulations. By

[129] Owen, *Economics of Uranium*, p. 91.

1975, uranium mining had become the number one political issue in Australia.[130] Just as the Australian government's leverage within the cartel was growing, its ability to control the domestic uranium industry was being sharply curtailed by its political need to respond to a wide variety of public concerns. Because the uranium industry in Australia was relatively new, the government was able to bring all the producers together and to formulate a coherent and cooperative national strategy. But because the entire industry was also so politically controversial, the government was ultimately unable to win domestic support for uranium mining, let alone for its participation in a cartel designed to regulate the entire international uranium market.

Finally, the story of the Canadians and the cartel provides the most glaring case of how the values attached to participatory democracy may run contrary to and impede any efforts at international cartelization. From the start, it seems, the Canadian government realized the political difficulties that its participation in any orderly marketing arrangement would encounter, and it therefore went to extreme lengths to structure its participation so as to keep it immune from domestic rebuke. The Ministry of Energy, Mines, and Resources was extraordinarily careful to create a legal trail that made participation in the cartel mandatory and that couched this participation in the language of national security and the long-term viability of a critical industry. The government also took unprecedented steps—before, during, and after the cartel—to ensure that a measure of secrecy was maintained and that knowledge of the cartel's operations was restricted to only a handful of individuals. Finally, the Ministry of Energy, Mines, and Resources even indicated its willingness to use its own national uranium stockpiles as a buffer of sorts and thus to accept the critical responsibilities of the cartel leader. The problem, however, was that domestic politics and deep-seated political values in Canada ran counter to these exceptional steps and ultimately rendered them inadequate to maintain Canada's participation in the cartel.

Canada simply had no institutional history of either business-government cooperation or intercorporate coordination. On the con-

[130] Paul Kelley, "The Uranium Men Discover They've Got a Lousy Image," *National Times* (Melbourne), August 16–21, 1976, p. 1.

trary, with the exception of the explicitly national Crown corporations, Canadian business was accustomed to competition and extremely wary of any official attempt to coordinate the activities of competing firms. As a result, most of the Canadian companies joined the government's program only under duress, and even during the operation of the cartel, they continued to distrust one another and even to sign secret, separate contracts with their preferred customers. Moreover, with the possible exception of Jack Austin, the officials who were actually running Canada's participation in the cartel were themselves extremely uncomfortable with the idea, especially with the secrecy it required. Throughout their tenure in the cartel, the Canadians were dogged by a sense of uneasiness and a fear of the possible legal ramifications. Although the participants were sincerely convinced that cooperation was in the best interests of both the uranium industry and Canada itself, they were still wary of their participation in an international marketing arrangement and worried that changing political conditions might make them subject to prosecution. Accordingly, they were all extremely careful to protect themselves from possible future prosecution by notifying everyone they thought should be notified and thus to leak the secret as they thought appropriate.

In the end, their fears were well-grounded. All the Canadian companies that had links to U.S. firms were made party to the Westinghouse suit and, especially in the case of Gulf Minerals Canada Limited, dragged through a humiliating and expensive federal inquiry in the United States. Soon afterward, in response to growing opposition from the Conservative party, the Liberal government launched a quasi-judicial review of the cartel that found "just cause" for criminal charges to be levied against all participants and charged two high-ranking officials of the Ministry of Energy, Mines, and Resources as "unindicted co-conspirators." Although all charges were eventually either dropped or settled out of court, the political and popular furor from which they arose is indicative of how incendiary the entire cartel issue had become in Canada and how deeply it disturbed the mainstream of Canadian public opinion. In particular, Canadians were concerned about the secrecy of the cartel. Despite official insistence that Canada's role in the cartel had been announced both publicly and diplomatically in 1972,[131] public opinion continued to regard the cartel as a covert activity and therefore something that tarnished Canada's long-standing aloofness from any such international arrangements. That Canada had participated in an effort to regulate world markets was not deemed particularly egregious; there were not even any debates on this in the House of Commons. But the fact that the government had acted "in secret" was perceived as a gross violation of an unwritten, yet deeply held rule of political conduct. Thus, the Canadian government was—and is—caught in a classic catch-22. The success of any cartel seems to be significantly enhanced by secrecy, and indeed I have argued that one of the reasons that the uranium cartel fell was its inability to keep secrets. Yet, public opinion and political values in Canada argue strongly against government involvement in any secretive international arrangements.

Finally, Canada's participation in the uranium cartel was vulnerable from the start to the changing whims of electoral politics. The cartel began when Jack Austin, a new political appointee, was able to garner enough political momentum to pass the regulations that legitimized and even compelled the companies' involvement. When Austin left, however, he took with him much of the motivating force, and new ministers and new governments passed their own, often contradictory regulations. Eventually, the entire matter became a parody of electoral and bureaucratic politics. Facing severe opposition from the Conservative party in an election year, the Liberal government pressed charges against all the Canadian companies, even though two of the companies were Crown corporations and thus official arms of the government and even though all the companies had been *legally required* to participate. In an even greater irony,

---

[131] In a press release dated October 14, 1977, the Honourable Alastair Gillespie, then head of the Ministry of Energy, Mines, and Resources, argued that "the notion that Canadian participation in the marketing arrangement was undertaken in secret is, quite simply, untrue" (EMR, Ottawa). The minister is correct. In fact, the Canadian government had informed the U.S. government of its participation in February 1972 (Letter of February 14, 1972, from the commercial counsellor of the Canadian Embassy, Washington, to the acting director of the Division of International Programs of the U.S. Atomic Energy Commission). Moreover, as mentioned earlier, the Paris meetings had been reported at some length by the *Toronto Globe and Mail*.

while the government in the form of the Department of Justice was launching a suit against Austin's deputies at EMR, the government in the form of the Treasury allocated funds to EMR to pay for the legal defense of the men.[132]

The immediate impact of these shifting political forces was to make it highly unlikely that Canadian uranium producers would ever again participate in any sort of government-sponsored cooperative endeavor. As one insider noted: "[The politics of the cartel's aftermath] left a very bitter taste in the mouths of the producers. There is no possible way that private producers in Canada would ever cooperate with Canada again. In fact, they won't do anything in a cooperative sense *forever*. . . . The logic [of the cartel] was so firm, so well-founded, but it was so distorted by the politics of the day."[133]

On an even more profound level, the fate of Canada's participation in the uranium cartel indicates the difficulty that democratic states will face whenever they attempt to bind themselves to international cooperative agreements. If, as in the uranium cartel, success on the international level depends on achieving a certain amount of secrecy and commitment among the members, then states for whom openness and opposition politics are important will be at a distinct disadvantage. And if, as in the Canadian case, they are particularly sensitive to public opinion and factional politics, they will be extremely hard-pressed to play the kind of game that cartel leadership demands.

[132] Personal interview, Toronto, May 11, 1989.
[133] Personal interview, Toronto, May 11, 1989.

CHAPTER FOUR

Howling like Wolves: Cooperation in the International Gold Market

On the surface, the gold market is an example of nearly perfect competition. There are over fifty producers and millions of buyers. The price fluctuates daily in accordance with shifts in demand, and a global market provides instantaneous communication between buyers and sellers.

Beneath the surface, though, the international market for gold is not quite as open and competitive as it appears. For years, two of the leading producers—the Soviet Union and South Africa—played a central role in shaping the market and steering the price of gold. Because the market is so vast and so active, the two producers were never able to exercise the type of control that we saw in the diamond market. They never had the power to set prices or regulate global supply. And they never embedded their relationship in a formal institution. There is no international gold cartel.

For years, however, there was a quiet arrangement between the Soviet and South African producers. It was a loose arrangement, to be sure, more differentiated and less adversarial than that which bound them in the diamond market. The arrangement was never designed to control the market but only to coordinate the market behavior of these two leading producers. And on these terms it succeeded remarkably well. By quietly cooperating, the Soviet and South African producers were able to maximize their own positions in the international gold market and minimize the likelihood of a significant decline in gold prices.

To a large extent, this cooperation is again attributable to structural conditions. Because the former Soviet Union and South Africa together produce about 45 percent of the world's gold, cooperation is in some sense a natural result of structure. Yet once again, structural criteria do not provide a sufficient explanation for cooperation. They cannot explain why the Soviets and South Africans succeeded where so many other firms and countries have failed. They cannot explain why Soviet and South African cooperation in the gold market was characterized by a peculiar and distinct division of labor. And they cannot explain why this cooperation began to falter with the breakup of the Soviet Union.

Instead, cooperation in the gold market can be explained only by reference to the cooperators themselves. Specifically, cooperation was facilitated by the high degree of centralization that marked both countries' gold mining industries and by the autonomous position of the industry within the state. In the former Soviet Union, the gold industry *was* the state; the government controlled all aspects of gold mining and marketing, and all decisions pertaining to gold were made by a small group of high-ranking officials. In South Africa, gold has long been produced by a handful of extremely powerful mining houses, all of which have a long history of cooperation with one another and with the state.

And thus the internal structures of both states yielded similar results: gold policy was made consistently, coherently, and apart from any competing pressures or internal opposition. Because they were autonomous, the leading players in the gold industry could allow their gold sales to be dictated by a joint concern for stability. They could act strategically in the market, making decisions with an eye to the long term and implementing these decisions without fear of domestic ramifications.

But if cooperation in the gold market was facilitated by the autonomy of the Soviet and South African producers, it was also vulnerable to a dissolution of this autonomy. In the late 1980s and early 1990s, the political changes sweeping South Africa and the Soviet Union quietly began to manifest themselves in the market. The changes were not dramatic. Prices did not plummet, stocks did not suddenly accumulate, and there was no formal cartel to tumble. But still there was change. The mutual restraint that had bound the Soviets and South Africans dissolved, and the Soviets in particular began to seek the short-term benefits of unilateral action. As long as they had autonomy at home, the Soviets were able to cooperate in the market, working with the South Africans to smooth the inevitable fluctuations in the price of gold and maximize the long-run interests of the major gold producers. Once this autonomy dissolved, however, cooperation gave way to chaos.

OPERATION OF THE INTERNATIONAL MARKET

In many respects, the gold market is one of the simplest markets in the world. Gold is a completely homogeneous product, easy to detect and impossible to copy. It has unique physical properties and has been prized for centuries as an object of beauty and a symbol of wealth. It is nonsubstitutable in most of its industrial uses and enjoys extremely high barriers to entry. Gold is difficult to find, expensive to mine, and very rare. Together, all the gold mined throughout history would occupy a space less than nineteen cubic yards.

Most critical, perhaps, the gold market is also marked by a high level of concentration. Although production is scattered across the globe, most producers are small, high-cost, and contribute little to the overall supply of gold. The bulk of the world's gold remains in the hands of a few very large producers. South Africa no longer dominates the market to the extent it did earlier in this century, but it remains the single largest source of gold, accounting in 1990 for approximately 30 percent of world production. The United States and the former Soviet Union each produce nearly 15 percent of the total, and Australia and Canada contribute another 20 percent. Together, the top five producers account for 75 percent of world production. Everyone else remains on the fringes.

On the supply side, then, the gold market is straightforward and ripe for cartelization. What makes matters more complicated is gold's lingering role as a monetary metal. Most of the gold market is composed of industrial demand. Indeed, the jewelry and electronics industries alone account for roughly three-fourths of total world demand. For these consumers, gold is a commodity like any other. It is a raw material to be bought, processed, and sold. The complication, though, is that there are other buyers in the gold market who do not share these same concerns. For them, gold is a very special kind of commodity. These consumers buy gold not to use it but to store and speculate in it. They purchase gold as a financial instrument rather than an industrial input.

This financial or speculative demand arose, of course, from gold's traditional role as a monetary metal. From 1717 to 1973, most of the world's currencies were linked in some way to gold, and the price of gold was fixed by the central banks that bought it. Gold was the currency in which all national debts were ultimately reckoned, and flows of gold from one nation to another were taken as an adequate representation of the financial relationship between the two. Under these conditions, nations went to the market to buy gold whenever an increase in their currency accounts permitted them the luxury of building up their reserves or whenever they wanted to protect themselves against an inflation in their own currency. Nations returned to the market as sellers whenever they needed to settle their international debts or had to raise funds to cover some domestic exigency.

Today, of course, the world's currencies float against one another and against gold. Gold prices fluctuate daily,[1] and central banks no longer dominate the international market. Yet gold retains a monetary function. It still serves as a medium of exchange between states and as an anchor for some currencies. It is also still the core of most national reserves. The United States, for example, holds over 70 percent of its total reserves in gold; Switzerland holds nearly 65 percent; and France, Italy, and the Netherlands each keep over 50 percent. Germany's gold reserves account for approximately 45 percent of its total reserves, and Britain's are just over 30 percent. The only major industrialized country that still keeps a relatively insignificant portion of its reserves in gold is Japan; and in recent years there has

---

[1] The official price of gold is still set daily in an odd ritual known as the "London fixing." Five people, each representing one of the major bullion houses, meet in the London offices of N. M. Rothschild & Sons. There, each seated before a miniature British flag, they haggle over the price of gold, phoning back when necessary to their trading rooms to gauge the level and direction of activity. Whenever members want to announce a change in their position, they raise a flag; when all the flags are down, the price of gold is "fixed." For more information on the fix and its members, see, for instance, "Fixing the London Gold Fixing," *Europa Star*, December 18, 1986, p. 228; and "Survey: Money and Finance," *Economist*, January 17, 1981, p. 4.

been much speculation about the possibility that Japan will become a major purchaser of gold.[2]

Even more important, though, gold's historical link to money remains a powerful force of sentiment in the market. Many people buy gold not because they need it for industrial or monetary purposes but because they simply trust in gold or fear the alternatives. Gold is still seen as a safe financial haven, a refuge from inflation, and a savings of last resort. In times of crisis and political turmoil, people still turn to gold, either as an investment vehicle or a physical means of transporting wealth. As a result, the gold market is affected by forces much broader than the usual shifts of supply and demand. It responds to changes in the price of oil, in the value of the U.S. dollar, and in the general economic indicators of the industrialized countries. It is also extremely susceptible to changes in the political environment: traditionally, gold prices have risen during times of crisis and declined during eras of peace. And, finally, the gold market is also affected by intangible shifts of sentiment. Like other investment options, gold is subject to trends, slipping in and out of fashion without any underlying rationale.

Together, the forces that impinge on the gold market make it an extremely complicated place. Gold deals are conducted all day, around the world, and by thousands of intermediaries. New options in gold loans, gold bonds, and gold-backed securities have drawn investors to the market, increasing speculation and magnifying price fluctuations. The gold market today is one of the most vibrant and volatile exchanges in the world. There are so many players and so many motives that no one can ever hope to control it or even to manipulate it beyond a certain small extent.

Still, despite its size and its idiosyncrasies, the gold market rests, as do all others, on a fundamental relationship between supply and demand. Gold is valued by banks, jewelers, and investors because it is heavy and shiny—and rare. The supply of gold has simply never been quite sufficient to go around. Thus, regardless of financial instruments and investor sentiment, the supply of newly mined gold remains a critical factor in the market. And the suppliers thus retain

[2] See Timothy Green, *The Prospect for Gold: The View to the Year 2000* (New York: Walker, 1987), pp. 120–21.

a significant potential to coordinate their behavior and influence the market.

For the most part, this coordination has not occurred. The American, Canadian, and Australian producers act alone, each mine working to boost its production and raise its profits. The Soviets and South Africans, however, have cooperated.

GOLD IN SOUTH AFRICA

To a large extent, modern South Africa was built on a base of gold. Although the lure of diamonds initially brought investors to the area and the state now boasts a full range of mining and manufacturing industries, the core of its economy has always been gold. In the early decades of this century, gold accounted for nearly 20 percent of South Africa's national income and over 60 percent of the country's foreign trade.[3] In 1980 it contributed over 68 percent of South Africa's exports and over $1 billion in taxes.[4] Less tangible, but just as critical, the development of the country has been intricately linked to the fortunes of its gold mines. It was the mines that first drew capital into the country,[5] the mines that created most of the country's infrastructure,[6] and the miners who played a key role in the creation of the state and the shaping of its domestic agenda.

The relationship between state and capital, between the government and the gold industry in South Africa, is thus a complicated one. Despite its critical role, the industry remains completely in private hands. Gold is discovered, mined, and processed entirely by private corporations. All the country's gold *sales*, however, are handled by a single government agency, the Federal Reserve Bank of South

[3] Leo Katzen, *Gold and the South African Economy* (Cape Town: A. A. Balkema, 1964), pp. 46 and 48, tables 8 and 9.

[4] See George A. Morgan, "The Mineral Industry of the Republic of South Africa," in *Bureau of Mines Yearbook*, vol. 3, 1987 (Washington, D.C.: Government Printing Office, 1989), p. 771, table 3, and p. 761. The exact tax figure is $1.2 billion.

[5] According to one estimate, gold accounted for over five million pounds worth of new investment per year between 1887 and 1910. See S. H. Frankel, *Capital Investment in Africa* (London: Oxford University Press, 1938), p. 95.

[6] For instance, in 1941 the Industrial and Agricultural Requirements Commission cited gold mining as "the mainspring of the Union's economic system." Industrial and Agricultural Requirements Commission, 3d Interim Report, U.G. 40-1941, para. 46, cited in Katzen, *Gold and the South African Economy*, p. 53.

Africa.[7] In practice, then, although private firms can gauge their levels of production in accordance with prevailing market prices and their own profit considerations, they themselves cannot shape the market, as all sales are routed through the state. This contradiction, however, runs both ways. Because gold is so central to the South African economy, the government in many ways is beholden to, if not indeed dependent on, the gold industry. With gold sales providing South Africa's major link to the international economy, the government does not want to risk damaging the health of the gold-mining sector or raising the ire of the gold producers. Thus the official separation between the public and private sectors is largely mitigated by the mutuality of their aims and by the economic leverage wielded by the industry.

In addition, the industry itself is highly centralized and tightly controlled. Ostensibly, there are a number of competing producers in the country. In practice, though, these producers are linked by a series of intimate ties and a history of coordination. They are also all linked in some way to one central firm—the Anglo American Corporation of South Africa. Ultimately, the story of gold in South Africa is the story of this corporation and the family that controls it, the Oppenheimers. To a considerable extent, it is Anglo which shapes the gold policy of the state and which, in conjunction with the other producers and the government, has been able to push the domestic industry away from competition and toward cooperation.

The Founding of the Rand

In 1886, gold was discovered on the Witwatersrand. It was not the first report of gold in the area. Indeed, since the 1850s, scattered deposits had been found littered around the Transvaal, an area that stretched from the Vaal River in the south to the Limpopo in the north.[8] These earlier deposits, however, had proved to be of only minor economic significance. The Rand was different.

Almost at once, it became clear that the Witwatersrand deposits

[7] There is one exception. Gold coins—Krugerrands—are sold by the Chamber of Mines.

[8] For a description of these early discoveries and the initial attempts at mining, see Owen Letcher, *The Gold Mines of Southern Africa* (London: Waterlow & Sons, 1936; New York: Arno Press, 1974).

extended farther and deeper than any other deposits in the world. By 1892, the value of gold produced in the Rand had already exceeded the value of South Africa's diamond production,[9] and by 1898 the Republic of South Africa had emerged as the largest producer of gold in the world, accounting for 27 percent of total gold output.[10] Nearly all this gold came from the Rand.

Getting the gold out of the Rand, however, was far more vexing that the numbers alone might suggest. In most of the other great gold rushes—in California, Alaska, and Australia—the gold was primarily alluvial, meaning that it was carried by water and could be retrieved simply by panning and sifting through the silt on the river bottom. The South African gold, by contrast, existed in reefs, layers of microscopic gold particles that stretched diagonally far beneath the surface of the Rand. What made the Rand astonishing was the sheer depth of these gold-bearing veins and the consistent quality of the gold metal they bore; what made the Rand so troublesome was that the deposits themselves had a surprisingly low gold content. None of the Rand gold existed in lodes, nuggets, or even pebbles. Instead, it occurred almost solely in "banket," a conglomerate of rock and minerals that contains just an invisible fraction of gold.

In mining terms, the composition of these reefs meant that new methods of crushing and extraction would need to be developed. In economic terms, it meant that mining would be possible only when done on the very largest of scales. From the start, therefore, gold mining in South Africa was destined to be dominated by big businesses. Unlike the gold rushes of California and Australia and even the early days of the South African diamond fields, gold mining on the Rand was never the province of the individual prospector or the small-time adventurer.[11] Rather, those who dug for gold were largely

[9] Katzen, *Gold and the South African Economy*, p. 44.

[10] A. C. M. Webb, "Mining in South Africa," in *Economic History of South Africa*, ed. Francis L. Coleman (Pretoria: Haum, 1983), p. 179. There are numerous accounts of these early gold days and of the creation of Johannesburg, often called the "City of Gold." See, for example, Eric Rosenthal, *Gold Bricks and Mortar: 60 Years of Johannesburg History* (Johannesburg: Printing House, 1946); Lawrence Neame, *City Built on Gold* (South Africa: Central News Agency, 1960); and William Charles Scully, *The Ridge of the White Waters* (London: Stanley Paul, 1912).

[11] In the very early stages, there was a rush of individual prospectors. Most, though, rushed to the areas that had been discovered before the major Rand, and many of them were working on behalf of larger syndicates or investment groups. See Webb, "Mining in South Africa," pp. 175–76.

the same people who had already made their fortunes in diamonds and who already commanded the heights of the South African economy.[12]

Even for the wealthiest investors, however, the Rand still posed intractable problems. The inaccessability of the ore meant tremendous start-up costs. To be profitable, the mines had to cover a considerable surface area and be sunk deep below the visible outcropping. The low gold content of the ore also meant that huge quantities of it had to be processed in a relatively short period of time. The mines, therefore, had to operate on a very large scale, and the miners had to be able to afford the most sophisticated methods of gold extraction.[13] Moreover, the scale and nature of these mines made them extremely labor- as well as capital-intensive. If they were to be profitable, the mines would need a huge and steady supply of cheap labor. Finally, these constraints had to be considered in the context of a fixed price for gold. Although the demand for the metal was virtually unlimited, the price for it was not. Thus mining gold made sense only if costs could be kept below a certain minimum level.

Juggling these various constraints quickly proved too difficult for most of the original mining companies. Between 1887 and 1932, six hundred gold-mining firms had established themselves on the Rand. By 1932, only fifty-seven remained, and even these continued to face tremendous pitfalls.[14] The Rand was indubitably the single greatest source of gold in the world, but making money from that gold was no simple matter. The only way to turn a profit was to

[12] There are some excellent biographies of these people and the role they played in the economic development of South Africa. See, for instance, Robert I. Rotberg, *The Founder: Cecil Rhodes and the Pursuit of Power* (New York: Oxford University Press, 1988); Geoffrey Wheatcroft, *The Randlords* (New York: Atheneum, 1986); and Sir Theodore Gregory, *Ernest Oppenheimer and the Economic Development of Southern Africa* (Cape Town: Oxford University Press, 1962).
[13] In 1887 two Scottish chemists discovered that gold could be extracted or "leached" from its ore by suspension in a weak cyanide solution. This new system of extraction proved very efficient on the Rand, but it demanded the creation of cyanide plants as well as special mills to crush the ore to sufficient fineness. See L. H. Gann and Peter Duignan, *Why South Africa Will Survive* (New York: St. Martin's, 1981), p. 146; and Webb, "Mining in South Africa," p. 180.
[14] Alf Stadler, *The Political Economy of Modern South Africa* (London: Croom Helm, 1987), pp. 50–51.

consolidate production, boost output, and keep costs—especially labor costs—as low as possible.

Consolidation and Collaboration

To a large extent, this looming need to reduce costs shaped the structure of the gold industry and laid the foundation of its subsequent development. At the same time, however, the methods that the industry chose also reflected the people who presided over the industry and the political climate in which they operated. Together, the structure of the market and the nature of its participants created a very peculiar, but very powerful, industry—an industry remarkable both for the cooperation that binds its producers and for the links it has forged with the state and throughout the national economy.

As the gold industry sank its roots deeper into the Rand, the movements toward consolidation became ever more pronounced. The shakedown that had begun in the earliest days of the mines picked up even greater speed over time, as high costs and virulent competition drove all but the largest and most powerful firms out of the business. This sort of consolidation was to be expected, of course, and represents little more than the natural evolution of firms in a competitive, high-cost industry. What happened next, however, was unprecedented: the surviving firms began to organize themselves into "groups," a corporate structure that was developed on the Rand and to which it still remains unique.

In many respects the groups were nothing but a sequential step in the consolidation process. As development of the mines was more and more a financial concern, it became clear that the miners also had to be businesspeople, skillful in finding investment capital as well as gold. What the groups did, therefore, was to take care of the business side of things. Each group was composed of a number of quasi-independent mines linked together and supported by a central finance house. This finance house did all the group's business: it covered the start-up costs, found the outside investors, and brought new mines into the network. The finance house could afford the initial expenses of sinking a mine and "proving" its gold. More important, it also had a large enough base of operations to woo overseas investors with the promise of high returns at low risk.[15] By organizing and presiding over groups, the finance houses could benefit from the largest economies of scale and offer these benefits in turn to the individual mines and mining companies that chose to participate in the group. Groups also provided their members with a central source of technical expertise and managerial advice. As described by one group leader: "The term 'group' has a wider meaning in the South African mining industry than its statutory definition. . . . The parent house not only administers companies that are not necessarily subsidiaries, but provides them with a full range of technical and administrative services, and is able to assist them in finding capital for expansion and development."[16] The parent, or finance house, thus buffered the independent firm not only from the cold winds of competition but also from the hassles of finance, management, and capital investment. All the firm had to do was to find gold, mine it, and allow the finance house to become its majority shareholder. Not surprisingly, most of the independent companies eventually decided to ally themselves with one of the major groups.[17] In many respects, therefore, the group system acted as a rational engine of consolidation. As one observer has noted:

> The Gold Mining Industry may claim to provide a working model of a "rationalized" industry. Through the group system of control of separate mining companies and the close cooperation of the whole industry . . . it has substituted for the blind selection by competition of the fittest to survive, a conscious and deliberate choice of methods, equipment, areas and personnel on the basis of an extremely detailed comparative study of results.[18]

[15] From as early as the 1890s, it cost up to $2 million to start a new mine, and most of this money was raised overseas, especially in Great Britain. By 1932, £200 million had been brought into the gold industry, of which £120 million came from abroad. See Webb, "Mining in South Africa," p. 182. See also Duncan Innes, *Anglo American and the Rise of Modern South Africa* (New York: Monthly Review Press, 1984), p. 54.

[16] Anglo American Corporation Annual Report, cited in David Pallister et al., *South Africa Inc.: The Oppenheimer Empire* (London: Simon & Schuster, 1987), p. 6.

[17] For more information on the group system, see John Martin, "Group Administration in the Gold Mining Industry of the Witwatersrand," *Economic Journal* 39 (December 1929): 536–52. See also Katzen, *Gold and the South African Economy*, pp. 9–11; and Innes, *Anglo American*, p. 56.

[18] Henry Clay, cited in Frankel, *Capital Investment in Africa*, pp. 81–82.

By the time the depression hit, the group system had become pre-dominant in the gold-mining industry, and nearly all the firms on the Rand were directly linked to one of the six major mining houses.[19] The gold industry had become completely dominated by major corporations, and it was these corporations that together controlled and directed the course of the industry.

Even as this consolidation was occurring, a second critical process was also underway. As the mining houses drew closer to one another, they also moved closer to the government of South Africa, voicing their preferences and exerting an ever greater influence over a broad range of economic and social policies.

Initially the producers turned to the government because they needed to reduce their wage bills. Because mining was so labor-intensive,[20] the producers realized that to increase their long-term profits, they needed to secure a large, reliable, and inexpensive labor force. The obvious choice for this force, of course, was the native blacks. But bound by custom to their land and their own occupations, most of the blacks had little interest in working in the mines and no real incentive to do so. What the industry began to do, therefore, was to pressure the government to pass laws that would compel the blacks into the mines and force them to accept certain industrywide wage standards. In 1890, for instance, the industry's association, the Chamber of Mines, informed the Kruger government that "private enterprise has repeatedly failed in attempting to organize and maintain an adequate supply of Kaffirs [blacks]. The task must be undertaken by the public authorities, and the Chamber trusts that the Government will lend it their indispensable assistance."[21]

At first the state kept its distance, leaving the producers to launch their own efforts at organizing and controlling the available labor

[19] Five of the houses—Rand Mines, Gold Fields of South Africa, Johannesburg Consolidated Investment, General Mining and Finance Corporation, and the Union Corporation—were founded in the 1890s. Anglo American joined the network in 1917, and Anglo-Transvaal Consolidated Investment was created in 1933. In 1971, Thomas Barlow & Sons acquired Rand Mines, forming the new Barlow Rand Ltd., and in 1980, Union Corporation and General Mining were merged into a single company, Gencor.

[20] During the first two decades of the industry's operation, labor costs accounted for approximately 60 percent of the industry's total costs. Innes, *Anglo American*, p. 50.

[21] Chamber of Mines, Second Annual Report, 1890, p. 61. Cited in ibid., p. 58.

supply. Between 1895 and 1900, however, the government passed a series of laws—such as the Pass Law and the Master and Servant Act—that increased the mine owners' control over their work force and reduced industrywide wages for black laborers.[22] The two most critical acts were probably the Glen Grey Act of 1894 and the Natives Land Act of 1913. By providing for a system of individual land tenure, the first of these measures ensured that certain segments of the black community would become landless. By putting geographical restraints on the lands that blacks could purchase, the second measure worked to enforce racial segregation and to use economic incentives to push the natives into the labor force. Or as the initial recommendation for the act argued: "It cannot but be an advantage to the natives to be induced without compulsion to become more industrious. Economic pressure and the struggle for existence will be felt by many of them at no very distant date and an industrious people will be better fitted for such conditions."[23]

This is not to argue that the mining houses and the government were working in complete cahoots or that the gold producers are to bear the sole blame for the creation of South Africa's apartheid system. On the contrary, the government also passed a number of economic measures that impinged on the miners' profitability, and there was also considerable support for apartheid among the middle- and working-class Boers. Still, it is hard to deny the role that the mining houses played in the creation of a segregated work force and hard to disagree with one South African scholar who concludes that "it was the mining industry, and particularly gold mining, which rapidly and profoundly transformed the social and political structures of colonial South Africa."[24]

Even more important to this study, the relationship between the government and the mining industry that was forged at the turn of the century laid the foundations of a symbiosis that has existed ever since. The two sides do not always work in tandem, and the government has on occasion passed legislation that is injurious to the indus-

[22] Innes, *Anglo American*, p. 61.
[23] Report of the South African Native Affairs Commission, 1903–1905 (1905). Cited in ibid., p. 67.
[24] Stadler, *Political Economy*, p. 37. This view is also expressed by Innes, *Anglo American*, and Pallister et al., *South Africa Inc.*

try's interests. For the most part, however, on matters pertaining to mining the government has followed the industry's lead, letting the Chamber virtually set its own policy and incorporating these measures into law as necessary. Presumably, the government does not always agree with the mining industry. In recent years, in fact, the industry has moved much faster than the government toward desegregation and has been openly critical of the government's policies in this area. But where matters of mining are concerned, the pattern that was laid a century ago persists: the industry leads, and the government, even if reluctantly, is brought along.

The South African gold industry, therefore, has long been characterized by consolidation, coordination, and cooperation. Rather than competing with one another, the great mining finance companies have forged powerful bonds between themselves and with the South African government. Domestically, the mining houses operate by coordinating their activities and presenting a unified front to the labor market and to the government. Internationally, their combined strength makes them the single largest player in the gold market. Part of the gold producers' success can be traced, no doubt, to the structure of the gold-mining industry and in particular to its cost constraints and scale economies. But part of it must also be credited to the peculiar characteristics of the producers themselves—to their history of personal friendships, their tradition of interlocking holdings, and especially to the actions of their most powerful member, the Anglo American Corporation.

The Role of Anglo

Since its founding in 1917, the Anglo American Corporation of South Africa has been a major player in the political and economic life of South Africa. The company was initially formed to bring new capital into the country and to invest in the goldfields of the Far East Rand. From the start, however, the company's ambitions reached far beyond the Rand. Its founder, Ernest Oppenheimer, explicitly planned to use Anglo as a vehicle to gain control over the entire gold-mining industry on the Rand and then to expand into diamonds and throughout the South African mining sector.[25] He stated in 1920: "The right

[25] As early as 1917, Oppenheimer wrote to one of his associates that "the first object I have in mind is to secure for our company a fair share in the business offering on

policy for this corporation to pursue is to investigate any attractive industrial proposition that presents itself and not merely confine its activities to mining enterprises. The Anglo American Corporation should be, and is, ready and anxious to play its role in the industrial development of South Africa."[26]

Oppenheimer's ambitions were not surprising, especially given the spirit of the times and the gold rush mentality that still permeated South African society. What was surprising, though, was the speed with which Oppenheimer laid his plans and attained his objectives. In 1919, Anglo American took over the Rand Selection Corporation and assumed leadership of the group with which Rand Selection had been associated. Just ten years later, Oppenheimer also triumphed in diamonds, taking control of the entire DeBeers Corporation and replacing the London-based buyers' Syndicate with his own Diamond Corporation.[27] By 1932, the South African minister of mines was publicly denouncing Oppenheimer as "the center of the whole diamond industry" and a man who could "juggle, manipulate and deal with all the diamonds he pleases."[28] Still, Oppenheimer continued to push himself—and Anglo—deeper and deeper into South Africa's economic infrastructure, gradually taking hold of South Africa's most critical mining industries.[29] When Ernest Oppenheimer died in 1957, he left behind an empire that controlled nearly all the

---

the Far East Rand. Once this is accomplished I shall steadily pursue the course of bringing about an amalgamation of Consolidated Mines and Rand Selection with our own company. . . . Taking all the facts into account, it does not seem too optimistic to think . . . that we shall be able, within a reasonable time, to bring about a willing combination of the three Eastern Rand holding companies, which would straightaway make us the most important gold group in Johannesburg.

"There is, moreover, no reason why our new company should not grow in other directions than in gold development. It may for instance play a part in the diamond world. What South Africa wants is enterprise and money and I believe our new company will supply both." Letter from Ernest Oppenheimer to W. Honnold, May 25, 1917, cited in Gregory, *Ernest Oppenheimer*, pp. 86–87.

[26] Quoted in Anthony Hocking, *Oppenheimer and Son* (New York: McGraw-Hill, 1973), p. 95.

[27] See Chap. 2.

[28] South African *Hansard*, March 2, 1932, cited in Pallister et al., *South Africa Inc.*, p. 33.

[29] In 1928, Anglo had formed a holding company to invest in Rhodesian copper; by the end of the war, it was producing nearly half of the area's copper ore. Likewise, in the later 1920s the corporation formed Potgietersrust Platinum Mines and soon become the main producer on the world's richest platinum field. See Hocking, *Oppenheimer and Son*, pp. 108–11.

world's diamonds, was the single most important player in the gold market,[30] and produced 24 percent of the South Africa's uranium, 43 percent of southern Africa's coal output, and 51 percent of the copper in Northern Rhodesia.[31]

Much of this new activity did not bear the direct imprimatur of Anglo. Rather, it was launched by and tied into an increasingly complex web of subsidiaries and holding companies. Within this network, firms generally fell into one of four categories: group subsidiaries, administered associates, controlled associates, and related companies.[32] The firms were ultimately linked to Anglo and were under the ultimate control of the Oppenheimer family.[33] Moreover, in the gold-mining industry, even those firms that remained independent found themselves somewhat under Anglo's sway. Anglo, for instance, has a 41.3 percent holding in Johannesburg Consolidated Investment (JCI), and Anglo's sister company DeBeers holds an additional 9.1 percent, effectively giving the Anglo network a majority share in JCI. Anglo also has a 10.8 percent share of Gold Fields of South Africa (GFSA) and a 28.9 percent holding in Consolidated Gold Fields (Consgold), the London mining house that in turn holds 48 percent of GFSA.[34] Anglo also has small holdings in Barlow Rand and Gencor.[35] As Anglo emerged as the dominant player in the industry, the outlying players simply accepted its leadership and con-

---

[30] In 1958, Anglo took a controlling interest in Central Mining and then merged it with two other British companies to form Charter Consolidated. Soon afterward, Anglo also gained control of Johannesburg Consolidated Investment, one of the original powerhouses in the gold-mining industry.

[31] R. B. Hagart, "The Changing Pattern of Gold Mining Finance," *Optima* 2 (December 1952): 6.

[32] I am borrowing these terms from Pallister and his colleagues. See *South Africa Inc.*, pp. 214–60, for a survey of these companies today.

[33] Many people have tried to sketch the entire Anglo network, but no one has yet been completely successful. It is said that only the Oppenheimers themselves truly understand the myriad connections that constitute their total holdings. Two of the best sources on Anglo's structure, however, are Pallister et al., *South Africa Inc.*, and Innes, *Anglo American*. The latter contains a particularly interesting list of 656 companies that are within the Anglo group.

[34] Anglo's holding in Gold Fields is via Minorco, its Bermuda-based subsidiary. It was Minorco that Anglo used in 1989 when it tried to wrest full control of Consolidated Gold Fields. See Peter Schmeisser, "Harry Oppenheimer's Empire: Going for the Gold," *New York Times Magazine*, March 19, 1989.

[35] See Timothy Green, *The New World of Gold* (London: Weidenfeld & Nicolson, 1981), p. 33.

tinued to play by the established rules of the industry's game. Institutionally, Anglo established its position by virtue of its economic control and its near domination of the powerful Chamber of Mines.[36] In practice, its position was also cemented by a tradition of oligopolistic cooperation in the South African gold industry and by a sheer lack of external pressures on its operations in the gold fields and on the gold market.

By the 1970s Anglo had become the single most important player in the South African mining sector and probably in the entire economy as well.[37] In addition, Anglo had also become one of the most important *political* forces in South Africa. Part of this expansion into politics was personal. Following the pattern set by Cecil Rhodes and other great "Randlords," both Ernest Oppenheimer and his son Harry had been vigorously involved in politics. Ernest was a member of Parliament and twice served as mayor of Kimberley. Harry also served in Parliament for a while and then broke away in 1959 to become a major force behind the newly created Progressive party.[38] Moreover, as one might expect, the Oppenheimers simply had friends in high places. Many of South Africa's highest-ranking politicians have been personal friends of the family, former Anglo executives, or both. Even more important, though, Anglo's position was a direct

[36] Officially, the Chamber is composed of over one hundred representatives from a variety of mining interests. In practice, however, the main decisions are made by two small groups. By virtue of its wide presence in all the mining areas, Anglo has always been a considerable factor in both executive groups and thus in the decisions of the Chamber. See Pallister et al., *South Africa Inc.*, pp. 139–40.

[37] In 1976, for instance, the top five mining houses in South Africa were all Anglo companies, and with the exception of chrome and manganese, Anglo had a virtual monopoly over all South Africa's most important commodities. In manufacturing, too, Anglo was important, with either a controlling or substantial minority interest in five of the top ten concerns. Anglo also had interests in seven of the country's top twenty banks, and it owned one of the three largest life insurers. Overall, Anglo not only controlled the country's three top market leaders—Anglo American itself, De-Beers, and Amgold, a subsidiary—but also ten of the top fifteen ranking concerns, and it had minority shares in three of the others. See Innes, *Anglo American*, and Anthony Sampson, *Black and Gold* (New York: Pantheon, 1987), p. 102.

[38] The Progressive party was founded largely by liberal professionals who believed that the issue of race was central to South African politics and that to survive, South Africa would have to develop an alternative to apartheid. At this early stage, though, Oppenheimer was *not* arguing for a total end to segregation in the country but rather for the critical modifications that would allow the country to continue its economic growth without bearing the moral outrage of the international community.

result of its economic power. Because the firm controlled so many of South Africa's most critical minerals and so large a percentage of its total capital, it was only logical that the government and Anglo would, occasionally, be forced into a working partnership. Thus it was Anglo that developed South Africa's critical uranium industry and, after the 1960 Sharpeville massacre, Anglo that joined the government in stemming the flight of capital from the country and providing massive support for state loans.[39]

This is not to claim, of course, that Anglo has ever worked for the South African government. On the contrary, Anglo's power has been a constant source of irritation to the government and an occasional subject of outrage. In 1951, for instance, a member of the South African Parliament argued that Harry exercised "a greater influence than . . . any man in South Africa has ever had."[40] And in 1962, the prime minister complained that Harry "has political aims; he wants to steer things in a certain direction. . . . He can secretly cause a good many things to happen. In other words, he can pull strings with all that monetary power and with this powerful machine which is spread over the whole country he can, if he so chooses, exercise an enormous influence against the Government and against the State."[41]

The point is that as much as the government may dislike the private ambitions or personal politics of the Oppenheimer family, it simply cannot ignore the economic clout of the Anglo network, nor can it afford to put any shackles on Anglo's myriad operations. Quite simply, Anglo is the backbone of the South African economy and a political force in its own right. As an article in the Johannesburg *Sunday Times* explained it: "The fact, of course, is that it is Mr. Oppenheimer and men like him who make the wheels go round in South Africa, who provide it with the sinews of war and enable it to withstand the assaults of the world. Basically, it is they who keep the Government in power—and the Government knows it."[42]

---

[39] On March 21, white police officers killed sixty-nine protesters at Sharpeville, near Johannesburg. Hundreds of others were also wounded in the Sharpeville massacre. Pallister et al., *South Africa Inc.*, p. 62.

[40] Quoted in Hocking, *Oppenheimer and Son*, p. 247.

[41] Quoted in ibid., p. 369.

[42] Quoted in ibid., p. 370. Or as Gavin Relly, then chairman of Anglo, put it more bluntly, "The government knows that they would fiddle with Anglo at their peril." Quoted in Sampson, *Black and Gold*, p. 191.

On all sides, therefore, Anglo is bolstered by strength and buffered from opposition. It is the leader of the South African gold producers and the voice of the industry. It does not directly control all the gold-mining companies, and it cannot command them. It can, however, act as a powerful hegemon, presiding over a cooperative arrangement and setting the course for its other members. Anglo's role in gold, meanwhile, coupled with the place of gold in the South African economy, has put the corporation in an enviable position vis-à-vis the South African government. Any constraints that the government puts on Anglo will simultaneously serve to constrain, and perhaps even damage, the innermost workings of the South African economy. The government clearly recognizes this—and so does Anglo.

And thus it is not surprising that the South African government has traditionally kept Anglo and the entire gold industry at arm's length. The Federal Reserve Bank sells the country's gold, but it does not make gold policy per se or enforce any specific obligations on the gold producers. Rather, South Africa's gold policy is largely determined by the coordinated efforts of its producers and shaped and implemented under the watchful eye of Anglo. Presumably, Anglo could use its position to serve a variety of different ends. What it has done almost exclusively, however, is to work toward the long-term health and stability of the gold market. Over time, of course, many of the company's policies have changed. Its initial embrace of apartheid as a means of securing a cheap and reliable labor force, for instance, has been modified to reflect its new conviction that apartheid will mean only growing unrest in South Africa and increasingly damaging sanctions from the international business community. It has modified its policies toward its own work force, improving the living conditions of its black miners and spending considerable sums of money to finance black education and vocational training.

One policy, however, has never changed: Anglo has always believed that prosperity rests with orderly marketing, that the producers will always do better by cooperating than by competing. Anglo has thus used its position to cement its ties to the other mining houses and to contain any competitive practices that might endanger the stability of the market or the prosperity of the industry. Anglo's hegemony, in short, is directed largely toward the maintenance of cooperation. Because it carries such weight in South Africa, it has been able to squelch any interference in its own affairs and preside over a closely knit group of the country's gold producers. And because South Africa, in turn, carries such weight in the gold market, it has been able to act as a stabilizing force in the market and extend its cooperation toward the second largest producer, the former Soviet Union.

THE DEVELOPMENT OF THE SOVIET GOLD INDUSTRY

Unlike in South Africa, where gold mining has always been a private concern, gold in Russia was long an affair of the state. Just as the tsars owned all the country's mines and claimed their output in two annual dispatches, so too did the Bolsheviks establish a state monopoly over every aspect of the gold industry and trade. Throughout the tenure of the Soviet state, gold was regarded as belonging solely to the state, and it was the state alone that could determine the conditions under which gold was mined, purchased, and sold. There were no independent voices in gold—no prospectors who struck it rich, no companies that built their fortunes on the metal. No firms competed for shares of the domestic market and no bureaucracies struggled to exercise their jurisdiction over the industry. Instead, there was only the state, guiding the development of the industry, controlling the direction of foreign trade, and covering all of its activities in a heavy shroud of secrecy.[43]

For decades the Soviet Union was a central player in the international gold market. Quietly, the Soviet leadership cooperated with Anglo American in a joint venture that allowed both parties to maximize their returns from gold and safeguard the long-term stability of the market.

[43] Starting in 1938, all information relating to the Soviet gold industry was classified as a state secret, and no data were released concerning the level of gold production in the Soviet Union, the quantity of gold sold on the market, or the size of the Soviet Union's gold reserves.

The Evolution of Soviet Gold Policy

Before the legendary California gold rush of 1848, Russia was the world's primary source of gold. Gold had been found in the hills of Armenia and the rivers of Siberia for as long as anyone could remember, and for centuries Russian mines had provided the tsars with a valuable source of revenue. The most spectacular finds, however, occurred in the early 1840s and set off the world's first gold rush in the area of the Yenisei River. By 1847, Russia led the world in gold production, accounting for at least three-fifths of newly mined gold in the world.[44] In 1884, even after the discovery of gold in California and the Klondike, Siberia was still producing more than a quarter of the world's gold.[45]

The coming of the revolution and the civil war, however, forced the gold industry to a halt, and by the time the Bolsheviks consolidated their power, the gold industry had slipped out of favor and into obsolescence. The mines were troublesome to discover and expensive to operate, and in the disarray that faced the new Soviet government, they hardly seemed a priority. Moreover, ideologically the Bolsheviks opposed the use of gold as a medium of exchange. Gold, they held, was the symbol of capitalism, and it was in pursuit of gold that capitalism's most grievous offenses had been committed. In the most explicit statement of his views on gold, "The Importance of Gold Now and after the Complete Victory of Socialism," Lenin wrote:

When we are victorious on a world scale I think we shall use gold for the purpose of building public lavatories in the streets of some of the largest cities in the world. This would be the most "just" and most educational way of utilising gold for the benefits of those generations which have not forgotten how, for the sake of gold, ten million men were killed and thirty million maimed in the "great war for freedom," the war of 1914–1918 . . . and how, for the sake of the same gold, they certainly intend to kill twenty million men or to maim sixty million in a

[44] Green, *New World of Gold*, p. 4.
[45] Michael Kaser, "The Soviet Gold-Mining Industry," in *Soviet Natural Resources in the World Economy*, ed. Robert G. Jensen et al. (Chicago: University of Chicago Press, 1983), p. 574.

war, say, in 1925, or 1928, between Britain and the U.S.A., or something like that.[16]

Despite these proclamations, though, Lenin was clearly aware that the Soviet Union could not yet afford to disdain all transactions made in gold and that the economic viability of the new state rested heavily on its ability to use the gold reserves of the state to finance critical purchases from the West. Thus Lenin modified his opposition to the use of gold by reasoning that

> however "just", useful or humane it would be to utilise gold for this purpose [public lavatories], we nevertheless say that we must work for another decade or two with the same intensity and with the same success as in the 1917–1921 period, only in a much wider field, in order to reach this stage. Meanwhile, we must save the gold in the R.S.F.S.R. [Soviet Union], sell it at the highest price, buy goods with it at the lowest price. When you live among wolves, you must howl like a wolf.[17]

Indeed, during these early stages of the battle, gold was a vital commodity for the Bolsheviks. The Soviet ruble was worthless in international trade, and the Soviet government owed millions of dollars in old foreign loans in addition to its current needs for imported technology and energy. Gold was the only currency available to pay the bills.

Bearing this fact in mind, the Bolsheviks were careful to keep a tight guard over all gold supplies in the country. In May 1920, the Politburo informed the Soviet commissar of trade that any agreements he concluded in gold currency would first have to be endorsed by the Politburo.[48] In public, Lenin decried the lack of gold in the country, admitting that the available reserves were not even sufficient to cover the Bolsheviks' favored program of electrification.[49]

[16] V. I. Lenin, "The Importance of Gold Now and after the Complete Victory of Socialism," November 1921, in *Collected Works*, vol. 33 (Moscow: Progress Publishers, 1970), p. 113.

[17] Lenin, "Importance of Gold," pp. 113–14.

[48] Lenin, "Letter to L. B. Krasin," May 8, 1920, in *Collected Works*, vol. 44, p. 375. Krasin was one of Lenin's chief foreign representatives and the man most directly responsible for overseeing Soviet commerce during this period. See Adam B. Ulam, *The Bolsheviks* (New York: Collier, 1965), pp. 485–86.

[49] Lenin, "Speech at a Meeting of Activists of the Moscow Organisation of the R.C.P. (B)," December 6, 1920, in *Collected Works*, vol. 31, p. 455.

"It is absolutely necessary," he wrote in 1920, "to economise gold to the utmost."[50]

Despite the shortage of gold, little thought was paid to the development of the Soviet gold industry, and official opinion continued to maintain that gold would lose its value under a collectivist system.[51] Instead, party economists remained convinced that Soviet exports of timber, furs, and grains would be able to generate sufficient hard currency earnings. By the end of the decade, however, the Soviet Union was facing a severe balance-of-payments crisis. Grain exports, once the major source of foreign earnings, had plummeted, a victim of both a worldwide slump in agricultural prices and a serious decline in Soviet agricultural production between 1927 and 1929. Meanwhile, a prospector had found gold on the Aldan River in eastern Siberia, which tempted more than twelve thousand miners to rush to the tiny Siberian village of Nezametny.

By September 1927, the pressing need for hard currency had forced the government to rescind its earlier aloofness from gold and invest state funds directly in the development of the gold industry. The Fifteenth Party Congress of December 1927 called for "an increase in the mining of gold in the country" to improve the foreign trade balance.[52] Soon afterward, A. P. Serebrovsky was put in charge of gold mining, and the entire industry was transferred to Narkomfin, the commissariat of finance.[53] But even these changes were minor. Gold was still not labeled a priority industry for the Soviet Union, and exports of other raw materials were still considered the best means of generating the foreign currency that the country so desperately needed.

Josef Stalin, however, had different ideas. During the late 1920s, he had become intrigued with the California gold rush and its impact on the development of the American West. He read the work of Bret Harte, an American author who described the great gold rushes of the late nineteenth century and credited them with having

[50] Ibid.

[51] John D. Littlepage and Demaree Bess, *In Search of Soviet Gold* (New York: Harcourt, Brace, 1937), p. 24.

[52] KPSS v. Rezolyutsiyakh (1954), ii, p. 456. Cited in E. H. Carr and R. W. Davies, *Foundations of a Planned Economy, 1926–1929*, vol. 1, pt. 2 (London: Macmillan, 1969), p. 715.

[53] *Torgovo-Promyshlennaya Gazeta*, October 26, 1927. Cited in Carr and Davies, *Foundations*, p. 715.

pushed the United States to its Pacific frontier. At this time, Stalin was becoming concerned with the growing Japanese threat to the east; with so much of Asiatic Russia underdeveloped and virtually unpopulated, it was a logical target for Japanese expansion. Gold, Stalin reasoned, might change that. If the known gold fields of Siberia could be developed and expanded, they would attract the human resources that Siberia lacked. If the gold mines proved successful, they would act as catalysts for other mining ventures and for the service industries that would inevitably be created around them.[54]

Admittedly, gold still smacked of capitalism, and a gold rush of any sort carried the connotations of individualism and get-rich-quick schemes that were an anathema to the socialist mind. But, on the other hand, as one eyewitness recalls: "Here was a huge region, sparsely settled and all the more vulnerable to attack, which might be filled up with abnormal rapidity, as the western regions of the United States had been after 1849, if only a gold rush were started. And Stalin knew that there was plenty of gold lying around in the Soviet Far East almost completely neglected by its theoretical owner, the Soviet government."[55] And he continues: "When it became a choice between expediency and socialist principles, the Communist authorities decided for the measures which seemed practical. The threat from Japan made them more disposed to compromise with their theories."[56]

There is also another, less savory, objective that may have motivated Stalin's interest in the goldfields of Siberia. According to some historians, Stalin built the gold industry with a full-blown conception of what the mines of Kolyma and Magadan would become. He planned to use forced labor to run the mines and then to rely on the harsh conditions of Siberia to dispose of the millions of "class enemies" who might threaten his vision and his power.

Still, the Siberian camps were not the only prong of the government's gold program. The search for gold and the push for settlement began in the southern regions of Uzbekistan, the traditional

[54] Stalin's words to this effect are quoted by A. P. Serebrovsky, *On the Gold Front*, and cited by Kaser, "Soviet Gold-Mining Industry," p. 560.
[55] Littlepage and Bess, *In Search of Soviet Gold*, p. 27 (Littlepage was the eyewitness).
[56] Ibid., p. 130.

source of Russian gold. In 1927, the government created an over-arching gold trust, the Glavzoloto, "to combat embezzlement in the gold industry, eliminate small industry, and insure the influx of gold to the national treasury."[57] Under the leadership of Serebrovsky, a vast system was established to map the geological potential of the entire country and coordinate all mining activities. Glavzoloto became the central agency of the wide-ranging network, with various regional subordinates responsible for production in their areas. Independent prospectors were organized into groups called artels and commissioned to search for gold on behalf of the state. Hundreds of Soviet students were sent to the Leningrad Geological Institute to be trained as mine engineers, and thousands of outlawed farmers and kulaks were transported to the mining regions and taught the rudiments of mining. Throughout, the industry made liberal use of Western technology and capitalist tactics. Several American mining engineers spent years working closely with Serebrovsky and the Gold Trust, organizing the industry according to Western models.[58] An entire fleet of boats, rafts, trucks, and planes was purchased for the exclusive use of the gold industry. Separate telephone lines and a radio network were built to connect the vast reaches of the gold territory. All workers connected to the gold industry were paid in special gold rubles that allowed them access to a privileged chain of "Gold Trust" stores.[59]

By the middle of the 1930s, the Soviet gold rush was in full swing, and gold production had surpassed its prerevolutionary levels. According to Western estimates, total Soviet gold output rose from 53 metric tons in 1931 to 124 or 131 tons in 1934.[60] From 1937 to 1946,

[57] *Little Soviet Encyclopedia*, 1930. Cited in Silvester Mora, *Kolyma: Gold and Forced Labor in the USSR* (Washington, D.C.: Foundation for Foreign Affairs, 1949), p. 60. Here the author refers to the Gold Trust as the *Soyuzzoloto*. Most other sources, however, use the term *Glavzoloto* that I have also adopted. The full name is *Glavnoye upravleniye zoloto-platinovoi promyshlennosti*, or Main Administration for the Gold and Platinum Industry.

[58] See Littlepage and Bess, *In Search of Soviet Gold*.

[59] Ibid., p. 125.

[60] Arthur Z. Arnold, *Banks, Credit, and Money in Soviet Russia* (New York: Columbia University Press, 1937), p. 416, estimates that Soviet gold production rose from 52.8 to 130.6 metric tons over this period. Estimates from the United States Mint, cited by Harry Schwartz, in *Russia's Soviet Economy*, 2d ed. (Englewood Cliffs, N.J.: Prentice-Hall, 1954), p. 484, range in fine ounces from 1,655,725 (53.2 tons) to 3,858,089 (124.1 tons). See Kaser, "Soviet Gold-Mining Industry," p. 560.

the focus of the industry switched northward and eastward, as the fury of the Stalinist purges kept the gold camps of Siberia supplied with approximately thirty-eight thousand prisoners a year.[61] During this period, the administration of the camps was transferred to the NKVD, the Soviet security police, and gold production seemingly began to level off in 1938, when the camps' punitive objectives apparently overrode their production goals. Simply put, it was easier to let the prisoners die.

Whether or not Stalin created the Siberian gold camps with the conscious intention of using them as the receptacle for his purges, the dual effects were the same. The cheap human labor of the gulag built the Soviet gold industry and provided millions of dollars worth of gold for the Soviet state. At the same time, the gold mines rid the state of millions of "class enemies" who had incurred Stalin's wrath. Numerous accounts have described the horrendous conditions that prevailed in the gold camps during the time of the Stalinist purges,[62] but it is beyond the scope of this book to deal with these histories at any length. It will suffice to conclude that life in the camps was almost unbearably harsh. Millions of innocent people perished—but gold was produced. It was produced, indeed, in nearly record quantities, providing the Soviet government with a seemingly bottomless source of reserves and restoring the Soviet Union to a preeminent position in the international gold market.

Soviet Gold on the International Market

The outbreak of war brought an end to the great purges and a lessened importance for the Soviet gold industry. All available human resources were needed for the war effort, and the availability of lend-lease from the United States helped to reduce the Soviet Union's foreign currency needs. But the gold rush had left an indelible mark on the Soviet economy. Not only had it served Stalin's objectives of populating the Far East and disposing of the purges' vic-

---

[61] Estimates of the number of people sent to the gold camps vary widely, compiled as they are from prisoners' accounts. See Mora, *Kolyma*, and Robert Conquest, *Kolyma: The Arctic Death Camps* (London: Macmillan, 1978).

[62] See, for instance, Robert Conquest, *Kolyma*, Silvester Mora, *Kolyma*, and Aleksandr Solzhenitsyn, *The Gulag Archipelago* (New York: Harper & Row, 1974–1978).

tims, but it had also revealed the vastness of the Soviet Union's gold resources and the value of gold for easing the country's balance-of-payments problem. By 1954, the Soviet Union was producing nine billion ounces of gold a year, accounting for 4 percent of total world gold sales. Gold had become a critical element of the national economy and the basis for all Soviet trade with the West.

When the Soviets first entered the market in the 1950s, they were rather unsophisticated traders. They sold their gold in large quantities, at one time, and always through a select handful of London-based bullion houses.[63] Until 1968, of course, such behavior made perfect sense. As long as gold was fixed at thirty-five dollars an ounce and the Bank of England was willing to buy whatever gold it was offered, there was really no other way for the Soviets to sell their gold and no reason why their gold sales should ruffle the market. Between 1953, the year Stalin died, and 1965, it is believed that the Russians sold at least twenty-nine hundred tons of gold, seriously depleting their reserves in the process.[64] After 1968, however, the creation of a two-tier market in gold meant that the Bank of England was no longer available to absorb all the thirty-five-dollar-per-ounce gold on the market. Recognizing this, the Soviets began to diversify their gold-selling operations. They established their own bank in London, the Moscow Narodny Bank, and instructed it to sell Soviet gold to a wide array of dealers. When the gold trade began to shift its focus from London to Switzerland, the Soviets shifted too, moving their gold operations to the newly created Wozchod Handelsbank in Zurich. Gradually they began to spread their sales over an ever-widening field, never relying on any constant group of dealers and refusing to follow any consistent pattern of operations.

The Wozchod made no secret of the fact that its buy-and-sell orders were coming directly from the Vneshtorgbank offices in Moscow. At the same time, however, Wozchod never operated as a sim-

[63] Confidential interview, London, June 1988.
[64] Michael Kaser, in *Gold 1971* (London: Consolidated Gold Fields, 1972). Cited in Green, *New World of Gold*, p. 67. In 1965, the Soviets suddenly stopped exporting gold, and for five years, they remained completely absent from the market. They returned in 1971, selling approximately ten tons a month through Zurich bankers. Reportedly the Soviets added approximately $1 billion worth of gold to their reserves during their time away from the market. See Radio Free Europe Research, "Soviet Gold Sales Resumed after Five Years," *USSR: Economy*, March 3, 1971.

ple extension of the Soviet sales plan. Instead, it quickly became one of the most skilled and adept of the international gold houses.[65] By playing one broker off another, hedging its own positions, and keeping a careful eye on the regional gold markets, the Wozchod reportedly was able not only to market all the Soviet gold but also to secure a slightly-higher-than-market price for most of the gold it sold.[66] The Wozchod also became the channel through which the Soviet authorities attempted to maintain the world price of gold. When gold prices began to falter, the Wozchod would quietly step back into the market and, using funds lent by the Vneshtorgbank, buy gold in sufficient quantity to send prices upward again.

In 1984 the Wozchod was disbanded, and the Soviets moved their sales operations back to Moscow.[67] The style of operations, however, remained exactly the same. The Soviets continued to do business through a wide variety of foreign banks and trading firms, dealing in all the available gold instruments and "playing the market" to its fullest potential.[68] And they continued, quietly and secretly, to coordinate their deals with their ostensible rivals, the South Africans.

WORKING TOGETHER

In November 1980, Gordon Waddell went to Moscow. Waddell, who was then chairman of Rustenberg Platinum, an executive director of Anglo American, and Harry Oppenheimer's former son-in-

---

[65] See, for instance, Craig Forman, "Soviet Bank's Zurich Office Is Linchpin of Bid to Be a Bigger Player in Markets," *Wall Street Journal*, August 28, 1990, p. A6.

[66] Green, *New World of Gold*, p. 68.

[67] The bank was disbanded after its manager (a Swiss citizen) became involved in a complicated scheme of buying back on the forward market gold that the bank had sold. When the manager neglected to roll over a particular contract, the bank was suddenly short of a huge sum of money. The exact sum was never revealed, but industry sources put it in the range of $200 to $400 million. In the aftermath of the scandal, the manager was put in jail, the Wozchod was closed for good, and the Soviet Vneshtorgbank stepped in to handle all international gold operations.

[68] For a description of how the Soviets operated on the world market, see "Our Gold—How We Trade It on the World Market," Interview with E. P. Gostevoi, vice-chairman of the board of the USSR Bank for Foreign Economic Activity, *Izvestia*, October 24, 1989. Condensed text translated in *Current Digest of the Soviet Press*, November 22, 1989.

law, was spotted by a BBC correspondent while at the Bolshoi with Sir Albert Robinson, a senior Anglo executive, and two Soviet officials. The "sighting" set off a flurry of activity in the diamond and gold markets, as Soviet and Anglo officials hurried to deny any links between them even while journalists were trying to prove them.[69] Within the discreet world of the gold-trading community, however, Mr. Waddell's visit came as no surprise. Indeed, most of the inside members of the community had long ago acknowledged that the Soviets and the South Africans were involved in some form of an "orderly marketing arrangement."[70] They understood that the two sides met frequently, if quietly, to discuss their common strategies in the market and to ensure that neither one acted so as to contradict the other's aims.

For years, these meetings were surrounded by a distinct atmosphere of secrecy and skullduggery, and rumors abounded at the fringes of the industry and in the popular press. In content, however, it seems that the meetings were straightforward. According to industry insiders, the Soviets and South Africans simply met to coordinate their behavior in the market. Both sides wanted to ensure that they acted in tandem, regulating the supply of gold so as to keep prices high and speculation under control.

Their arrangement was never embedded in a formal institution,

---

[69] A BBC documentary, for instance, urged that South Africa and Russia were "linked together by chains of gold." This same documentary cited *Izvestia* as vowing that "our country has no contacts of any kind with South Africa, the racist citadel of apartheid" and quoted South African prime minister P. W. Botha as claiming that his people were fighting against a "total onslaught by Soviet communism." Transcript of "South African Gold and Diamonds: The Kremlin Connection," Panorama, BBC-1, April 6, 1981. Similar allegations appear in Michael Cockerell, "The Clandestine Partnership of South Africa and the USSR," *Listener*, April 9, 1981; François Soudan, "L'axe Pretoria-Moscou," *Jeune Afrique*, January 7, 1981, pp. 32–33; and "South Africa: The Soviet Connection," *Nation*, March 7, 1981, p. 263. In response to these claims, an article in Izvestia (February 16, 1981) stated in part: "The whole world knows that the Soviet Union has opposed the policy of apartheid resolutely and consistently, and that the Soviet Union, unlike Western countries, strictly observes the United Nations decision concerning the economic sanctions against the racist regime.

"The attempt to place the blame at some other's door and to accuse the Soviet Union of mythical trade contacts with South Africa is as groundless as the inventions about 'aggressive designs of the Soviets' in the south of Africa. A lie no matter how twisted still remains a lie."

[70] As one analyst argued, there is simply "no question that there is collusion" between the two producers. Confidential interview, London, July 1988.

nor did it entail any production quotas or allocation schemes. Instead, cooperation revolved around a commitment to mutual restraint and a shared responsibility for smoothing any significant fluctuations in the world price of gold. Specifically, the Soviets and South Africans agreed not to act unilaterally in the market. They agreed to use their gold sales strategically, stockpiling production as necessary and resisting the temptation to treat gold as a means of meeting short-term financial demands. In addition, it appears that they worked out a convenient system for joint regulation. Neither party, of course, could dictate the price of gold. But they could use their position in the market to *influence* the price and reduce its volatility. To do this, the system relied on a distinct division of labor between the producers. Basically, the South Africans used their gold sales to set the tone for the market. Selling solely through their Federal Reserve Bank,[71] the South Africans could gauge their sales fairly precisely, boosting them when prices were high and stockpiling whenever prices fell below a certain point. With nearly 40 percent of total world production under its control,[72] the bank could exert a tremendous influence on the direction of gold prices.

The one thing the bank could not do, though, was to purchase large quantities of gold on the open market.[73] And this is where the Soviets came in. While the South Africans provided the "hard core" of world gold supplies, the Russians "played it at the top."[74] They were, in other words, the speculators. Unlike the South Africans, the Soviets always seemed to enter the market erratically. Sometimes they would sell huge lots of gold through one source; sometimes

[71] All mines in South Africa are required to sell their gold directly to the South African Reserve Bank, which in turn sells the gold on behalf of the South African Ministry of Finance.

[72] The South African share of world production has varied somewhat over the course of the past few decades and began to decline in the late 1980s. Still, even as late as 1991, South Africa accounted for nearly 30 percent of total world production. See Gold Fields Mineral Services Ltd., *Gold 1992* (London, 1992), p. 21.

[73] From time to time, the South African Reserve Bank enters the market to support the price of gold. Because its foreign exchange reserves are limited, however, it usually has chosen not to intervene too frequently and instead to rely on its gold sales to influence market trends. See Green, *Prospect for Gold*, pp. 121–23.

[74] Dr. Chris Stals, spokesperson for the South African Reserve Bank, as quoted in David Marsh and Bernard Simon, "Gold: The Game Hots Up," *Financial Times*, October 26, 1981, p. 16.

they would disappear entirely from the market. Customarily, these dips and rises were explained by reference to the Soviet Union's hard currency needs. According to this explanation, the Soviets sold gold to earn the hard currency they needed to import critical items such as grain. Soviet sales increased, it was postulated, whenever a particularly bad harvest forced the leadership to increase its purchases of foreign grain. There is, to be sure, some truth in this argument. But it still fails to explain the pattern of Soviet sales.[75] There is no apparent correlation between bad harvests and high gold sales. In fact, Soviet gold sales actually fell during some of their worst harvests.[76] In addition, the hard currency theory cannot explain why the Soviets were also the most active speculators in the gold market, why they entered not only to sell gold but also, and just as often, to buy it. Indeed, the Soviets would often "turn over" (buy and sell) approximately ten to fifteen times the volume of gold they actually produced in a year.[77] They would sell huge amounts of gold forward and structure complex pricing options that allowed them to take advantage of shifts in foreign exchange rates as well as movements in the gold price.[78]

To a certain extent, the Soviets were probably using these financial instruments to increase their own profits. But they were also using them to stabilize the market. While the South Africans set the supply side of the equation, the Soviets worked on both demand and supply. By buying as well as selling in the market, the Soviets could smooth the edges of price fluctuations and counteract any sudden shifts in the market. For example, whenever gold prices hit a "break

[75] In 1985, for instance, a market study by Shearson Lehman/American Express concluded that gold sales represented only a marginal source of foreign exchange reserves for the Soviet Union and that the Soviets' net trade totals over time were "random." David Williamson and Sarah Fromson, London Metals Research Unit, Annual Review of the Gold Industry 1984–1985, Shearson Lehman/American Express, February 1985.

[76] One glaring example is 1975. In that year, Soviet grain imports nearly quadrupled, while the net value of their gold sales apparently fell by over 30 percent. Calculated from Shearson Lehman/American Express study, p. 73, table 4-2.

[77] Confidential interview, London, July 1988. For more on Soviet tactics in the market, see "Bank Official Describes Gold Trading Operations," Interview with E. Gostev, chairman of the Bank for Foreign Economic Activity, *Pravda* (Moscow), March 9, 1990, p. 7.

[78] Marsh and Simon, "Gold," p. 16.

point"—a price above or below a long-term price trend—the Soviets would spring into action. If gold prices suddenly fell below the general downward price trend, the Soviets would enter the market as massive buyers of gold, single-handedly pushing up demand for the metal and thus reversing the price drop. Similarly, when prices rose steeply above the trend, the Soviets would plunge into the market as sellers, temporarily flooding the market with gold and pushing prices down to their more normal long-term range.[79] In this fashion, the Soviets could in effect fine-tune the market, dealing with exigencies before they became emergencies. Together with the South Africans, they worked to stabilize the market, forsaking short-term gains for the long-term viability of the industry.

To a certain extent, this sort of cooperation is both predictable and natural. One could even argue that the structure of the gold market made it inevitable. Even without explicit coordination, the Soviets and the South Africans were likely to act in a similar fashion—selling their gold when prices are high, stockpiling when prices fall, and working always to maintain a certain level of stability. In these terms, cooperation seems to be nearly embedded in the structure of the system.

Once again, however, the structural explanation alone does not suffice. In the first place, comparable structures in other markets do not necessarily lead to similarly cooperative arrangements. More important, the relationship between the Soviet gold agencies and Anglo American was more than a coincidence of mutual interests. Until 1990, the producers met regularly to coordinate their actions, they refrained from competing with one another for lucrative long-term contracts, and they worked out a sophisticated system by which to divide their responsibilities in the market. The arrangement that existed between them was undeniably flexible, informal, and concealed. It was also, however, an example of cooperation among competitors.

[79] This pattern was confirmed to me in confidential interviews conducted in 1987 and 1988.

THE FACTORS OF COOPERATION

What made cooperation attractive to the Soviet and South African gold producers were the long-term benefits it offered. What made it possible, though, was the particular nature of the industry in each country. In the former Soviet Union, the domestic gold industry was strictly hierarchical and completely centralized. All regional gold-producing enterprises were directly linked to the national gold agency and hence to the Ministry of Nonferrous Metallurgy.[80] Each individual enterprise met its production targets through the operation of fourteen regional administrations, or zolotos.[81] On the international side, all operations fell under the sole domain of the Bank for Foreign Economic Affairs. Before 1990, gold policy in the Soviet Union was made at the highest levels of government, without the risk that it would ever be undermined by the actions of other individuals, firms, or competing internal agencies. Gold policy was never subjected to popular opposition or scrutinized by public officials. Rather, the central agencies involved had full control over their affairs and full authority to manage Soviet gold in the international marketplace. The capitalistic characteristics of the industry, therefore, were only apparent vis-à-vis the outside market. Domestically, the Soviet gold authorities faced no competitive pressures, no overarching profit considerations, and no division of their authority.

Likewise, the gold industry in South Africa has long been highly centralized and rationalized. All gold sales are made by the Federal Reserve Bank, which means that the course of South Africa's involvement in the international market is directed entirely by a single autonomous agency. In addition, even the ostensibly independent production side of the industry is, in fact, highly consolidated and cooperative. The producers are all linked to one another and to the

---

[80] Like most Soviet agencies, the gold agency was periodically renamed and reshuffled. From 1927 to 1976 Glavzoloto was the primary agency, despite being divided into two regional agencies from 1957 to 1965. Then in 1976 Glavzoloto was replaced by Soyuzzoloto, a national industrial administration. As with most Soviet reorganizations, the change from Glavzoloto to Soyuzzoloto did not significantly affect the way the agency operated or the people it employed. See Kaser, "Soviet Gold-Mining Industry," p. 557; and P. F. Lomako, "On the Road Set Out by Great October," *Tsvetnye Metally* no. 10 (1977): 4, 11.

[81] See Rae Weston, *Gold: A World Survey* (New York: St. Martin's, 1983), p. 167.

state. The leader of the group, the Anglo American Corporation of South Africa, is largely invulnerable to both hostile take-over and internal pressure. In most cases, therefore, it can make its decisions free from any fear of their short-term costs. These decisions are then gently imposed on the entire industry and become, in effect, the gold policy of South Africa. The state does not interfere at this stage, and the producers never get publicly involved with the bank's conduct of foreign sales. Under the leadership of Anglo American, then, the industry can act as a cohesive whole, removed from any competing domestic pressures and able to act definitively in the international market. In both the Soviet and the South African industries, therefore, domestic autonomy facilitated international cooperation.

Once this cooperation was under way, moreover, it was eased by the ability of both parties to negotiate consistently and in secret. In South Africa, all negotiations were conducted by a small group of people working under the auspices of one firm. In the Soviet Union, an elite cadre of officials handled all international contacts in the gold market. Similarly, both the Soviets and the South Africans were long able to conduct their affairs out of the glare of public scrutiny. The Soviets in particular took great pains to conceal their dealings in the market. The country never reported its gold reserves to any international agency and until recently never faced the international ramifications that usually befall a state when it buys or sells large quantities of gold. All Soviet data pertaining to gold were highly confidential, and most transactions were hidden through a variety of intermediaries. As a result, no one ever really knew what the Soviets were doing in the market.[82] Their production was concealed, their sales were concealed—and so was their cooperation.

Meanwhile, the Anglo American Corporation is also distinctly able to conceal its operations from its shareholders. Its vast network of

[82] Western estimates of Soviet gold productions and sales always ranged widely. For example, in 1961, estimates of Soviet production ranged from $300 million a year to $750 million and estimates of reserves anywhere from $4 billion to $9 billion. See Oscar L. Altman, "The Role of Gold in the Soviet Economy," *Optima* 11 (September 1961): 135. More recently Kaser has cited the wide discrepancies between his figures and those calculated by the Central Intelligence Agency and Consolidated Gold Fields. See "Soviet Gold-Mining Industry," pp. 584–88.

subsidiaries and associates means that monies can be passed from one firm to another and that short-term transactions are easily hidden. In addition, Anglo benefits from a nearly unprecedented level of corporate secrecy and a strong tradition of obedience from its internal ranks. Any moves that Anglo makes, therefore, and any deals that it strikes can be kept private. In this way, the firm is able to consolidate its holdings and work with its apparent competitors without attracting undue attention.

Finally, until about 1990, both the Soviet Union and the Anglo American Corporation had a tremendous ability to bear the short-term costs of cooperation and cover the losses that occasionally befell them as a result of their restraint in the market. Anglo American had a remarkable reserve of surplus capital and a very real ability to move profits and losses from other parts of its corporate empire. The Soviets had gold reserves of undisclosed proportions and a ruble that was not convertible on world markets. Even major transactions in the gold market had little direct impact on the domestic Soviet economy. And the domestic economy, in turn, imposed no constraints on Soviet activities in the gold market or Soviet cooperation with the South African producers.

FREE FALL: GOLD IN A POST-SOVIET WORLD

All this changed, of course, when reform hit the Soviet Union. As was the case with diamonds, the opening of the Soviet state robbed the gold industry of the autonomy it had enjoyed for so long. Like everything else in the former Soviet Union, gold policy suddenly became a topic of public debate and a subject of widespread scrutiny. Gold deposits, meanwhile, were eagerly claimed by the republics and regions in which they were located. For several years, the Soviet authorities struggled to carve out a special niche of protection for the gold sector. Stressing its strategic and financial importance, they urged that gold needed to remain under high-level centralized control. Their efforts, though, were in vain. By 1990, Soviet gold policy was already in a shambles. Any vestiges of cooperation and restraint were gone, replaced by a mad dash to sell, steal, and smuggle what was once Soviet gold.

In 1988, Soviet gold production, like Soviet diamond production, was included in Gorbachev's wide-sweeping movement toward reform. The industry was reorganized and placed under the newly created Directorate of Precious Metals and Diamonds (Glavalmazzoloto). Officially, the reorganization was designed to liberalize and modernize the industry. In practice, however, the effect (as with diamonds) was actually to make the industry more centralized than it had been previously and to place it more directly under the control of the Soviet Council of Ministers. Glavalmazzoloto clamped down on the gold-prospecting cooperatives known as artels, convicted more than two hundred officials and workers for crimes related to gold, and maintained a policy of complete secrecy with regard to the gold industry.[83]

Very quickly, though, the structures of control began to falter. Even as Soviet officials were publicly debating the merits of a gold-backed ruble, Soviet citizens were rushing to buy gold from state-owned jewelry stores, and Soviet gold was beginning to seep into world markets. The troubles began in the mines, as workers for the first time began to demand higher wages, better living conditions, and easier access to consumer goods.[84] Many of the independent artels also staged their own strikes, claiming that low state procurement prices were making their operations increasingly unprofitable.[85] Meanwhile, nearly all state mines were struggling under their own problems. Machinery was breaking down, spare parts and fuel were in short supply, and the central authorities could no longer provide them with investment funds. In addition, the mines were feeling the first twinges of democratization. Suddenly, workers were leaving in search of better jobs, and citizens' groups were protesting the environmental impact of many mining ventures. And in the southern republics, outbreaks of ethnic violence threatened to dis-

[83] See Richard M. Levine, "Glasnost, Perestroika, and Soviet Gold," *Minerals Today* (March 1990): 8–12.

[84] The protests began in 1989 and culminated in a series of strikes during the spring of 1991. See Leyla Boulton, "Moscow Adopts Hard Line on Mine Strike," *Financial Times*, March 21, 1991, p. 6.

[85] Gold Field Mineral Services Ltd., *Gold 1991*, p. 28; and Pavel Lunyashin, "A Beggarly Share of the Gold in the Sack," *Rabochaya Tribuna*, October 2, 1991. Reprinted and translated in Foreign Broadcast Information Service, October 10, 1991, p. 36.

rupt the entire economy.[86] As a result of these difficulties, Soviet mine production fell sharply in 1990, dropping twenty-five tons from its 1989 total and relegating the country to third place among world producers.[87]

Sales, however, actually increased. In fact, during the first quarter of 1990, the Soviets shipped approximately three hundred tons of gold to the West, thus matching their 1989 total in just three months and sparking fears in the market of widespread dumping.[88] And so the Soviets' behavior seemed to cut both ways. Turmoil in the country meant that production would almost certainly decrease. But at the same time, it increased the likelihood that the government would be forced to sell gold in order to meet its increasingly urgent financial demands.

This confusion was further exacerbated in August 1990, when the Presidium of the Russian parliament declared its sovereignty over all resources on Russian soil and declared invalid all Soviet contracts for the sale of gold.[89] Over the course of the next year, the gold-mining industry—like much in the former Soviet Union—remained in limbo. The old structures of control had clearly stopped functioning, but nothing solid emerged to take their place. In May 1991, Glavalmazzoloto launched a last-ditch effort to maintain unity. Calling for its own denationalization, the agency suggested that all former state enterprises be converted into joint-stock companies, with 85 percent of the stock to be turned over to the enterprise collectives and their local republics.

Presumably, this plan could have worked to preserve the structure of the industry. But in the turmoil that surrounded the events of August 1991, it simply disappeared. After the failed coup and the rapid disintegration of the Soviet Union, all gold-mining enterprises were placed under the jurisdiction of their local authorities. There

[86] As early as March 1990, Soviet officials had conceded that ethnic problems were affecting Soviet gold production. See *The Powell Gold Industry Guide and International Mining Analyst*, 1st ed. (Portland, Maine: Reserve Research Ltd., 1990), p. 4.

[87] Gold Fields Mineral Services Ltd., *Gold 1991*, p. 28.

[88] See, for instance, "Price Rally in Sight as Reds Scrape the Gold Barrel," *Johannesburg Star*, June 20, 1990.

[89] This resolution came in direct response to the Soviet-DeBeers deal. See Celestine Bohlen, "Soviet Zone Strives for Sovereignty and Diamonds," *New York Times*, August 15, 1990, p. A3.

was no longer a central authority to purchase gold or oversee its sale.[90]

The final blow came in September, when a leading official revealed that Soviet gold reserves amounted to just 240 tons, or less than one year's average production.[91] Western analysts, who had long estimated Soviet reserves as somewhere between 1,000 and 3,000 tons, were shocked. No one seemed to know where the gold had gone.

Slowly it emerged that much of the gold had been sold in a frantic effort to meet the demands of the tottering Soviet state. According to various official sources, the Soviet government sold roughly 600 tons of gold between 1989 and 1991, using it to cover a hard currency trade deficit that had exceeded $6 billion in 1990.[92] Domestically, news of the sales released a torrent of popular outrage. In a typical pronouncement, *Izvestia* intoned, "The cynical selling off of the homeland's reserves was conducted in the name of preventing the conversion of the Soviet economy to capitalism and defending the ideals of socialism, but in actual fact it was done to conceal the government's own inertia and its inability and unwillingness to introduce market mechanisms."[93] Other allegations went even further, claiming that most of the Soviet gold had actually been stolen by high-ranking party officials. According to reports published in London and Moscow, around $4 billion worth of gold left Moscow during the spring of 1991, most of it ferried through Switzerland and bypassing normal export channels.[94] Some of this gold may well have

---

[90] E. Guseynov, "The Soviet Gold Concepts No Longer Exist," *Izvestia*, October 4, 1991, p. 7. The article goes on to state that "entire elements of this gold . . . concern are disappearing today during the course of converting the branch's enterprises over to republic subordination, with consequent destruction of the technological chains and economic contacts. The strange market in which our economy appears to have been abandoned in recent years is disorganizing the work of the gold industry." Moreover, even at the republic level control was breaking down. In Russia, for instance, the leading gold agency, Rossalmazzoloto (successor to Glavalmazzoloto), was increasingly being challenged by newly formed independent companies.

[91] See, for instance, "Estimate on Gold Worsens Outlook for Soviet Union: Official Cites Vast Drop," *New York Times*, September 30, 1991, pp. A1, A7.

[92] See Mikhail Sarafanov, "No Gold, No Illusions," *Delovie Lyudi* 18 (December 1991): 24.

[93] I. Demchenko, "Who Sold Our Gold, and Why," *Izvestia*, September 30, 1991. Translated and reprinted in *Current Digest of the Soviet Press*, October 30, 1991.

[94] Dan Atkinson and Mark Milner, "Soviet Gold Bullion Worth $4 Billion Secretly Moved Out of Country," *Guardian* (Manchester), September 11, 1991, p. 1; and

been official Soviet transfers abroad. But some of it also seems to have been destined for the private accounts of former Soviet officials. During the summer and fall of 1991, substantial quantities of gold, platinum, and palladium were allegedly smuggled out of the Soviet Union through airport customs stations.[95] All of the metals were shipped in small quantities and destined for financial centers such as London, Zurich, and Frankfurt.[96] None of it could be traced directly to official transactions. Accordingly, many analysts—both Western and Soviet—believe that Communist party officials simply helped themselves to their country's reserve assets once they realized the extent of the turmoil let loose by reform. Once the August coup was over, these officials stopped worrying about their allegiance to the party and concentrated instead on securing their own future in a post-Soviet system. Thus, following in a long line of disposed leaders, they cleaned out the coffers before they left. According to one estimate, at least 60 tons of gold, 8 tons of platinum, and 150 tons of silver were hidden abroad at the behest of Communist party officials.[97]

As of this writing, there is no way to confirm whether these amounts are accurate or even if smuggling did, in fact, occur. In light of the available evidence, however, it seems entirely plausible. There was chaos in the country, an erosion of all control in the gold industry, and a mysterious shrinkage of Soviet reserves. In addition, smuggling helps explain the odd behavior of the gold market through-

---

"Where Is the Gold Jinni Hiding? What They Think in London," *Pravda*, September 24, 1991, p. 2. Translated and reprinted in Foreign Broadcast Information Service, October 2, 1991, p. 45.

[95] See "Over a Month and a Half, at Least Five Tons of Gold and Platinum Has Been Sent Out of the Country, By Whom and For Whom, No One Knows," *Izvestia*, November 15, 1991. Translated and reprinted in *Current Digest of the Soviet Press*, December 18, 1991; and "Gold Smuggling Operations Uncovered at Airports," from the "Vesti" newscast, Moscow Russian Television Network, June 5, 1992. Translated in Foreign Broadcast Information Service, June 12, 1992, pp. 55–56.

[96] E. Guseynov, "The Shipping of Gold and Platinum Abroad: The Situation Is Becoming Clearer, But Questions Remain," *Izvestia*, November 26, 1991. Translated and reprinted in *Current Digest of the Soviet Press*, January 1, 1992.

[97] Vladimir Kvint and Natalia Darialova, "Man in the Shadows," *Forbes*, October 28, 1991, p. 120. Mr. Kvint, who worked in the Soviet gold industry, also contends that gold was a major factor in the August coup attempt. According to his account, the real leader of the coup was Oleg Shenin, secretary of the Central Committee of the Communist Party and the man who controlled the party's purse strings.

out 1990 and 1991. Theoretically, gold prices were set to soar during
this period. With the production increases of the 1980s at last level-
ing off and industrial demand high, most analysts had predicted a
significant increase in the price of gold. With turmoil in the Soviet
bloc and war in the Persian Gulf, their predictions rose even higher,
because political uncertainty in either of these regions has historically unleashed a rush to gold.[98] This time, though, the rush never
came.

Even during the height of the Gulf War, gold prices rose only
momentarily and then quickly slipped back to their pre-invasion
level.[99] The market stayed sluggish for the rest of the year, driving
investors away and confounding the "gold bugs," who kept predicting its imminent rebirth.[100] Undoubtedly, many factors were at work
in the market. Gold in the 1990s was being buffeted by low inflation
rates, active currency markets, and a host of new investment opportunities.[101] But the strange happenings in the former Soviet Union
were also a major factor in gold's desultory performance. As the
country dissolved, it lost control over its gold industry. Gold, which
for decades had been so strategically produced and sold, began to
flow freely—and then frenetically—from the state. It flowed from
the central authorities who now needed desperately to salvage their
hard currency position. And it flowed from the fringes, as independent republics, prospectors, and frightened officials rushed to satisfy
their own short-term needs.[102] From the start, Soviet cooperation in

[98] See, for instance, Kathryn M. Welling, "Ready to Reclaim Its Luster—Gold Could
Be the 'Sleeper' Investment of the 'Nineties," *Barron's*, July 15, 1991, pp. 27–29; and
Kenneth Gooding, "Gold Price to Reach $700, Says Gengold," *Financial Times*, Decem-
ber 18, 1990, p. 28.

[99] See "Gold Plunges as Gulf Hopes Rise," *Financial Times*, January 20, 1991, p. 15.

[100] See Lauren Chambliss, "Is Gold Dead?" *Financial World*, March 19, 1991, pp. 58–
59; "Gold, Platinum Confound Bulls," *Jewelers' Circular-Keystone*, April 1991, p. 46;
and "What Is This Thing Called Gold?" *Economist*, September 1, 1990, p. 69.

[101] See Dana Milbank, "Gold Loses Traditional Role as a Hedge in Times of International Crisis, Economic Downturns," *Wall Street Journal*, December 24, 1990, p. 24.

[102] In September 1991, Edward Gostev, deputy head of the Bank for Foreign Economic Affairs, offered an apt description of the effect of the "wildcat" gold sales.
"Hasty and uncoordinated activities," he warned, "can very easily spoil the gold market and lead to a fall in prices." Quoted in Anthony Robinson and Kenneth Gooding,
"Gold Hits 5-Year Low after Fresh Middle East Selling," *Financial Times*, September
12, 1991, p. 32.

the gold market had been a rather fragile affair, marked primarily by the restraint that Soviet officials had been able to display. And once this restraint was gone, so too were any prospects for cooperation in the international gold market.

CHAPTER FIVE

Stockpiles, Speculators, and the International Silver Market

Unlike the other cases in this book, the story of silver contains no covert meetings, no hidden documents, and no quiet corporate rendezvous. There are no rules, either explicit or implied, by which the producers attempt to regulate the market, and no institutions to maintain whatever cooperation might emerge. There is, in short, no cartel in the international silver market, and to the best of anyone's knowledge, there never has been. Silver is the cartel that isn't and the market in which, despite the existence of the most conducive structural factors, producer cooperation has never even been attempted. The story of silver, therefore, is not the story of a cartel that failed but of a cartel that never was, a short story of what *didn't* happen, and an effort to understand the forces that impeded it. Compared with the other cases, silver is the nonbarking dog. But as with many such dogs, the silence alone is revealing.

Most central, the silver case emphasizes the extent to which internal characteristics influence the producers' ability to cooperate and thus effectively determine whether a cartel is formed. In our other cases, not only were all the structural criteria in place, but there were also at least two major producers with the will to join in a cooperative endeavor and the wherewithal to bear the internal costs of the cooperation. In the silver market, by contrast, cooperation has been impeded by the producers' persistent inability to reconcile their external desire for long-term cooperation with other, more immediate domestic concerns.

In particular, producer cooperation in the silver market has been rendered virtually impossible by the fact that the largest player in the market—the United States—historically has been forced to abstain from any attempt at market collaboration. Part of the United States's reluctance has been due to the country's deeply held division between business and the state. Part is also due, no doubt, to an ideological distaste for cartels of any sort. But most of the reluctance results from the domestic politics that have surrounded the question of silver since the late nineteenth century and the domestic interests that have shaped and dominated U.S. silver policy. The problem is not simply that the United States is an open or decentralized economy. Indeed, as this chapter demonstrates, silver in the United States has historically been affected as much by official decree as by market forces, and the U.S. government has played a key role in regulating the entire domestic industry. The problem, in fact, is not that the government cannot speak for the industry but rather that the government has been completely dominated by the industry's demands. Indeed, although silver policy in the United States has largely been set and controlled by the government, the policy has for the most part reflected the momentary interests of the individual producers and bears the mark of the competitive pressures that forged it. Silver policy changes along with the desires and political clout of its constituents. It often falls under the jurisdiction of officials who had no part in creating it and have no vested interest in implementing it. These internal vacillations and frictions mean that silver policy is only as stable as the coalition that forged it. Once the coalition has dissolved, the policy will be ignored, discarded, or replaced.

From an external perspective, this pattern of behavior makes the United States a wholly unreliable partner. Because its external policy is subject to shifting internal whims and coalitions, it is largely unable to make credible external commitments. And because it cannot make credible commitments, its ability to participate in cooperative endeavors is severely hampered. Thus, although there is a central voice for silver policy in the United States and a logical point from which collaboration with other silver-producing countries could be expected to flow, this voice has been largely captured by its individual components, and short-term and parochial interests have completely outweighed the collective logic of cooperation.

Admittedly, the inability of the United States to cooperate should not necessarily doom the prospects for collaboration among the other producers. The United States, after all, is just one of several large players, and as the uranium case demonstrated, the cooperative game can be played very well in its absence. In the silver market, however, the other producers have not been able to overcome the tremendous obstacles to cooperation created by the United States and its domestic priorities. Some of them have had to deal with their own domestic constraints and inability to bear the costs of cooperation. Others who may have been willing to join a cooperative venture have not had the resources necessary to initiate one. In each case, though, it was internal institutions and priorities that shaped the country's propensity to cooperate and internal characteristics that precluded the formation of a producers' cartel.

THE RESTLESS METAL: THE INTERNATIONAL MARKET FOR SILVER

One of the most notable features of the silver market is the degree to which it has been plagued by violent shifts in supply, demand, and price.[1] Of the eight precious metals,[2] silver has traditionally suffered the greatest fluctuations in the market and has experienced the most volatile price swings. The price of silver rose dramatically, for instance, in the mid-1970s, climbing 556 percent between 1972 and 1979. Then, swept up in a speculative fervor, the market collapsed, and prices fell from forty-eight to eleven dollars per ounce in just seven weeks. Although this boom-and-bust cycle was perhaps the most violent in silver's history, it was by no means the first. Indeed, the market for the "restless metal" has been erratic since 1875.[3]

Most descriptions of the silver market explain this volatility as an inevitable result of the market structure and of the peculiar nature of silver itself. The silver industry is anarchic, analysts argue, be-

[1] I have borrowed the phrase in the heading from Roy W. Jastram, *Silver: The Restless Metal* (New York: John Wiley, 1981).

[2] The term "precious metals" usually refers to gold, silver, and the six metals that comprise the platinum metals group.

[3] Jastram, *Silver: The Restless Metal*, p. 157.

cause the structure of the market facilitates chaos and precludes order. The market is naturally volatile, and the same structural forces that cause this volatility also block the prospects of producer collaboration.

This argument is well bolstered by the fact that there is not and never has been any significant cooperation in the silver market. What I argue here, however, is that this logic may be mistaking cause and effect: the market may be volatile *because* there has been no cooperation among producers and thus no concerted efforts to impose order on the existing chaos. And the absence of cooperation is due not to any structural obstacles but to the internal characteristics of the leading producers and their perpetual inability to implement the domestic conditions that are a prerequisite to external collaboration.

As we shall see below, there are indeed some quirks in the structure of the silver trade that would seem to increase the volatility of the market and limit the possibilities for cooperation. The presence of these quirks, however, does not change the underlying structure of the market, one that contains all the central conditions for cartelization. To begin with, silver production is and always has been highly concentrated. Geologically, nearly all the world's silver is located in the Americas, primarily in a mountainous band stretching from western Canada to Peru. Four countries in this region—Canada, the United States, Mexico, and Peru—account for over 50 percent of total world production. With the addition of the former Soviet Union, the five countries produce fully 62 percent of the world's newly mined silver.[4] The remainder comes primarily as a by-product of various base-metals mining and is scattered throughout the world. Only Australia, Chile, Japan, and Poland qualify as substantial fringe producers.[5]

[4] The silver industry has always been highly concentrated. In 1929, U.S. interests controlled 66 percent of the mine production in the world, while British capital controlled an additional 21 percent. See Y. S. Leong, *Silver: An Analysis of Factors Affecting Its Price* (Washington, D.C.: Brookings Institution, 1934), pp. 68–71.

[5] Calculated from Robert G. Reese, "Silver," *Minerals Yearbook*, vol. 1, *Metals and Minerals*, United States Department of the Interior, Bureau of Mines (Washington, D.C.: Government Printing Office, 1987), p. 870, table 14 (hereinafter cited as Bureau of Mines Yearbook). South Africa produces only six and a half million troy ounces, or 1.6 percent of total world production.

Even more important, perhaps, each of the major producers has a history of strong centralized control over the silver industry. Though the mechanisms vary from country to country, in each state there is a sturdy connection between the producers and the central policymakers, and the government has considerable leeway in setting a national silver policy. To be sure, the mine producers in most of these countries are completely separate from the state and operate as independent private enterprises. As we shall see, though, a history of governmental intervention in nearly all these countries has meant that the producers are still intimately bound to the state and that the state maintains the capacity to affect the activities of the producers under its jurisdiction. High concentration, therefore, is paired in the silver market with a fair amount of centralized authority in each of the major producers, creating the opportunity for unified action in the market and improving the prospects for effective international cooperation.

In addition, the prospects for a silver cartel are enhanced by the metal's virtual nonsubstitutability. Currently, over 90 percent of annual silver production goes for industrial uses, mainly photographic development, electronics, tableware, and catalytic converters.[6] In some of these industries, silver can be replaced by other materials. Stainless-steel flatware will be substituted for silver if prices go too high, and silver jewelry has a wide variety of potential substitutes. In most of its industrial uses, however, silver is the critical component and is therefore virtually nonsubstitutable. The photographic industry, for instance, uses approximately 200 million ounces of silver a year to produce light-sensitive films and papers covered with a thin layer of silver halide salt.[7] For years, Eastman Kodak, Fuji Photo, and Agfa-Gevaert (the three major film manufacturers) have attempted to create a substitute for silver halide or to invent an electronic means of imaging that would replace the chemical reaction

---

[6] Production here refers to annual mine production. See Bureau of Mines Yearbook, p. 851, table 1. See also Thomas Patrick Mohide, *Silver*, Ontario Mineral Policy Background Paper no. 20 (Ontario: Ministry of Natural Resources, 1985), pp. 215–62.

[7] For a description of how silver reacts with light to produce a photographic image, see W. J. Streeter, *The Silver Mania: An Exposé of the Causes of High Price Volatility of Silver* (Dordrecht: D. Reidel, 1984), pp. 138–39.

that now occurs when light strikes the silver-coated film and reproduces the image as a photograph. To date, however, no economically viable substitute has been found, leaving the photographic demand for silver very high and the film industry at the mercy of shifts in the international silver market. Likewise, silver's suitability as an electrical conductor makes it and its alloys a preferred medium for many electrical contacts. In addition, because silver can be inserted into the human body without any harmful effects, there is a small but critical demand for silver in dentistry, surgery, and pharmacology.[8] Although none of these industries is truly strategic, all of them are vital components of normal industrialized economies and are largely dependent on silver. Once again, then, the producers are in a potentially enviable position, and a key structural prerequisite of cooperation is in place.

Finally, cooperation in the silver market should be facilitated by the overall demand inelasticity of silver. The basis of this inelasticity, as noted above, is the industrial market and the fact that most silver is either used in products for which it has no close economic substitute or in which silver comprises an insignificant portion of the total cost.[9] There is no definitive means of measuring the industrial elasticity of silver and no way of calculating the price at which industrial consumers would be forced to switch. Most estimates, however, gauge the price elasticity of industrial silver to be quite low.[10]

On top of this industrial inelasticity come the more intangible demands for monetary and speculative silver, demands that are rooted in silver's long history as a form of money and in the value many people place in silver as a source of wealth. Governments regularly issue commemorative silver coins, for instance, and people regularly collect and hoard them. In India and parts of the Middle East, women customarily carry their wealth in the form of silver and gold jewelry, using their necklaces and bracelets as both a display of pros-

[8] See Mohide, *Silver*, p. 235.

[9] D'Arcy Banister and Richard W. Knostman, *Silver in the United States*, Bureau of Mines Information Circular 8427 (Washington, D.C.: Government Printing Office, 1969), p. 28.

[10] See, for instance, Charles River Associates, "Economic Analysis of the Silver Industry" (Cambridge, Mass., September 1969), pp. 3–58 (hereinafter referred to as CRA); and Jastram, *Silver: The Restless Metal*, p. 152.

perity and a hedge against personal misfortunes. In the markets of the West, moreover, many silver "bulls" fervently believe that silver is the single best shield against inflation and that the metal will eventually regain its role as the currency of choice.[11] These speculative and monetary demands are difficult to quantify and predict, but they play a tremendous role in the overall market for silver. Together, demand from India and the Middle East accounts for a consistently high portion of total international demand, and it soars even higher during times of political unrest or economic uncertainty. Meanwhile, the bulls continue to prod demand in the commodity markets of the West.[12] In fact, the extremely high prices that might potentially put a dent in industrial demand are likely to have precisely the opposite effect on the speculative demand, thus giving credence to the argument that silver is a profitable investment and perpetuating a speculative frenzy.

As a result, the producers face a fairly inelastic demand curve. All that they need to do—and what a cartel would clearly allow them to do—is to regulate their own sales so as to stabilize the market and prevent sharp vacillations in either price or supply. Specifically, to reap the benefits inherent in their market position, the large producers need to adopt cooperative measures that would allow them to keep their joint sales within an optimal range—the range at which supply is sufficient to keep shortages from occurring and prices from soaring upward but not so abundant as to flood the market and depress prices. In short, they need to form a cartel. With a cartel or with any form of strategic cooperation, the producers could take advantage of their structural assets and avoid some of the more dangerous pitfalls of the market. Without such cooperation, the market will tend toward its more volatile extremes, and the producers will pay the price.

Just how steep this price can be was vividly illustrated in the "silver crisis" of 1979–80.[13] In March 1980, a rumor that had long been

[11] See, for instance, Paul Sarnoff, *Silver Bulls* (Westport, Conn.: Arlington House, 1980), esp. pp. 171–78.

[12] Most recently, the Hunt fiasco demonstrated the lengths to which the bulls will go to buy silver.

[13] The story of the Hunts and their effort to corner or "squeeze" the silver market in 1979–80 is the biggest recent event in the market. Yet because this story is basically

circulating in the market became a reality. Urged by their own belief that silver was destined to regain its role as a monetary and perhaps even a scarce strategic metal, the Hunt brothers of Texas began speculating in silver futures and buying physical silver by the ton. As the extent of their activities became known, the market's worst fears were realized. The Hunts' investment in silver futures created a speculative fever that pushed silver prices steadily upward. At the same time, the fact that the Hunts had physically taken their silver out of the United States meant that the silver "shorts"—investors who had purchased contracts to *sell* silver at a fixed price at a future date—were left with the prospect of having to buy silver from the Hunts, at prices the Hunts alone could control. There simply was not enough physical silver left to fill all the contracts that had been signed.

This sudden and drastic shortage wreaked havoc in the market. As prices soared to $48 per ounce in January 1980, everyone was either scrambling to find silver or to sell it. Industrial users began to recycle whatever they could, small high-cost mines opened across the United States,[14] people sold their family heirlooms,[15] and the large producers expanded production. Individuals who had never dealt with silver before were suddenly active in the market and selling whatever they could. Inevitably, though, the wave of supplies overwhelmed the speculative frenzy, and silver prices plummeted. In December 1980, silver was selling for $16.39 per ounce; by June 1982, the per-ounce price had sunk to $4.88. As the market crashed, many of its most recent entrants simply took their profits and left. For the large producers, however, it was not so easy. They were often locked

---

unrelated to our primary interest—the organization of the silver *producers*—it is not covered at any length in this chapter and is instead included only insofar as the speculation that ensued affected the overall market for silver. For three interesting, if polemical, accounts of the Hunt story, see Streeter, *Silver Mania*; Sarnoff, *Silver Bulls*; and Stephen Fay, *Beyond Greed* (New York: Viking Press, 1982). See also Alan Trustman, "The Silver Scam," *Atlantic Monthly*, September 1980, pp. 70–81; and Roy Rowan, "A Hunt Crony Tells All," *Fortune*, June 30, 1980, pp. 54–60. For the Hunts' own version, see "Price Volatility in the Silver Futures Market," U.S. Senate, Hearings before the Subcommittee on Agriculture, Nutrition, and Forestry, 96th Cong., 2d sess., May 1 and 2, 1980, pp. 182–226.

[14] See Jerry Ruhl, "A New Gold and Silver Rush," *Venture*, December 1980, pp. 16–18.

[15] "To the Melting Pot," *Time*, February 4, 1980, p. 68.

into expansion plans or production schedules based on higher-priced silver, and they now had to face the longer-term economic consequences of an oversupply guaranteed by their (and their competitors') increased production.

By the mid-1980s, lower prices had brought a nearly 50 percent reduction in silver recycling.[16] But the large mines, having committed themselves to expansion during the boom times of the late 1970s, had significantly increased their production and thus were driving prices and profits steadily downward.[17] Remarkably, this oversupply was occurring even as industrial demand for silver was rising and was predicted to rise even more.[18] Had the producers been able to work together, even if only to hold back some of their new production, they could have allowed prices to slip slowly back upward. Instead, they flooded the market and paid the consequences.

In retrospect, many of these consequences could have been averted if the producers had been able to coordinate their activities in the market; they could probably have been minimized if the producers had ever established a cooperative mechanism for using stockpiles or production quotas to regulate the market and limit the sudden entry of additional silver. The obvious question, then, is why the major silver producers have never joined forces to regulate the market. The tools, it appears, are all there. The puzzle is why they have never been used.

Traditionally, two answers to this puzzle have been suggested, both of which are derived from the structural quirks mentioned earlier. Specifically, the quirks refer, first, to silver's role as a by-product metal and, second, to the existence of a secondary market. Both these factors exert a considerable influence on the silver-mining industry, and both serve to skew some of the price relationships of the market. Neither, though, is so important as to undermine the more

[16] See "Study Shows Silver Gap Closing," *Financial Times*, November 19, 1985, p. 36a.

[17] Between 1979 and 1985, production increased 25 percent. See Stefan Wagstyl, "Silver Seen Losing Its Glitter," *Financial Times*, November 29, 1985, p. 28b; and "Surplus Keeps Prices Low," *Financial Times*, September 8, 1986, p. 13c.

[18] See, for instance, "Study Shows Silver Gap Closing," p. 36a; "Decline in Western Silver Surplus," *Financial Times*, February 17, 1983, p. 32; "Higher World Demand for Silver Likely," *Financial Times*, May 15, 1984, p. 36b; and "The Silver Bugs May Be Ready to Swarm," *Business Week*, December 1, 1986, p. 126.

basic structure of the silver market, and neither should in any way preclude the possibility of cooperation among the silver producers.

The first of these arguments centers on the fact that, unlike most metal commodities, silver is produced primarily as a by-product of other metals. Only 40 percent of U.S. silver production, for example, and 30 percent of Mexico's comes from silver mines.[19] The rest is produced along with copper, lead, zinc, and gold. Known as by-product or coproduct silver, this silver usually occurs in small proportions relative to the dominant metal and is, therefore, a prisoner to its production. In economic terms, then, silver production does not and indeed cannot respond immediately to changes in the demand for or price of silver. Instead, the output of silver is determined by the demand for the base metals with which silver is mined.[20] As a result, the usual connections between demand, supply, and price are somewhat skewed in the silver market. A decline in the silver price will not necessarily induce a curtailment of production, unless the decline reflects a general fall in the price of all metals. By the same token, small price increases will have very little effect on the majority of the producers, who will not agree to risk their overall production schedules just to earn slightly greater profits on the relatively small amount of silver they produce.[21]

The second source of disruption in the silver market and the second market-based explanation of silver's discord lies in the fact that newly mined silver is not the only source of silver supply. Instead, there is a rather significant "secondary" market that also affects the overall supply. This market is composed primarily of silver consumers who, under certain economic circumstances, will be sufficiently motivated to recycle their silver and offer it for sale. Under normal conditions, the secondary market is reserved for major silver users such as the commercial photography industry, which routinely recovers some of the silver used in its chemical processes and recy-

---

[19] Firoze E. Katrak and Robert H. Pittman, "The Non-Communist World Market for Silver," *Metal Bulletin Precious Metals Survey*, 1982, p. 43.

[20] See Mohide, *Silver*, p. 118; and Leong, *Silver: An Analysis*, p. 84.

[21] "Relatively" here means relative to the other base metals. For more information on the ways in which silver's position as a by-product affects the relationship between price and supply, see CRA, pp. 4–42. For the relationship between price and supply, see Leong, *Silver: An Analysis*, pp. 68–71.

cles it for its own use.[22] In addition, though, the secondary market is also composed of outside sources of supply such as coin melting and "dishoarding." In normal times, people tend to hold on to their silver coins, jewelry, and flatware and to view them only as consumer items or personal possessions. But when prices hit extraordinary heights, a "melting point" is reached, and old silver comes flooding back onto the market. This avalanche distorts the supply side of the market because it opens up a new and potentially unlimited source of "production."

According to some analysts, the impact of this secondary market, coupled with silver's awkward position as a by-product metal, is sufficient explanation for the notable lack of cooperation in the market. Cooperation, they argue, is doubly unlikely; first, because these structural quirks make the market more volatile and, second, because they cause supply to be influenced by several factors that are completely beyond the producers' control. The problem with this argument, however, is that it refers only to the market under the most extreme conditions. Most of the secondary market is composed of industrial users and commercial recyclers, who basically produce a steady amount of silver regardless of price and thus do not really interfere with the normal workings of the market.[23] In fact, the secondary market becomes important only when prices soar suddenly upward, thus bringing new players onto the scene and disturbing the existing relationship between supply and demand. The point to remember, however, is that price increases of this magnitude are relatively rare. Most of the time the silver flatware remains in the cupboard, the women of India continue to wear their silver jewelry, and the mine producers control the supply side of the silver market.

In practice, then, the secondary market imposes few constraints on the day-to-day operations of the mine producers and need not

---

[22] Although there are no wholly reliable figures for this additional source of supply, a recent Bureau of Mines report indicates that scrap silver accounted for approximately 6 percent of the total silver consumed in the United States in 1991. See *Silver*, United States Department of the Interior, Bureau of Mines (Washington, D.C.: Government Printing Office, 1992), table 1, p. 11.

[23] Jastram, *Silver: The Restless Metal*, p. 147. See also The Silver Institute, *World Silver Survey 1950–1990* (Washington, D.C.: The Silver Institute, 1990), pp. 19–20. This report also states that "silver held in inventories . . . has had virtually no impact on the market over the past few decades."

present any barriers to cooperation. Indeed, if the producers were able to cooperate, they would also likely be able to moderate the price shifts that trigger the secondary market. All they need do is regulate the supply of newly mined silver so as to keep prices above the level of their own costs but below the point at which secondary silver would flood the market.[24] Admittedly, cooperative price targeting is no easy task. Yet as previous chapters have demonstrated, it is a classic function of cartels and something that can be achieved relatively painlessly by the right kind of producers in the right sort of circumstances. In the silver market, then, it may very well be that a lack of producer cooperation has exacerbated the very conditions that permit the secondary market to exist at all.

Likewise, there is no reason why silver's status as a by-product metal should necessarily preclude cooperation. Even if outside factors influence the amount of by-product silver that is produced in any given period, they need not have any effect on the amount of silver that is *sold*. In other words, even producers of by-product silver could act strategically in the market, selling from stockpiles in accordance with market trends and using their collective stockpiles to regulate the market. Once again, this is no easy task, but neither is it impossible or unprecedented. Most cartels rely to some extent on the collaborative management of stockpiles, and all depend on the strategic restraint inherent in such management. If the producers could exercise enough restraint to separate the sale of silver from its production, then their potential control over the market would be vastly enhanced and strategic cooperation would be entirely possible.

Thus, although both the secondary market and the by-product problem have undoubtedly left their marks on the silver industry, neither condition is central to the market itself, and neither necessarily excludes cooperation. Instead, both these quirks may actually be exacerbated by the historical absence of cooperation in the market and by the chaos that prevails instead. To explain the lack of cooperation, then, we need to look elsewhere.

Specifically, we need to look once again at the domestic level and

---

[24] In 1984, Streeter calculated that a price of fifteen dollars per troy ounce would be high enough to bring increasing amounts of secondary silver onto the market and that at twenty dollars the market would be flooded. See *Silver Mania*, pp. 211–13.

at the various internal characteristics that have prevented the major silver producers from reaping the collective benefits of collaboration. We need to understand how internal politics created barriers to external cooperation and how the domestic priorities of each state influenced its relationship with the others. In short, we need to explain why some producers may be unable to cooperate even under conducive structural circumstances.

THE UNITED STATES

In the context of this study, the most important explanation of the lack of producer cooperation in silver is the behavior of one of the major producers, the United States. Not only has the United States shown no interest in any type of cooperative action, but in the process of placating its own domestic silver interests, it has also managed to disrupt the entire market and worsen the longer-term interests of the producers themselves. This behavior on the part of the U.S. government cannot be dismissed solely as economic irrationality or as an inability to perceive the potential benefits of market cooperation. Rather, as was the case with Canada and uranium, it reflects the special difficulties that cooperation poses for diverse and fragmented democracies.

The problem with silver is not decentralization and diffuse powers. On the contrary, as the U.S. government has traditionally assumed the responsibility for setting national policy on silver, it has made itself a powerful presence in the market and an obvious point of national authority and coordination. If the United States were ever interested in participating in an international silver cartel, it is likely that an agency of the U.S. government—such as the Treasury Department—would be able to lead the U.S. contingent and discipline all the producers in its ranks. A lack of centralized authority, then, does not appear to be the obstacle preventing the United States from external cooperation. Instead, the obstacle seems to lie in the fact that this authority has long been subject to the shifting whims and demands of a small but powerful minority.

Specifically, silver policy in the United States has emerged from a distinctly political process in which the majority of the government and the population, who deal only rarely with silver and have little personal interest in its fate, have been arrayed against the silver producers and their representatives, who care passionately about silver and have done their utmost to keep the metal in the national spotlight and protected by federal programs. The battle, like many in the United States, has thus pitted a silent majority against a small but committed minority. And as in many battles of this type, the minority has prevailed.

Even more important, though, the minority here has not been able to work toward its own collective long-term interests or to maintain a consistent set of policies and demands. Rather, it has tended to focus on the most immediate of concerns, putting the short-term demands of individuals before the long-term interests of the industry. From time to time, of course, bureaucrats or policymakers in one of the relevant agencies have recognized the long-term prospects of the market and the benefits that international cooperation would bring. But although these people had the power to implement policies, the content of these policies was set by the silver lobby. Thus, those with the ability to take a broader perspective were effectively precluded from setting policy and were instead forced to implement the policies dictated by the narrower and more immediate whims of a politically committed minority.

As a result, silver policy in the United States seems, from the outside at least, to be completely arbitrary, if not indeed irrational. Because the U.S. government must constantly use its power in the market to respond to the silver politics of the moment, it is robbed of its ability to take a longer-term view and make the credible commitments that are central to any cooperative venture. Other nations that might have been eager to collaborate with the United States in the silver market have been turned away by American power in the market and by the apparently arbitrary and self-serving ends to which it has customarily been directed. Thus, rather than using its authority to regulate the silver market to the collective benefit of the producers, the United States has convinced its would-be allies that it is not to be trusted in the market and that any international commitment it makes is subject to the demands of its own domestic politics.

The Silver Bloc and the "Crime of '73"

The question of silver no longer attracts either widespread public interest or extensive official attention. The public at large cares about silver only on those rare occasions when selling the family heirlooms becomes profitable, and the government gets involved only when speculation gets out of hand or when financial considerations rekindle interest in selling some of the nation's vast stockpiles of silver. For the most part, silver issues and silver policies pass unnoticed.

This has not always been the case. For more than a century, silver was a major issue in the United States, and silver policy was the subject of intense political debate. During this time, a skillful silver lobby was able to forge a powerful coalition in support of its own narrow interests and steer U.S. policy so as to best serve those interests. The immediate effect of this lobby was to force the United States to adopt a series of self-serving and occasionally even contradictory policies. The more lasting effect was to create an institutional precedent that disregarded any concern for the longer-term prospects of the industry and abandoned any hope for international cooperation in the market.

To understand why cooperation has been lacking for so long in the international silver market, we need to understand how the evolution of silver policy in the United States made its participation in a collaborative endeavor impossible and any cooperation at all unlikely.

As far as silver is concerned, the central event of the nineteenth century was the passage of the Coinage Act of 1873 and the political revolt it occasioned. The act was passed for a straightforward reason: to acknowledge that the United States was evolving toward a single gold standard and thus to phase out the existing bimetallic system by halting the minting of silver dollars. Although the act allowed existing coins to remain as legal tender, it effectively served to eliminate the free coinage of silver and place the United States on a de facto gold standard.[25] Initially, the Coinage Act passed and went

[25] The act did provide for the minting of several subsidiary silver coins, such as a trade dollar for use in commerce with the Orient. See Dickson Hammond Leavens, *Silver Money*, Cowles Commission for Research in Economics, Monograph no. 4 (Bloomington, Ind.: Principia Press, 1939), pp. 18–24.

into effect without inciting any real public interest, much less concern. The population had become accustomed to paper money, and because silver coins had been scarce for several decades, few consumers cared about their passing.

There was, however, one domestic group that saw its interests directly threatened by the act. The silver producers who had grown accustomed to selling their metal directly to the Treasury now faced the elimination of their major source of demand. Quickly, they organized themselves and pressured their fledgling state representatives to trumpet silver's cause in the Senate. The obvious problem, though, was that the silver producers were still too diffuse and the states too few in number to present any real opposition to hostile legislation such as the Coinage Act of 1873. What these states needed to do, therefore, was to forge a coalition with sympathetic interests that could be persuaded to rally to the cause of silver. And this is precisely what they did.

Specifically, the silver states were able to join with a number of domestic groups that were then clamoring for an increased money supply to ease the financial crisis that had beset large portions of the country in 1873 and 1874. Individually, neither of these groups had much hope of realizing their goals. Together, the forces of "silver money" and "cheaper money" presented a virtually undefeatable bloc. As Allan Seymour Everest describes it:

> The so-called "Silver Bloc" represented at various times 7 or 8 states, with 14 or 16 senators committed to a specific program. They were only a minority. Therefore, early in their collective career in Washington, they thoroughly learned the art of politics. The lesson they assimilated and applied was the mathematics of combination: if eight mining states want to sell their silver at a good price, and 20 agricultural states want more and cheaper money, the combination of 28 states would command a majority of the Senate.[26]

By 1876, this combination had chosen the Coinage Act of 1873 as the target of its joint attack. Arguing that massive defaults in the silver industry would put large chunks of the West at the mercy of

---

[26] Allan Seymour Everest, *Morgenthau, the New Deal, and Silver: A Story of Pressure Politics* (New York: King's Crown Press, 1950), p. 3.

their eastern creditors, the senators demanded protection for the silver industry and restitution of the wrongs imposed by the "Crime of 1873." The silver bloc, later described as "one of the most efficient, sophisticated, and ruthless in the nation,"[27] had been born.

The bloc scored its first victory in 1878, passing the Bland-Allison Act over President Hayes's veto. Under the act, silver dollars (which had been effectively demonetized in 1873) were once again to be treated as legal tender. Moreover, the government was directed to purchase and coin at least $2 million worth of silver each month, and the president was ordered to assemble an international conference to work toward the reestablishment of international bimetallism.[28] Over the next twelve years, the U.S. Treasury would purchase about 291 million ounces of silver, or about 60 percent of U.S. production.[29] These efforts notwithstanding, the world price of silver continued to decline, and the silver bloc continued to lobby for unlimited free coinage. In 1890, it succeeded in passing the Sherman Act, directing the U.S. Treasury to purchase 4.5 million ounces of silver a month at $1.29 per ounce. The Treasury would pay for the silver with notes that were to be redeemable in coin and legal payment for all debts. For all practical purposes, silver had been remonetized.

More important, perhaps, the Sherman Act also established several critical precedents: that the U.S. government was responsible for the economic well-being of its silver producers, that the government would effectively set the U.S. market price for silver, and that the U.S. Treasury would act as a buyer of last resort. The bloc had triumphed, not just in achieving remonetization but also in establishing a pattern whereby the U.S. government would regulate the domestic silver market to serve the immediate interests of the silver producers. And thus the economic reasoning that had launched the Coinage Act of 1873 was largely reversed by 1890 and replaced by a political logic of an entirely different sort.[30]

[27] John Gunther, *Inside U.S.A.*, p. 183, cited in Everest, *Morgenthau, the New Deal, and Silver*, p. 172.

[28] Leavens, *Silver Money*, pp. 38–39.

[29] F. W. Taussig, *The Silver Situation in the United States* (New York: Putnam's, 1893), pp. 75–78.

[30] Although the Sherman Act was repealed by President Cleveland in 1893, the question of silver continued to dominate the national agenda. In 1894, William Jen-

The London Economic Conference and
the Silver Purchase Act of 1934

In the late nineteenth century, the question of silver was largely a domestic issue, and the silver policy of the United States carried few international ramifications. By the start of the twentieth century, however, the scope had widened. The United States had become one of the largest producers and consumers of the metal, U.S. producers were selling more of their silver abroad, and the U.S. government was becoming more involved in the monetary affairs of many of its allies. As a result, U.S. silver policy began to set the tone for the entire international market. In particular, because the U.S. market for silver was so large, the price set by the U.S. Treasury had a tremendous impact on the world price and on the well-being of the entire industry.

By the 1920s, the United States had the opportunity to play the role of benevolent hegemon in the silver industry. It had the market power, the centralized authority, and a considerable amount of political influence with the governments of the other major producing states. Had it chosen to do so, the United States was ideally positioned to launch a cooperative arrangement between the producers and preside over the orderly management of the market. As it turned out, however, the United States only went halfway. Realizing the power inherent in its political and economic position, the U.S. government did become increasingly involved in the international silver market. But rather than using its position to encourage cooperation, the United States continued to look inward, serving the immediate needs of its producers and disregarding both the international effects of its policies and the long-term ramifications for the industry.

Between 1918 and 1924, the silver industry had flourished under the provisions of the Pittman Act, under which the Treasury sent a

---

nings Bryan ran for the presidency on a pro-silver platform and won 48 percent of the popular vote. In one of his most quoted speeches, he argued, "We will answer their demand for a gold standard by saying to them: You shall not press down upon the brow of labor this crown of thorns, you shall not crucify mankind upon a cross of gold."

portion of its vast silver stocks to India to ease that country's acute wartime shortage and, in turn, replenished itself by buying from U.S. producers at considerably above market prices.[31] When the war ended and the act ran out, the Silver Producers Association tried to ward off the effects of a postwar price decline by going to the Federal Trade Commission with a request to organize an export association. Ironically, though, the U.S. government held that any such association would be illegal because it would involve silver produced outside the United States and therefore have an effect on domestic prices.[32]

This repugnance for noncompetitive behavior, however, clearly did not extend to any protective measures adopted by the government itself. Over the next several years, the silver industry began once more to lobby vigorously for federal protection and for a return to the bimetallism that alone, they claimed, could solve the nation's deepening economic troubles.[33] By itself, the call for protection might have gone unheard at a time when so many groups were suffering. By linking the case for silver subsidies to the case for sound money, however, the silver bloc was again able to construct a powerful coalition on behalf of its own interests. By 1933, silver had once more become a passionate national issue, and President Roosevelt was under pressure from all sides to do something about silver. In particular, powerful factions in Congress were urging the president to use the upcoming London Economic Conference as an opportunity for the United States to spearhead an international agreement on the remonetization of silver.

For the representatives of the sixty-six nations assembled in London, the first issue of the day was currency stabilization; the subject of silver was treated as an "international joke" that had been placed on the agenda simply to placate the Americans.[34] As it turned out,

---

[31] See Leavens, *Silver Money*, pp. 145–50.

[32] See John Parke Young, "European Currency and Finance," Commission of Gold and Silver Inquiry, serial 7 (Washington, D.C.: Government Printing Office, 1925), pp. 17–21.

[33] The silver industry was struck particularly hard in the early years of the depression. In 1931, production in the United States was one-half of what it had been in 1925, and its value was one-fifth as great. Everest, *Morgenthau, the New Deal, and Silver*, p. 9.

[34] Ibid., p. 28.

however, the U.S.-sponsored silver memorandum was the only agreement to come out of the conference and one of the only international agreements on silver ever signed.[35] In its simplest form, the agreement was designed to regulate the entire market for silver, easing the fluctuations experienced by both producers and consumers of the metal and stabilizing prices. Under the agreement's terms, the governments of the five major silver-producing countries—the United States, Canada, Mexico, Peru, and Australia—promised not to sell any silver on the world market for a four-year period and instead to purchase a total of thirty-five million ounces annually. The United States's share was figured at nearly twenty-five million ounces a year, which left the other four countries just over ten million ounces to split among themselves.[36] For their part, the major buyers and holders of silver—China, India, and Spain—agreed not to release any of their own vast stocks onto the market.[37]

Basically, then, the silver agreement was a massive attempt to stabilize silver prices by sharply limiting the available supply. On the surface, at least, it resembled nothing so much as an officially sanctioned international cartel. Indeed, if the arrangement had functioned as planned, it would have institutionalized cooperation in the silver market. Moreover, it is interesting to note that the agreement represents the one occasion on which the United States exercised its ability to act as a hegemon and organize a cooperative venture. The United States agreed to bear the bulk of the costs for an arrangement that both soothed an international problem and served its own domestic interests.[38] For the moment, there seemed to be cooperation in the silver market, and the United States seemed to have assumed the burdens of leadership.

Initially, the agreement appeared to benefit all concerned. The

---

[35] For more information on the provisions of the agreement, see U.S. Congress, House, "International Monetary and Economic Conference, London, England," Hearings before the Committee on Foreign Affairs, 72d Cong., 2d sess., on H.J. Res. 536, January 10–11, 1933; and U.S. Department of State, Treaty Information Bulletin no. 47, August 31, 1933, pp. 17–21.

[36] Leong, *Silver: An Analysis*, p. 136.

[37] Some allowances were made for the repayment of war debts. See ibid., p. 137.

[38] This would support the "benevolent" view of the hegemon. See Duncan Snidal, "The Limits of Hegemonic Stability Theory," *International Organization* 39 (Autumn 1985).

silver-producing nations expressed their satisfaction with U.S. efforts, and silver prices rose steadily throughout 1933. By April 1934, all eight nations involved had conformed to the agreement's provisions and decided to extend their participation until the end of 1937.[39] The problem, however, was that U.S. participation in the agreement had never been much more than a thinly disguised effort to placate domestic silver producers.[40] There was no one in the government who was interested in the agreement for its own sake, and no one concerned about preserving it as a legal or political entity that was in any way distinct from the immediate demands of the silver bloc. Thus, when the silver producers decided that the London Economic Conference had not gone far enough in protecting their interests, the agreement was hastily discarded and its provisions ignored by the very people who had just negotiated them.

By January 1934, proponents of expanded protection for the silver industry had begun to push for legislation that would authorize the Treasury to begin massive purchases of silver. Despite Roosevelt's plea that no further measures be implemented until the effects of the London agreements became more obvious, several key senators continued to forge a pro-silver coalition by appealing to the similar interests of their colleagues from major cotton- and tobacco-producing states.[41] Meanwhile, popular pressure in favor of remonetization was also being fomented by such advocates as the radio priest Charles E. Coughlin and the broad-based Committee for the Nation.[42]

By the spring of 1934, Roosevelt had realized that he would have to strike a compromise with the silver bloc and accede to its persistent demands for increased government purchases of silver. This

[39] Everest, *Morgenthau, the New Deal, and Silver*, p. 32.

[40] In fact, U.S. efforts at the London conference were directed by Senator Key Pittman, a leading member of the silver bloc and a long-time defender of the silver industry in the United States.

[41] Everest, *Morgenthau, the New Deal, and Silver*, p. 37.

[42] In one broadcast, for instance, Father Coughlin urged his listeners to stop imitating England where "the liars and the Judases, the high priests, Annas and Caiphas were at work crucifying silver." See the Radio League of the Little Flower publications of sixteen lectures between October 1933 and March 1934 (cited in Everest, *Morgenthau, the New Deal, and Silver*, p. 38). Father Coughlin's objectivity in this matter became suspect, however, when a Treasury investigation revealed that his Radio League owned one-half million ounces of silver futures.

compromise took the form of the Silver Purchase Act of 1934, an act later described as "one of the most absurd packages of legislation that has ever been passed"[43] and, less dramatically, as "one of the most unusual, far-reaching, and ultimately futile pieces of legislation in the history of our country."[44] The provisions of the act were simple but expansive. They declared that the amount of silver held by the U.S. government should be increased until silver constituted fully one-fourth of the country's monetary stock. Effectively, this meant that every government purchase of gold would have to be matched by the acquisition of additional silver. To this end, the Treasury was authorized to commence an intensive silver-buying program.

The implications of the act were manifold. First, it virtually ensured that the U.S. Treasury would become the single greatest force in the silver market. Second, it perpetuated the practice of extensive governmental support for the domestic silver industry. And, third, it superseded whatever international commitments the government had made—or might choose to make—with regard to silver. Instead, passage of the act revealed that silver policy in the United States had become completely politicized and subject almost exclusively to the demands of the silver bloc. As F. H. Wemple notes, "Most probably the Act was passed more because the popular clamor for inflationary measures of any kind drowned out the more considered opinions of the monetary experts . . . than because of any clearly conceived government objective."[45] Similarly, a 1939 article in the New York *Journal of Commerce* declared that "the whole silver

---

[43] Streeter, *Silver Mania*, p. 28.

[44] F. H. Wemple, "The Silver Market," in Allison Butts and Charles D. Coxe, eds., *Silver: Economics, Metallurgy, and Use* (Princeton, N.J.: D. Van Nostrand, 1967), p. 41.

[45] Ibid., p. 40. It is particularly ironic that the silver act actually failed to achieve most of its stated objectives. Despite the Treasury's purchase of over two billion ounces of silver between 1934 and 1941, it acquired even more gold and thus never attained the stated proportion of one-fourth silver. Moreover, remarkably, during the time that the Silver Purchase Act was in operation, the market price of silver declined, slipping from forty-five cents per ounce in 1934 to thirty-five cents in 1939. Finally, the uncertainty created by the act, plus the promise of vast purchases that it offered, meant that many of the silver-producing and silver-hoarding countries offered more silver than usual for sale, thus pushing prices even lower and undermining the ostensible purposes of the act.

buying program was conceived in folly, and carried out with primary attention to the political considerations involved."[46]

In attending to the demands of the domestic industry, moreover, the U.S. government completely abandoned the commitments it had made at the London Economic Conference. In fact, passage of the 1934 act caused considerable damage to many of the nations that had just joined the United States in the silver agreement of 1933. China, for instance, was still on a silver standard in the 1930s and dependent on imported silver to fuel its economy. The Chinese desperately needed stability and certainty in the silver market. They had signed the London agreement enthusiastically, trusting that the limited government regulation it promised would stabilize the world market and ease their own domestic economic troubles. What they got as a result of the Silver Purchase Act, however, were silver prices that rose and fell—seemingly arbitrarily—at the hands of the United States.[47] In the winter of 1934–35, when China seemed on the brink of economic disaster, Secretary of the Treasury Morgenthau tried to initiate a program that would regulate U.S. sales to China and thus quell some of the agitation in the Chinese market. Even this program lasted for only two weeks. After that, Morgenthau was compelled by the silver bloc to terminate it. When the Chinese ambassador complained, Morgenthau could only advise him to speak to the members of Congress.[48]

In Mexico, too, the effects of the U.S. act were calamitous. Like that of China, Mexico's economy revolved largely on silver, although here the connection was due primarily to the country's role as a leading exporter of the metal. And like China, Mexico also treasured stability of silver prices above all and thus had been an eager participant in the London Economic Conference. Initially, Mexico stood to benefit from the Silver Purchase Act, as the higher prices it induced

[46] Quoted in Everest, *Morgenthau, the New Deal, and Silver*, p. 173. Everest also reports that the *New York Times, Herald Tribune*, and *Business Week* all regularly denounced the silver program, and he describes their "rage over the fact that a small group, by sticking together and making loud protests, could win a subsidy for the tiny silver industry and a profit for silver speculators" (pp. 173–74).

[47] Jastram, *Silver: The Restless Metal*, p. 100.

[48] Everest, *Morgenthau, the New Deal, and Silver*, p. 108. U.S. policy on this matter was further constrained by the State Department's persistent concern not to do anything that might alienate the Japanese.

increased the value of Mexico's exports. Beyond a certain point, however, the benefits of higher-priced silver changed dramatically into losses. At this time, the bullion value of the Mexican peso had been set at 71.9 cents an ounce. If the U.S. market price rose above 72 cents an ounce, therefore, the peso was worth more as metal than as currency. For several months, Mexico fared well. With the United States keeping silver prices in the range of 45 to 60 cents an ounce, Mexican exporters were making significant profits and helping to buoy the Mexican economy. In April 1935, however, the U.S. Treasury suddenly pushed the price of silver above 72 cents, thus driving silver coins out of circulation in Mexico and throwing the Mexican economy into a full-scale monetary crisis.[49] Eventually, Mexico was forced to ask the United States for aid. Ultimately, the Mexican government had to change the silver content of its coins.[50]

Indeed, throughout Latin America, countries that either produced silver or used it as a currency were caught off guard by the impact of the Silver Purchase Act. Because the United States was buying vast quantities of silver at a preordained price, it was impeding the free operation of the market and preventing a supply-induced price decline. Simultaneously, because it refused to coordinate its activities with the other producers, it was undermining their economies, most of which were based on a silver standard currency. Thus, as the Latin American nations hurried to issue new currencies and forbid the export of silver coins, they also petitioned the U.S. government directly, demanding compensation for the ill effects they had suffered as a result of U.S. policy.

The U.S. government was caught. On the one hand, it realized the damage it had wrought and, in an increasingly hostile international climate, wanted to ensure the political loyalty of its Latin American allies. On the other hand, the silver bloc had the domestic political clout to dictate continued Treasury purchases and continued high prices. The only option open to the government, therefore, was to ease the foreign impact of its policies: to help the foreign govern-

[49] The crisis of Mexican silver was "solved" temporarily when the United States, in response to the expropriation of American oil interests in Mexico, suspended all silver purchases from Mexico.

[50] For an extensive discussion of U.S.-Mexican negotiations on silver and oil, see Everest, *Morgenthau, the New Deal, and Silver*, pp. 79–96.

ments stamp new coins, slow the importation of existing silver coins, and buy these countries' silver at artificially high prices. The one thing that the Latin American countries truly needed but that the U.S. government would not do was to coordinate policy in the silver market. In the end, stabilization of the market fell completely by the wayside and no one benefited.

In time, the market and the U.S. public caught up with the silver industry, and a new coalition was forged. By the early 1940s, the increasing use of silver for industrial and military purposes had created a shortage of silver, and industrial users of the metal joined foreign governments in requesting that the U.S. Treasury release some of its vast stockpiles of silver for sale. The press quickly joined the attack, arguing against the absurdity of a government that urged its public not to hoard sugar, rubber, and gasoline but that itself continued to hoard a metal that was vital to the war effort.[51] One popular magazine even went so far as to label the activities of the silver bloc as "treason."[52] Even Secretary Morgenthau publicized his own opinion that silver purchases be ceased and that silver be made available to industrial consumers. The bloc, however, still refused to support any legislation that would have eased Morgenthau's position or made any American silver available for the war effort. Instead, all production in the United States was still bought directly by the Treasury and buried deep within its vaults.

By June 1943, however, the silver consumers had found their own political clout and gathered enough popular support to ensure their first victory over the silver bloc. Under the provisions of the Green Act, silver producers received a higher guaranteed price for their silver, but in exchange, the Treasury was permitted to sell or lease government silver to be used in the war effort.[53] In retrospect, though, the Green Act dealt little more than a minor blow to the silver producers or the silver bloc. Rather, throughout the 1940s, 1950s, and 1960s, the bloc continued to dominate U.S. silver policy and to wrest major concessions from the government with regard to silver purchases. The Treasury continued to buy far more silver

[51] *New York Times*, August 4, 1942. Cited in ibid., p. 137.
[52] Sylvia F. Porter, "Twelve Men against the Nation," *Reader's Digest*, November 1942, pp. 1–4.
[53] Wemple, "Silver Market," p. 44.

than it sold and to buy it all at highly inflated prices. Altogether, the Treasury acquired over three billion ounces of silver between 1933 and 1961, ten times more than it sold.[54]

The gross effect of these purchases was to put the entire world silver market at the mercy of the U.S. Treasury. The demand for and price of silver were no longer determined simply by market forces, much less by an international agreement between the countries most deeply involved. Rather, the parameters of the market were largely set by the vicissitudes of U.S. policy, which left other players to adjust as best they could. At the London Economic Conference of 1933, the United States had had the opportunity to preside over an international arrangement that would have stabilized the international silver market *and* would have ameliorated the plight of the domestic U.S. industry. Instead, prodded by the demands of a small but powerful minority, the United States adopted an independent course that divorced it from the international community and the longer-term interests of the silver market.

Silver Today

In 1967, Congress at last authorized the Treasury to stop redeeming silver certificates and to transfer to the national defense stockpile 165 million ounces of its own silver.[55] Since then, all U.S. citizens have been permitted to buy and sell silver at their own discretion, and silver has basically been treated as a commodity subject only to the normal fluctuations of the free market. Nevertheless, the history of U.S. regulation of silver has left several indelible marks that continue to affect the market and make cooperation between the producers highly unlikely. In the first place, the U.S. government still maintains a vast stockpile of silver and continues to deal with this stockpile as a political, rather than an economic, commodity. For example, whenever there is a motion afoot to sell some of the silver

[54] Ibid., p. 45. For additional data on the shape and extent of Treasury purchases, see CRA, pp. 2-23–2-38.

[55] For more information on this law, PL 90–29, see *Congressional Quarterly Almanac, 1967* (Washington, D.C.: Congressional Quarterly, 1967), pp. 676–78. Between 1960 and 1966 the U.S. Treasury had actually been a net seller of silver, keeping the market well supplied with bullion as it completed the withdrawal of silver from currency.

stockpile or to use it in the manufacture of commemorative coins, congressional supporters of silver are always quick to offer opposition or at least to impose restrictions on the quantities sold.[56] At the same time, though, the development of a speculative market in silver, coupled with the very real financial demands of the country, have also created some countervailing political forces that occasionally try to prod the government into disposing of some of its vast stockpile.[57] In either case, the size of the stockpile, together with the unpredictable policies that guide it, cause great uneasiness in the market. If the United States were ever to decide to sell off any significant portion of its stockpile, the market would be awash in silver, and prices would plummet. On the other hand, if political pressures were to force the United States into holding on to its stockpile forever, then the market could basically ignore those stocks and subtract them from its calculations of possible supply. As matters stand now, however, there is no way of knowing which of these conditions will prevail. And thus a shadow of uncertainty hangs over the entire market.

The U.S. stockpile could also serve as a stabilizing force for the entire market, but only if the U.S. government was willing to use it strategically, adding to it to support a declining world market and selling from it when prices threaten to rise too far and too fast. To date, however, the United States has given no evidence of a willingness to use its stockpiles in this fashion. On the contrary, the stockpiles that were created to serve the demands of domestic silver pro-

---

[56] For examples of congressional testimony against proposed legislation to dispose of any portion of the silver stockpile, see, for instance, testimony of Representative Larry McDonald, House, Hearings on H.R. 2603, H.R. 2784, H.R. 2912, and H.R. 3364 before the Seapower and Strategic and Critical Materials Subcommittee of the Committee on Armed Services, 97th Cong., 1st sess., June 2 and 4, 1981, pp. 33–42; Testimony of Senator James A. McClure, "Stockpile Legislation," Senate, Hearings before the Subcommittee on Preparedness of the Committee on Armed Services on S. 906, S. 1338, and S. 1823, 97th Cong., 1st sess., June 17, 19, and December 14, 1981, pp. 57–70; and Statement of William Griffith, "Gold and Silver Coinage Proposals," Senate, Hearing before the Committee on Banking, Housing, and Urban Affairs, 98th Cong., 1st sess., April 15, 1983, pp. 27–29.

[57] In 1981, for instance, the Reagan administration won congressional approval for a plan to earn $2 billion by selling 140 million ounces from the stockpile. See "Silver's Sinking Fortunes," *Business Week*, July 19, 1982, p. 156. For a reference to the lobbying efforts of the "bears," see Sarnoff, *Silver Bulls*, pp. 14–15.

ducers seem likely to be used by whatever group in the country sees its interest served by them and is able to rally enough political support for its cause. The policy that emerges from this process is thus shifting and unpredictable, making it nearly impossible for the U.S. government to commit itself to any long-term agreement and undermining the credibility of any commitments it might make.

Of course, it is not completely beyond the realm of possibility to imagine that the U.S. government might someday decide to join with the governments of the other major producing nations and agree, as they did in 1933, to manage their stockpiles in conjunction with one another. Given the nature of U.S. intervention in the past, however, and the vacillations that mark U.S. silver policy, any such cooperation seems highly unlikely.

THE OTHER PRODUCERS

The historical inability of the United States to cooperate should not necessarily condemn the entire international market to perpetual chaos. On the surface, at least, there is no reason why the other major producers could not cooperate with one another, counteracting at least some of the ill effects of U.S. policies. Admittedly, the United States has played the market with a heavy hand. Admittedly, a vast and concerted effort would be needed to neutralize its behavior and regulate the industry to the collective good of the other producers. Still, efforts such as these have been launched in other markets. OPEC arose even after decades of American dominance in the oil market, and the uranium cartel was a direct response to the U.S. Atomic Energy Commission's attempt to keep the international uranium market under its own control. The existence of one unruly player—even one big unruly player—is not by itself sufficient to squelch cooperation among the others.

The silver market, however, has suffered particularly from bad timing and domestic complications. For most of the past century, the United States and its policies were virtually untouchable, especially as three of the other major producers—Canada, Mexico, and Peru—were all too closely linked to the United States and too dependent on its political largesse to contemplate any direct affront in the market. But in recent years, the problem has been less the international power of the United States and more the internal impotence of the other producers. Internationally, these other producers are now in a position where they could conceivably lead a producers' cartel and challenge the United States's declining domination of the market. Internally, though, none of them is particularly well suited for the cooperative game. Mexico and Peru are hampered by their overwhelming debt and by the inability of their governments to resist the temptation of using surplus silver to ameliorate their countries' immediate financial crises. Canada lacks any central authority with interest in or concern for silver. And the former Soviet Union, although clearly able to collaborate, is left alone—unwilling to initiate cooperation with such an unlikely cast of participants. Thus, lacking any countervailing pressures, the market continues to be dominated by the unilateral policies of the United States and the anarchy they engender.

The Soviet Union

Of the other major producers in the market, the former Soviet Union was always the most likely participant in an international cartel.[58] It had a highly centralized authority system, leaders whose entrenched positions gave them the luxury of a long-term view, and, until recently, a nearly total lack of domestic opposition and internal factions. There were no independent silver producers, no independent consumers, and no group whose livelihood was determined by what the government chose to do with its silver. Instead, all silver in the Soviet Union was controlled and marketed by one central authority, thus making it entirely possible for the government to dispose of the metal as it wished, free from the constraints imposed elsewhere by interest groups, fragmented authority, or electoral politics. So, as they were in the diamond and gold cases, the Soviets were well positioned to engage in strategic manipulation and joint regulation of the silver market.

---

[58] The Soviet Union produced fifty-four million troy ounces of silver in 1990, or about 12 percent of total world mine production. The Silver Institute, *World Silver Survey*, p. 24.

To a certain extent, this is what we find. During the 1970s and 1980s, evidence suggests that the Soviets were operating in the silver market just as they did in gold, diamonds, and platinum. That is, they operated largely as speculators, trying to boost their export revenues by playing the relevant markets and intervening to keep prices as high as possible.[59] Periodically, the Soviets would buy significant amounts of silver from the open market, presumably in an attempt to bolster prices for their own exports. By purchasing silver, the Soviets could first hope to push prices back up or, even if that failed, simply save the silver and sell it at a profit when prices did eventually go back up. Such behavior would be completely in keeping with the idea of strategic marketing and would indeed be exactly the type of behavior mandated by an international arrangement designed to stabilize the market and keep prices relatively high.

The problem is that the Soviets never had any partners in the silver market. Even when they were playing the game strategically, no one else was joining in. In the gold and diamond markets, the Soviet Union was fortunate enough to have a partner who shared not only its interest in orderly marketing but also its ability to maintain the internal discipline and long-term commitment that is so critical to any international marketing arrangement. In the silver market, by contrast, there has been no one else to play the game.

Canada

For instance, one of its most likely partners—Canada—has never shown any interest in participating in an international arrangement in silver. Although the country is one of the largest producers of silver in the world[60] and its trade balance is largely determined by its mineral exports, it still has no central institution to deal with silver

---

[59] This view is supported by Streeter, who observes: "The Russians are among the best game players on the economic scene. . . . When the Russians start covertly buying silver in Zurich, their Swiss brokers know very well what is going on. For relatively minor sums they can influence the international silver market. The word is spread in the financial press; somebody is buying silver again. The price of silver moves up in response to the increased buying and expectation of further rises which again increases buying." See *Silver Mania*, p. 73.

[60] In 1990, Canada produced approximately forty-four million troy ounces of silver, or nearly 10 percent of total world mine production.

and no governmental agency with the power to set silver policy. Part of this apathy, it seems, is due to Canada's proximity to the United States and its traditional reluctance to take any international actions that might be perceived as interfering with its neighbor's policies. Part, too, may be due to the fact that Canada's political system shares many of the values and institutions of the United States and as the case of uranium suggested, some of these values and institutions may constrain the country's ability to participate in international marketing arrangements.

There are few precedents for Canadian participation in orderly marketing arrangements and a very real disinclination on the part of the Canadian government to become involved in any sort of international commodity cartel. In the case of uranium, as we have seen, Canada played an active role only when the situation had reached a crisis point and only when there was a group of individuals willing to expend the personal energy required. And even under these circumstances, Canada's participation was ill-fated and short-lived.

In the silver market, there is even less opportunity for the government to play a central role or exert any authority over the silver producers. Instead, all matters pertaining to silver mines and mining fall under the jurisdiction of the various provincial governments. These governments exercise control over the silver mines in their territory only insofar as they encourage investment, tax profits, and try to protect jobs.[61] Presumably, the provincial governments would encourage, or at least appreciate, any international measures that might help stabilize the market and improve the long-term interests of the silver producers. By themselves, however, none of these governments has the market share, the traditions, or the institutional base that would allow it to take even the most tentative steps toward international cooperation.

Mexico and Peru

By contrast, the last two major producers—Mexico and Peru—seem ideally suited for participation in an international silver cartel. Aside from their structural positions as leading producers, they also

---

[61] For an in-depth survey of one province's regulations concerning silver, see Mohide, *Silver*, pp. 183–89.

boast many of the internal characteristics identified thus far as being conducive to international cooperation. Both countries are major producers of silver, and both rely on silver to provide a large portion of their export earnings. The two are also relatively authoritarian countries, with a great deal of economic power vested in the central political authorities and only a handful of competing economic factions. On the basis of both structural and internal characteristics, we should expect Mexico and Peru to be both anxious and able to join in an international silver cartel.

As it turns out, however, neither Mexico nor Peru has taken anything but the most tentative steps toward cooperation in the silver market. Instead, a combination of political uncertainty and financial necessity has deprived the countries of the possibility of any strategic action in the market. Rather than being able to manipulate their resources to their own long-term advantage, both countries have been forced to comply with other extraneous demands and thus to undermine their own long-term revenues and the potential profitability of the entire international market.

In the terms of this study, the constraints on both countries are the direct result of "shallow pockets." Quite simply, neither Mexico nor Peru has had the resources that might have allowed them the luxury of strategic restraint. They have silver stockpiles and governments that have acknowledged their interest in using these stockpiles to shape the market so as to benefit all the producers. For the most part, however, the governments could not *afford* to use the stockpiles strategically, as they needed to sell the silver to meet more immediate economic needs and neglecting these needs would have threatened their countries' political stability as well as their own political power. And, thus, instead of using their stockpiles as part of a joint program of market regulation, both Mexico and Peru have sold silver erratically, eliminating any possibility of international coordination and further upsetting the stability of the market.

Since its first rich discovery of silver in 1546, Mexico has been one of the largest producers of silver in the world and one of the most important players in the international silver market. In 1990, annual production in the country was seventy million troy ounces, or approximately 15 percent of total world mine production.[62] Histori-

---

[62] The Silver Institute, *World Silver Survey*, p. 24.

cally, its percentage of the total has been even higher, and for much of the past three hundred years, Mexico has led the world in silver production. In purely economic terms, then, Mexico has always been a force on the international market and has always had the potential to exert a tremendous influence on the supply and price of silver. Even more critical, Mexico also has many of the internal political prerequisites of a successful cartel participant. For instance, the Mexican government appears to have created the domestic structures and institutions that would enable it to direct Mexico's participation in an international silver cartel. The country has a considerable public sector and a long and respected history of governmental intervention in the economy. The government has nationalized several key industries, guided the development of many others, and created a powerful central banking system under its close control.[63] In a wave of nationalism in the 1930s, it expropriated many of the foreign concerns then operating in the country and made clear that economic development would henceforth be under the control and guidance of the state.[64]

Historically, this proprietary concern has been particularly evident in the silver industry, as the government recognized both the importance of silver to its economy and the need for some kind of government-directed regulation in order to maximize silver revenues. Most important, the Mexican government appears to have acknowledged that long-term stability in the silver market could be ensured only through an international effort. As early as 1924, a special report commissioned by the government concluded, first, that the international price of bullion should be steadied and, second, that it would in fact be possible "to influence the silver market in this direction, without cost or hazard."[65] More specifically, the report noted:

[63] See William P. Glade, Jr., "Revolution and Economic Development: A Mexican Reprise," in *The Political Economy of Mexico*, ed. Glade and Charles W. Anderson (Madison: University of Wisconsin Press, 1963), p. 71.

[64] The most contentious event of this period was the expropriation of the U.S.-operated oil fields. See Raymond Vernon, *The Dilemma of Mexico's Development* (Cambridge: Harvard University Press, 1963), p. 76.

[65] Commission on International Exchange of the Republic of Mexico, "A Study of Monetary Systems as Effected by the Production, Consumption, and Sale of Silver Bullion" (Mexico City, 1924), p. 15.

It would certainly be impossible and unwise to try to control the price of any ordinary commodity in the market...; but in the case of silver, so far as its monetary use is concerned, the buyers, the Governments are in a position to regulate their purchases and even to agree to stop them temporarily if silver should advance over a certain price, which would endanger the monetary systems of the silver-using countries. . . . [T]hey are equally interested in counteracting a continued decline.[66]

Thus the report recommended a "meritorious experiment" that would establish a regular system of silver purchasing "by the Governments of certain countries" and urged that this system "would have a tendency to steady the price of silver bullion."[67]

To this end, Mexico was an enthusiastic supporter of the London Economic Conference, and even after the conference's provisions collapsed under the weight of the United States's independent behavior, Mexico tried to resolve its problems in the market through government-to-government collaboration with the United States. When these efforts proved limited, the Mexican government took the situation into its own hands and directed the Central Bank of Mexico (Banco Central) to enter the silver market in a concerted attempt to maintain a balance in the market and stabilize the price of silver.[68] In the late 1940s and into the 1950s, the bank thus "played" the market, buying when prices were low and selling from its own stockpiles when prices were high and in the process exerting a controlling presence over the entire market.[69] In return for its efforts, the bank (and the government) were assured of a more predictable world market for their silver exports and a more certain revenue stream. Had the bank been joined in its efforts by any of the other producers, it could potentially have laid the groundwork for a system of cooperative intervention in the market. As it turned out, however, even at the height of its buying operations, Mexico was acting alone, without any cooperation from the other major producers. Eventually, the Banco Central realized the futility of its actions and left the market in the hands of the predominant U.S.

[66] Ibid.
[67] Ibid.
[68] See Wemple, "Silver Market," p. 46.
[69] Mohide, *Silver*, p. 135.

Treasury. The bank continued to buy and sell silver, but no longer in a specific attempt to stabilize the market.

For several decades, then, Mexico had the internal ability to participate in cooperative ventures but found its efforts foiled by the overbearing power and contradictory goals of the United States. Although it wanted to cooperate, it found no easy means to do so and no feasible way of surmounting the obstacles created by U.S. policy.

More recently, however, the bank's inability to find international partners has been compounded and even surpassed by its own internal troubles and by the country's overwhelming need to use its stockpiles to reduce Mexico's debt burden. Although the government does not own any of the country's silver mines outright, it does maintain a controlling interest in several of the largest producers.[70] Through the bank, meanwhile, it maintains extensive silver reserves via monthly sales from Mexican refineries and, occasionally, from the spot market. This silver is mainly used to improve the country's balance of trade and pay down some of its foreign debt. Especially since 1982, when the Mexican currency system collapsed, the country has been in desperate need of foreign exchange—and silver sales, even at lower prices, are a major source of foreign exchange. Thus, any possibility of strategic marketing by the Mexican Banco Central has been precluded by its more immediate need to sell silver without regard for market conditions. As one dealer noted, "They can't afford to finesse the market."[71] Likewise, a 1985 market report concluded that its debt pressures would force Mexico to expand silver production and sales "almost regardless of cost."[72] In fact, Mexico's demand for silver has become so great that the government has been reluctant to allow mines to close, even when they are operating at a loss and their production is creating an oversupply that is pushing prices even lower. As one analyst has stated, the country "needs every ounce of silver it can get, for sale at any price it can get."[73]

[70] For instance, via the Comision de Fomenta Minera and Minera Frisco S.A. de C.V., the Mexican government controls 66 percent of the Minera Real de Angeles, the world's largest open-pit silver mine. See Mohide, *Silver*, p. 135.

[71] Quoted in Andrew Gowers, "Oversupply Pushes Silver to Near Four-Year Low," *Financial Times*, May 21, 1986, p. 32b.

[72] Cited in Wagstyl, "Silver Seen Losing Its Glitter," p. 28b.

[73] Mohide, *Silver*, p. 135.

Thus, despite the presence of conducive structural conditions in the market and a certain number of conducive internal characteristics, Mexico suffers from a very real inability to exercise the restraint so critical to any orderly marketing arrangement. Although the government has periodically recognized the need for producer collaboration in the silver market and probably has the domestic institutions that would facilitate its participation in any such collaboration, it does not have the resources that would allow it to take a long-term view in the market. As a result, it is unable to bear the costs of any cooperative venture in silver.

The problems that plague Mexico are echoed almost identically in Peru. Even more than in Mexico, the links between the state and silver production are strong, and the central government appears to have the power to guide the production and sale of the metal. In 1968, the largest mines in the country were taken over by the state, and the state-owned mining agency, Empresa Minera del Centro del Peru (CENTROMIN) remains the largest producer in the country. The problem, however, lies not with the government's ability to discipline its mining sector but rather with its own tremendous need for foreign currency. Like Mexico, Peru has been saddled with a tremendous debt burden since the mid-1970s and is thus compelled to use its silver reserves to pay off some of its foreign creditors. In 1983, for instance, the Central Bank of Peru was forced to sell nearly 290 tons of its silver reserves to accommodate the restructuring of its international debt.[74] The following year, the bank sold another 62 tons. The effect of these massive sales, of course, is to drench an already-overstocked market and send prices even lower. In the process, Peru's own revenues, along with those of the other producers, suffer. Still, the country appears to have little choice in the matter. Every once in a while, the government threatens to drive the price of silver up by curtailing its own sales,[75] but its insatiable demand for currency has always driven it quickly back to the market.

---

[74] Ibid., p. 125.

[75] For instance, the country restricted its sales in June 1982 but restored them by September of that year. See ibid. Then again in 1987, Peru announced a suspension of its silver sales that was never actually implemented. See Stefan Wagstyl, "Silver Springs to Life as Prices Rise Nearly 100%," *Financial Times*, April 28, 1987, p. 38.

In the short run, at least, there seems to be little chance that either Mexico or Peru will be able to escape from its dilemma. Both countries stand to benefit from cooperation: if they could manipulate the new supply of silver, they could stabilize the market, prevent oversupply, and push silver prices higher, boosting the value of their own exports. At the same time, though, both countries have such immediate financial needs that they cannot even afford to hold back their silver, much less engage in any kind of cooperative restraint. Instead, they are not only using their stockpiles in a less-than-strategic fashion but they are also expanding production and sales.[76] From the outside, it is easy to argue that Peru and Mexico are behaving in a completely irrational way. By increasing their production when prices are low, they are only competing with each other in a saturated market and undermining their profits over the long and medium term. From an inside perspective, however, it is just as easy to see that the rational choice may simply be impossible.

LOST OPPORTUNITIES AND MISSING SPARKS

Looking at the silver market today, it is difficult to see how any kind of cooperation could ever be possible. Prices fluctuate wildly and often without any discernible pattern, the producers periodically flood the market with sales from their huge stockpiles, and sporadic bursts of investment activity make another speculative frenzy a constant possibility.[77] There is not the slightest hint of collaboration among any of the major producers and no evidence of strategic behavior. Instead, the market seems inherently anarchic, subject only to the changing demands of its industrial consumers and the shifting whims of the speculators.

In retrospect, though, there is nothing about the silver market

---

[76] A surge in world production from 1980 to 1985 has, for example, been attributed largely to expanded production from debt-strapped Mexico, Peru, and Chile. See "Surplus Keeps Prices Low," *Financial Times*, September 8, 1986, p. 13c.

[77] In 1987, for instance, a rush of trading sent silver prices up by nearly 100 percent, feeding speculation that the bearish market had suddenly turned bullish. See Wagstyl, "Silver Springs to Life," p. 38; and "Silver Bugs May Be Ready to Swarm," p. 126.

that necessarily condemns it to anarchy. In fact, the market has always contained all the structural characteristics conducive to producer cooperation. What has been missing, though, is a willingness by the producers to expend the energy and take the risks demanded by any cooperative arrangement. There have been plenty of opportunities for cooperation in the silver market, but no one has been able to seize them.

In particular, opportunities have been lost through a bizarre combination of bad timing and absent partners. For nearly a century, cooperation was rendered unlikely by the self-centered policies of the United States and the havoc they wreaked in the market. It was made impossible by the absence of any other players with the willingness and domestic wherewithal to bear the costs of initiation and risk the anger of the United States. In 1933, the London Economic Conference could easily have provided the foundation for a long-term relationship among the silver-producing nations. The system of mutual restraint that it installed would have created one of the most benign and beneficial cartels of all time. Instead, the hegemonic cooperation established by the conference was quickly supplanted and destroyed by the unilateral actions of the hegemon. And once the hegemon had defected, none of the other players were able to organize cooperation in its absence.

From that point on, the United States was such a tremendous force in the market that any countervailing intervention by the other producers was virtually impossible. Acting under the direction of the silver bloc, the U.S. Treasury was buying vast quantities of silver at artificially inflated prices. Any actions by the other producers would have seemed useless, if not counterproductive. Thus, rather than carving out their own agreement or even attempting to view the market in a strategic fashion, the other producers simply allowed themselves to trail in the wake of the United States.

Eventually, the United States changed its course. Domestic coalitions shifted, priorities changed, and the power of the silver bloc declined. Still, the precedent had been established. Vulnerable to the demands of its own internal factions, the United States was clearly unable to participate in any international arrangement that would affect its domestic policies regarding silver. Moreover, the huge stockpiles that it had amassed were still subject to the conflicting desires of the executive branch and the silver bloc. The manner in which these stockpiles might be disposed, therefore, would remain a *political* issue, not amenable to either international negotiation or strategic planning.

Even more important, the position that the United States had occupied for so long could not easily be filled by any of the other producers. First, none of them had any experience in spearheading international economic initiatives or in leading international cartels.[78] And, second, by the time the way was cleared for a new leader, the two most obvious candidates—Mexico and Peru—were descending into economic crises that limited their spheres of permissible action and precluded them from using their silver stockpiles as anything but a short-term salve.

What the story of silver reveals, therefore, is not just the importance of internal characteristics in explaining the presence of cooperation among competitors. In addition, it also emphasizes the extent to which cooperation requires an initial spark to ignite it. Even if the correct structural conditions are in place and the producers possess the most conducive internal characteristics, cooperation will not emerge by itself. Rather, it must be prodded and cajoled, and somewhere along the line, one of the players must accept the responsibilities of initiation and maintenance.

This is one of the subjects to which we shall turn in the final chapter.

---

[78] The one partial exception to this statement might be Canada, which was the major player in the uranium cartel.

CHAPTER SIX

The Internal Sources
of Cooperation

If nations want to exist in a world of competition and conflict, they will have to pursue cooperative policies from time to time. And if scholars want to understand the process by which order is forged from anarchy, they must begin by examining what it is that allows nations to cooperate. In this book I have tried to elucidate the question of cooperation by scrutinizing one of its tidiest and most comprehensible forms: the international cartel. As in cooperation generally, cartels are characterized by a continuous strategic interplay between the participants and are vulnerable to the constant threat that one of the members will abandon the agreement in favor of unilateral goals. When cartels are in place, they are evidence that cooperation is occurring; when they break down or fail to emerge, cooperation is being prevented. Thus, by studying the conditions under which cartels are either nurtured or destroyed, we can begin to understand the general phenomenon of cooperation and the factors that facilitate it.

The central observation of this book is that cooperative behavior among producers is not determined solely by the structure of the market in which they operate. If it were, then all four markets, which bear similar structural characteristics, would exhibit similar patterns of cooperation. Instead, the four cases vary greatly: we see a formal and highly successful cartel in the diamond market, sophisticated but informal collaboration in gold, a failed cartel and subsequent anarchy in uranium, and little evidence of any cooperation in silver. Clearly, market structure alone cannot determine the extent of cartelization. At best, structural variables are the necessary but still insufficient precursors of cooperation.

Admittedly, some of the variation in the markets may be attributed to the idiosyncrasies and quirks that characterize each one. Still, it is hard to argue that these peculiarities by themselves *determine* the extent of cartelization and harder still to distinguish the extent to which they may actually be a *result* of the cooperation that has prevailed. As the potential for recycling exists in all four markets, for instance, it cannot be the mere threat of secondary supply that has prevented a cartel in the silver market. Likewise, it is hard to argue that cooperation in the uranium market has been hampered by the extent of governmental intervention because in two of the other markets—diamonds and gold—it is precisely the close relationship between the government and the private sector that has facilitated cooperation. Where my four cases are concerned, there seem to be no specific features of the market that predetermine the extent or form of cooperation.

Accordingly, the cases imply that although structural analyses may be extremely useful in helping us to understand the underlying dilemma of cooperation among competing producers, they cannot explain why some producers are more able than others to create and sustain cooperative agreements. Structural approaches may point to the central importance of commitment, credibility, and retaliation, but they cannot tell us what *kinds* of producers will be able to make credible promises and threats and how they will be able to implement them.

Cartels form, I argue, not only because a market is predisposed to joint action but also because at least two major producers have certain internal characteristics that enable them to initiate and maintain a cooperative relationship. Specifically, I present three levels of explanation. First, I suggest that autonomous competitors—those with the power to discipline and command their own factions—will be best able to make the commitments that enable them to participate in and perpetuate cooperative endeavors. Second, I argue that autonomy is determined primarily by internal factors. And, third, I indicate that insofar as the initiation and maintenance of cartels entails a continuous process of bargaining, it will be best managed by those producers who are able to keep the circle of negotiators small, the rules flexible, and the power to retaliate as strong as possible.

It follows that to understand cartels, we must examine not only the external structure of markets but also the internal characteristics of producers. Analogously, to understand cooperation more broadly, we need to consider the internal characteristics of the competitors as well as the structure in which they are arrayed.

THE INTERNAL SOURCES OF COOPERATION

Cartels, Cooperation, and Internal Autonomy

One of the most important elements of cartels and of international cooperation in general is the ability to make credible commitments. Cooperation entails a constant process of bargaining and negotiation. Every settlement reached represents deals struck and compromises made. The first prerequisite of cooperation is that the competitors have an interest in cooperative outcomes and a willingness to make the necessary compromises. The second is that the competitors have the ability to implement these compromises at home, that is, that they can fulfill internally the promises they made at the international level. If they cannot deliver on these promises, then the commitments become worthless, and the cooperative arrangement is doomed. For cooperation to proceed, therefore, each competitor must be able to convince the others of its ability to commit itself to the agreement and to abide by its terms. If the competitors cannot follow through on their commitments, then any given settlement will fail.

The ability to make both credible commitments and believable threats is therefore critical to the initiation and maintenance of cooperation. It is also an ability derived largely from the *internal* characteristics of the competitors involved, as credibility is determined largely by the competitor's ability to control its internal factions and thus to implement the internal ramifications of an agreement. In other words, not all competitors are equally capable of making credible commitments. Rather, it appears that certain types of competitors are most likely to initiate cooperation and most capable of maintaining it. They are the ones who enjoy a great deal of centralized and nondisputed control, who have the power to discipline their internal factions and drive them toward a well-defined objective. They are competitors who are best described as autonomous, possibly even as authoritarian. They can cooperate at the international level because they can act autonomously at home.

The cooperation that has marked the diamond and gold markets, for instance, can be attributed directly to internal conditions in the former Soviet Union and in South Africa and particularly to the centralized and unrivaled power that before 1989 had traditionally been enjoyed by key decision makers. Specifically, the evidence presented in this book suggests that cooperation in the diamond and gold markets has been facilitated by the extent of centralized power that existed in both the Soviet Union and South Africa and especially by the autonomy enjoyed by those individuals who participated in and set policy for the markets. In the Soviet Union, all diamond and gold operations were controlled by the relevant foreign trading office. These offices set prices, fixed production quotas, and handled all foreign trade. There were no independent producers concerned about prices, no independent jewelers worried about supply, and no speculators eager to profit from market fluctuations. With few exceptions, there were not even domestic consumers for these products.[1] To be sure, the trade offices were constrained and may even have been commanded by the higher powers of the state and its need for hard currency exports. Still, whatever commands they received were coming from one central source and were rarely, if ever, contradicted or compromised by competing interests. The agencies that handled diamonds and gold had complete autonomy in their spheres of activity. They could set policy without outside interference and implement this policy without fear that it would cause domestic unrest.

As a result, whenever a Soviet trading agency entered into an external agreement, its partners could be confident that the agency's position would not be compromised or amended by other interests within the Soviet Union. Under these circumstances, international cooperation proved relatively easy and cartels entirely possible. The

[1] One exception is gold wedding bands, which were always available to Soviet consumers.

costs of participation—the costs of stockpiling or of occasional production cuts—could be borne without much difficulty because there were few groups in the country that would be specifically and disproportionately affected and even fewer that would protest against the costs. Similarly, as both the Soviets and their partners knew that the trading agencies had the requisite power, there was little question about their ability to commit themselves to a cooperative agreement and thus less distrust and suspicion on both sides of the partnership. Because the Soviets had the internal power to implement any domestic policies relating to diamonds and gold, they also had the ability to participate in the international regulation of these markets.

Still, as the lack of cooperation in the silver market demonstrates, it takes more than one producer to forge a cartel. What made cooperation possible in diamonds and gold was that the other major player in both markets shared the same powerful attributes. As in the former Soviet Union, the South African corporations have been able to participate in commodity cartels largely because of the centralized authority they command and the discipline they are able to maintain in their own ranks.

As detailed earlier in this book, DeBeers and Anglo American have long been joined to and protected by a vast corporate conglomerate. All firms in the network are linked to one another and, ultimately, to the top of the corporate pyramid and the Oppenheimer family. The "empire" is effectively controlled by its center and remains resistant to outside pressures and internal squabbles. In most modern firms, power is divided by a system of independent divisions, and decisions are made to suit the various, sometimes even competing, interests of the component parts. In the Oppenheimer companies, by contrast, very little decentralization has occurred. Integration remains the guiding principle, and control resides firmly at the top. Although all the firms are officially public, so much of each one's shares are, in fact, owned by its sister corporations as to make hostile takeovers nearly impossible; as the *Economist* notes, cross-shareholdings make the Anglo group "effectively bid-proof."[2] Fi-

---

[2] "The Oppenheimer Empire: South Africa's Family Affair," *Economist*, July 1, 1989, p. 60.

nally, because of the disproportionate role that the "empire" plays in South Africa's economy, it has been virtually free from governmental interference.

Like the Soviet trading agencies, the Oppenheimer companies have been able to enjoy a nearly uncontested position. Because they have their own ranks under such tight discipline, they are able to implement the policies they desire and impose the costs they must. Because they can act autonomously in their own sphere without having to share decision-making authority or worry about competing claims to power, they can make credible commitments on the international level. In short, because they have the internal power they need, they can create the external agreements they desire.

In the international silver market, by contrast, any possibility of U.S. cooperation was precluded by the need to placate the domestic silver lobby. Whenever U.S. officials tried to negotiate on the international level, their positions were constrained by the very precise demands of domestic producers. Likewise, Australia's participation in the international uranium cartel was delayed and distorted by environmental groups, and Canada's involvement in the uranium market was characterized by a constant tension among government agencies, private firms, and electoral politics. In these cases, the principal participants lacked the ability to impose sufficient costs on internal factions or to override the narrow interests of a politically active group. As a result, the principal participants could never commit to an international agreement that required internal sacrifices. And as cooperation generally requires at least some short-term sacrifices, this lack of internal power effectively made cooperation impossible.

We repeatedly find cases in which the autonomy of the producers proved instrumental in determining the success of a cartel or a producers' agreement. From 1931 to 1941, for instance, an international cartel in tin was held together largely by the efforts of the Dutch, who ran their industry in the East Indies as a virtual monopoly with close links to the government.[3] The aluminum cartel of

---

[3] See John Hillman, "Bolivia and the International Tin Cartel, 1893–1941," *Journal of Latin American Studies* 20 (1987): 83–110, and Hillman, "Malaya and the International Tin Cartel," *Modern Asian Studies* 22 (1988): 237–61.

1901 to 1908 was led by Alcoa, which already enjoyed a monopoly position in the North American market and such a high level of vertical integration that it was essentially "freed from dependence on any outside interest."[4] And the International Sugar Agreement of 1953 was dominated by the Cubans, whose tightly run system of huge plantations linked directly to the government allowed them to exercise tremendous restraint in the international market and act in effect "as the world's buffer stock."[5]

When the international steel cartel was organized in 1926, each of the national participants explicitly recognized the need to reorganize its domestic industries into centralized and closely knit combines. Great Britain broke with its long-standing tradition of free trade and individualism to establish a cartel-like arrangement under the auspices of the British Iron and Steel Federation. And the United States granted an exception under its prevailing antitrust laws to permit the formation of the Steel Export Association of America, which was designed to "meet foreign competition through establishing uniform terms and contracts for export sales, standardizing weights and qualities and the collection and exchange of information regarding foreign markets."[6] Finally, and in a very general sense, it seems safe to conclude that countries that have historically fostered strong industrial cartels—Nazi Germany, prewar Japan, and modern-day Switzerland, for example—have also tended to have systems of centralized power and limited checks and balances.[7] Countries need not

[4] George W. Stocking and Myron Watkins, *Cartels in Action: Case Studies in International Business Diplomacy* (Buffalo, N.Y.: William S. Hein, 1991), pp. 216–73. The other members of the cartel—the Aluminium Industrie A.G. of Switzerland, the British Aluminium Company, and two French concerns—were also large and well-funded businesses with uncontested monopoly positions.

[5] Albert Viton, "Towards a New I.S.A.," *F. O. Licht's International Sugar Report*, May 1983, p. 28. See also Jock A. Finlayson and Mark W. Zacher, *Managing International Markets: Developing Countries and the Commodity Trade Regime* (New York: Columbia University Press, 1988), pp. 128–33.

[6] Stocking and Watkins, *Cartels in Action*, pp. 192–211.

[7] On Germany, see Rudolf K. Michels, *Cartels, Combines, and Trusts in Post-War Germany* (New York: Columbia University Press, 1928); and R. J. Overy, *The Nazi Economic Recovery, 1932–1938* (London: Macmillan, 1982). On Japan, see Johannes Hirschmeier and Tsunehiko Yui, *The Development of Japanese Business, 1600–1973* (Cambridge: Harvard University Press, 1975), pp. 146–227; and Chalmers Johnson, *MITI and the Japanese Miracle: The Growth of Industrial Policy, 1925–1975* (Stanford: Stanford University Press, 1982). On Switzerland, see Jean Ziegler, *Switzerland Exposed*, trans. Rosemary Sheed Middleton (London: Allison & Busby, 1978).

be dictatorships, of course, to participate in international cartels, but they do appear to need an internal structure that centralizes power to some extent and thus minimizes the risks of defection.[8]

Similar constraints would seem to apply to the prospects of cooperation in the broader political realm. Even when a government sees cooperation as being in the nation's best interest and even if it is willing to pay the occasional costs of cooperation, it simply may not have the power to impose these costs on its population. For instance, a high-level U.S.-Japan textile agreement fell apart in 1970 when the textile industry in Japan refused to accede to the arrangements that the government had negotiated.[9] More recently, monetary coordination among the Western allies has been repeatedly compromised by the inability of the countries' finance ministers and central bankers to "sell their promises to politicians at home."[10] And in the United States, even the most delicate and finely tuned arms control agreements have been routinely scrutinized by a range of domestic groups and modified or blocked by those with different ideological viewpoints or contrary political agendas. Overall, cooperation among competing states will be affected in part by the internal structures of power within each country and by the extent to which these structures constrain the government's ability to make credible commitments at the international level. As a German finance minister once bluntly observed, "The limit of expanded cooperation lies in the fact that we are democracies, and need to secure electoral majorities at home."[11]

[8] This type of defection is labeled "involuntary" by Robert D. Putnam. See Putnam, "Diplomacy and Domestic Politics: The Logic of Two-Level Games," *International Organization* 42 (Summer 1988): 427–60.

[9] See I. M. Destler, Haruhiro Fukui, and Hideo Sato, *The Textile Wrangle: Conflict in Japanese-American Relations, 1969–1971* (Ithaca: Cornell University Press, 1979), pp. 140–57.

[10] See Peter T. Kilborn, "Dollar Unity in Jeopardy," *New York Times*, May 11, 1989, p. 29.

[11] Gerhard Stoltenberg, quoted in *Wall Street Journal Europe*, October 2, 1986, as cited in C. Randall Henning, *Macroeconomic Diplomacy in the 1980's: Domestic Politics and International Conflict among the United States, Japan, and Europe*, Atlantic Paper no. 65 (New York: Croom Helm for the Atlantic Institute for International Affairs, 1987), p. 1.

Autonomy and the Ability to Punish

A similar relationship between internal autonomy and credibility is also evident in the ability of competitors to threaten effectively at the international level. Here, as with commitment in general, words are worthless unless backed by the likelihood of action. Threats of punishment will deter defection only if they are credible, that is, if they convince the would-be defector that defection will prove extremely costly and thus not worth any rewards it might obtain. For threats to be credible, however, the threatener must demonstrate the internal ability to go through with the promised punishment. To threaten, a principal participant must be assured of a fairly high level of internal consensus.[12]

All the cooperative producers that emerge from the case studies—the former Soviet Union, DeBeers, and Anglo American—fit that criterion. The same centralized control and immunity from internal discontent that allowed them to deliver their commitments and absorb internal losses also enabled them to threaten and punish externally. When the Israelis and the Zairians began to break the rules of the diamond game, DeBeers lashed out at once, squeezing them out of business even at the cost of some of its own short-term profits. Similarly, whenever the Soviets suspected that their interests in the gold markets were being compromised by one of the other links in the network—the American mining engineers, for example, or the Wozchod Handelsbank—they responded quickly and thoroughly, punishing the offenders and cutting them out of the market. Even if such retaliatory moves were rare, they were still sufficient to create the perception of the Soviet government and the DeBeers–Anglo American network as having both the power and the will to punish.

By contrast, when none of the cartel members are able to play the role of enforcer, the prospects for cooperation diminish rapidly. In the uranium cartel, for example, a series of punishments was estab-

---

[12] For an excellent discussion of this point, see John S. Odell, "International Threats and Internal Politics: Brazil, the European Community, and the United States, 1985–1987," in Peter Evans, Harold K. Jacobson, and Robert D. Putnam, eds., *Double-edged Diplomacy: International Bargaining and Domestic Politics* (Berkeley: University of California Press, 1993).

lished but never implemented. Although all participants realized the necessity of retaliation, none were willing or able to carry it out in practice. Even one of the most flagrant violations of the rules—RTZ's arrangement to sell two hundred tons of uranium—went unpunished; the company's representative was sent away for a while to avoid further embarrassment, but the company itself received little more than a slap on the wrist.

The importance of a "punisher" is also apparent in other cases of successful cooperation. Saudi Arabia has often acted as a hegemon within OPEC, drawing on its tremendous reserves to flood the market and punish defectors.[13] And before the formation of OPEC, the largest of the Seven Sisters would frequently take it upon themselves to impose discipline on the smaller members of the oil industry.[14] Nor is the enforcer phenomenon peculiar to commodity cartels. Evidence suggests that the OECD Export Credit Agreement was cemented in 1986, when the United States created a $300 million "war chest" and made clear its intention to retaliate against all countries that offered credits in violation of existing accords.[15] Likewise, the "United Nations" probably would not have launched its attack against Saddam Hussein's Iraq in the winter of 1991 without the obvious initiatives of the Bush administration. In these cases, we find one competitor who is both willing and able to bear the actual costs of punishment. We find, in other words, a hegemon.

What distinguishes this hegemon is not just its power relative to the other members of the agreement. Rather, the hegemon is also

[13] See James D. Alt, Randall L. Calvert, and Brian D. Humes, "Reputation and Hegemonic Stability: A Game-Theoretic Analysis," *American Political Science Review* 82 (June 1988): 445–66. The authors also demonstrate the means by which punishment, if applied strategically, can establish a reputation for the hegemon that serves to lower the overall cost of punishment or coercion.

[14] For instance, the London Committee, composed of the three largest producers, was empowered under a 1934 "Draft Memorandum of Principles" to "in general do all things necessary toward the proper functioning of [the] arrangement." *International Petroleum Cartel*, Staff report to the Federal Trade Commission, submitted to Subcommittee on Monopoly of the Select Committee on Small Business, U.S. Senate, August 22, 1952 (Washington, D.C.: Government Printing Office, 1952), p. 265. See also Theodore H. Moran, "Managing an Oligopoly of Would-Be Sovereigns: The Dynamics of Joint Control and Self-Control in the International Oil Industry Past, Present, and Future," *International Organization* 41 (Autumn 1987): 575–607.

[15] See Andrew M. Moravscik, "Disciplining Trade Finance: The OECD Export Credit Arrangement," *International Organization* 43 (Winter 1989): 199.

distinguished by its *internal* power, or autonomy. The hegemon can threaten because it has the internal ability to punish. It does not fear that its sanctions will be overturned by domestic opposition or that its threats will be rendered inoperable by domestic constraints. Thus the Saudis, like DeBeers, make excellent hegemons because everyone knows that their threats will never fall prey to involuntary defection.

In other cases, hegemony is made considerably more tenuous by domestic constraints that impede the ability of the would-be hegemon to threaten convincingly. The United States is a dramatic case in point. At many times during the postwar period, the United States proved itself a hegemon of remarkable strength, sponsoring a wide range of international institutions and eagerly enforcing the rules embedded within them.[16] Simultaneously, though, the United States has proved on numerous occasions to be completely incapable of issuing credible threats or imposing sanctions on those who violate international agreements. It has had very little luck, for instance, in punishing violators of the GATT or in compelling compliance with the export restrictions embedded in CoCom.[17] This pattern of inconsistent hegemony could be due, of course, to a general erosion of U.S. power or to a relative lack of U.S. leverage in certain sectors. What seems equally plausible, however, is that the ability of the United States to play the role of hegemon depends heavily on the array of domestic constituencies affected. If the costs of the threatened punishment are low or diffuse, threats will be more credible and more readily employed. The United States can threaten relatively easily, for example, to withdraw foreign aid or send in the Marines. Because these punishments do not impose undue penalties

[16] For a description of U.S. institution building during the postwar period, see Robert O. Keohane, *After Hegemony: Cooperation and Discord in the World Political Economy* (Princeton: Princeton University Press, 1984), pp. 135–50.

[17] In the most famous case involving CoCom—Toshiba's 1987 sale of submarine-quieting technology to the Soviet Union—the offense was finally and loudly punished. For three years, Toshiba was forbidden to sell its products to the U.S. government. But even here it is interesting to note that the "punishment" was significantly watered down by an intensive lobbying effort undertaken by Toshiba's many associates within the U.S. business community. See Robert A. Rosenblatt, "Intense Lobbying Cools U.S. Anger at Toshiba," *Los Angeles Times*, May 1, 1988, IV-1; and Carla Lazzareschi, "Toshiba Enlists Unlikely Allies in Battle," *Los Angeles Times*, October 26, 1987, IV-3.

on any specific domestic group, they tend not to raise the ire of the population at large. Even when there is disagreement with the executive's actions—as with the threat of sending U.S. troops to Lebanon, Panama, or Iraq—the discontent tends to be sufficiently disaggregated so as not to undermine the power of the threat. By contrast, U.S. threats have been far less potent whenever following through on them would mean imposing real hardship on a particular domestic sector. Whenever the U.S. executive threatens to punish trade violations by cutting back on imports or imposing quotas, for instance, it encounters opposition from adversely affected groups.[18] Steel quotas are opposed by car manufacturers, semiconductor tariffs by computer manufacturers, and textile quotas by clothing manufacturers. U.S. farmers have repeatedly protested grain embargoes against the Soviet Union, and economic sanctions of any sort are routinely opposed by exporters who serve the target markets.[19] Lacking internal force, such threats lose external credibility.

The ability to threaten and punish, therefore, cannot simply be created by the members of an institution. Nor can it be easily mimicked or adopted. Rather, the capacity to retaliate depends on the particular traits and assets of the competitors involved. DeBeers can punish offenders in the diamond market because it has enormous reserves, tight control over its own operations, and a distinct lack of political, financial, and ideological constraints. Most other participants in commodity cartels are not so lucky. They do not have the unfettered resolve that would allow them to suffer in the short term to preserve the sanctity of a long-term venture. These are characteristics that come directly from the internal structure of the competitor. They cannot merely be implanted or institutionalized. But without them, enforcement will be exceedingly difficult and cooperation thus unlikely to survive.

The Shifting Length of Shadows

Cooperation depends on valuing the future. It means taking risks or relative losses in the short run in the hope of fostering joint gains

[18] In fact, as John Odell reports, whenever the U.S. executive orders trade retaliation, industries are given the opportunity to object to the inclusion of any particular products. See "International Threats and Internal Politics."

[19] For a classic story of how U.S. export interests constrained the ability of the U.S.

over the longer term. It means recognizing that the shadow of the future is long and then waiting for the benefits that iteration will bring. I suggest, however, that the shadow of the future may be less important than an individual decision maker's own perception of it. Seen from a structural perspective, the shadow adheres to the overall situation of the competitors. From an internal approach, the relevant shadow is attached to the principal participant from each side.

In practice, this means that cartels will be more easily created when the principal participants are confident of their own longevity and even more so when the players have a personal interest in the maintenance of long-term stability and profits. In the diamond and gold cases, for instance, we saw how intimately the fortunes of the markets have been linked with the personal fortunes of the Oppenheimer family. Since Oppenheimer founded Anglo American in 1917, control of the corporate empire has passed easily from one family member to the next. At no point in any of these transitions have questions been raised about successors or the extent of their power; it has simply been acknowledged that the Oppenheimers are the sole legitimate leaders of the conglomerate. Even the secondary echelons of the Oppenheimer corporations are, and always have been, extremely stable. Several of the top men are relatives of the Oppenheimers; many are close personal friends. Thus the entire conglomerate has always been led by individuals who have a vested interest in its long-term prosperity and who know that they personally will be around to enjoy the fruits of their labors.

All this could change, of course, if South Africa were to erupt in the large-scale political turmoil that many predict. Certainly, not even the Anglo empire could emerge unscathed from a civil war, a revolution, or the imposition of a radical left-wing regime. Anything that threatens the long-term viability of South Africa will also threaten the corporations that are based there and thus could force even the Oppenheimers to reevaluate their prospects for the future.[20]

Even so, for years the Anglo companies have managed to stay one step ahead of the political changes that they see imminent. They

government to win alliance support for its 1981 embargo against the Soviet Union, see Bruce W. Jentleson, *Pipeline Politics: The Complex Political Economy of East-West Energy Trade* (Ithaca: Cornell University Press, 1986).

[20] See Roger Thurow, "Golden Goose: Forces It Unleashed Now Threaten Future of Anglo American," *Wall Street Journal*, July 30, 1990, pp. A1, A6.

have always been a relatively liberal voice in the country and have pioneered social and educational programs among their work force. They have also been on the forefront (again, relatively) with respect to desegregation, aggressively bringing blacks into the ranks of management. Thus, although they have not escaped periodic bouts of labor unrest, neither have they been singled out as symbols of repression or potential targets of nationalization. More to the point, perhaps, the companies also have a fair amount of leverage over any government that might come to power. Quite simply, they own or at least control massive chunks of the country's infrastructure, including most of its mineral resources. Regardless of its political leaning, the leadership of South Africa is going to be dependent to some extent on the Anglo corporations if for nothing else than technical expertise.[21] Even a radical government might be tempted to woo the Anglo empire rather than to destroy it. This has already been the case in Namibia, Botswana, and Zimbabwe, where even fairly radical black governments have chosen to maintain tight economic relations with DeBeers and Anglo rather than risk the economic disruptions of nationalization.

And, finally, if all else fails, the companies appear prepared to move their operations abroad. Already, in an effort to avoid the full brunt of anti-apartheid sanctions, DeBeers has established a major subsidiary in Lucerne, Switzerland; and Anglo has been slowly acquiring both tangible and financial assets abroad.[22] South Africa may be changing, but the Anglo companies and the Oppenheimer family do not appear to be at any great risk of losing their global position or the long-term vantage point it affords them.

Likewise, until the dramatic events of 1989, power in the former Soviet Union had always been a long-term prospect. Soviet leaders remained in power until death, and most Soviet bureaucrats stayed in their positions (or in closely related positions) throughout their

[21] Note here the case of Namibia. After years of high-level politicking and guerrilla fighting, Namibia finally won its independence in 1990 and installed as president a former Marxist guerrilla leader who had led the fight against South African control. The country's relationship with DeBeers, however, was unaffected, and DeBeers still owns and runs the vast undersea mines at Oranjemund.

[22] See Peter Schmeisser, "Harry Oppenheimer's Empire: Going for the Gold," *New York Times Magazine*, March 19, 1989, pp. 32–43.

entire careers.[23] A similar rigidity of power was also evident at the lower levels of officialdom. Typically, bureaucrats in the Soviet Union stayed put, moving vertically rather than horizontally within the ministries and usually confining themselves and their careers to a narrow field of focus. This tendency was particularly evident in the more specialized and technical agencies, since the leadership needed to capitalize on whatever expertise was available. It is not at all surprising, therefore, that Soviet trade officials were eager to enter into agreements that maximized long-term rewards. For example, a bureaucrat in the state gold-trading company had good reason to be interested in the long-term prospects of Soviet gold and little incentive to do anything that might sacrifice the future of the agency for the promise of short-term rewards. This bureaucrat could afford to take a long-term perspective and to participate in cooperative arrangements such as cartels that simultaneously look to the future and depend on the ability of all their members to do likewise. Moreover, even when the bureaucrats themselves switched positions or left agencies, the Soviet bureaucratic system was structured to minimize the effects of personnel changes. Because all decisions had to be approved and integrated into a much broader plan, policies tended to become standard operating procedures, and an innovation begun by one bureaucrat became a routine to be followed by his successor. Even when a particular official's shadow was shorter than he might have liked, the agency's shadow tended to be long enough to compensate.

This changed, of course, with the events of 1989 and the subse-

---

[23] For instance, between 1959 and 1979, not a single minister in the Soviet Union was shifted from one portfolio to another (except for a small number who were promoted to major coordinating committees such as Gosplan). See Jerry F. Hough and Merle Fainsod, *How the Soviet Union Is Governed* (Cambridge: Harvard University Press, 1979), p. 386. Elsewhere, Hough also finds that "the pattern of stability in the ranks of the most senior industrial and construction administrators is striking." See Hough, *The Soviet Prefects: The Local Party Organs in Industrial Decision-Making* (Cambridge: Harvard University Press, 1969), p. 75. In a related context, Timothy J. Colton describes the "strangle-hold" that older officials were able to maintain throughout the Soviet political elite and the difficulties that the younger generation faced in trying to nudge them out of their positions. See Colton, *The Dilemma of Reform in the Soviet Union* (New York: Council on Foreign Relations, 1984), pp. 46–49. See also Frederick C. Barghoorn, *Politics in the USSR*, 2d ed. (Boston: Little, Brown, 1972), pp. 173–75.

quent breakup of the Soviet Union. From the start, liberalization meant a dissolution of central authority and a fundamental change in the perceptions and perspectives of the state trading agencies. As Soviet enterprises were gradually permitted to register for independent trading rights, they became less dependent on the internal hierarchy of the state and more concerned about their own short-term cash flows.[24] Bureaucrats who had long looked to the system to safeguard their own futures were suddenly very uncertain about the future and forced by events to focus their efforts on the present. As legislation gave way to economic and political turmoil, these shrinking time horizons were compounded by the tangible uncertainties of the breakup. As the former Soviet republics scrambled to lay claim to their own resources, the all-union enterprises were replaced by a hodgepodge of new and inchoate agencies. Some were hastily formed by the new republican governments, some were the renamed branches of the old trading agencies, and many existed only in name. The old structure of centralized control collapsed entirely, although its remnants were still visible—and still relatively powerful—in the new Russian republic.

Under these circumstances, we should expect people to discount the future very heavily and to put their efforts into the present. Who cares about long-term prospects, after all, when daily survival becomes a chore and all systems of promotion disintegrate? Accordingly, we should also see a crumbling of long-term outside arrangements, especially those that impose short-term costs.

And, indeed, this is what appears to have happened. In the gold market, the dissolution of internal controls seems to have led to a dismantling of the Soviets' tacit cooperation with the South Africans. After years of exercising great restraint in the market, Soviet officials began to behave far less cautiously. Individuals who had access to gold began to dump it on the market, using the proceeds to pave their own way through times of great economic uncertainty. Clearly, the country as a whole would have been better off if its gold reserves had been hoarded and if gold prices had been allowed to float as high as the international market would permit. Individuals, however, had far different objectives and far shorter time frames. And

[24] See, for example, *Economist*, "Bolshoi Bang," July 15, 1989, p. 69.

as these time frames shrank, so too did their propensity for international cooperation.

A similar pattern appears to be emerging, albeit more slowly, in the diamond market. Initially, DeBeers was able to forestall what it correctly guessed would be the consequences of a Soviet breakup. By physically removing the diamond stockpiles from the country and extending such an irresistible loan, it helped to keep the traditional diamond agencies in control. As demands for local autonomy mount, however, centralized authority is rapidly being splintered into a number of smaller and less-organized units. As the interests of these units become increasingly focused on the short term, we should expect to see them breaking from the cartel and choosing instead the immediate benefits of unilateral action.

Although less dramatic, the constraints of short-term pressures are also evident in a number of other cartel cases. We saw, for example, how Canadian and Australian officials were constantly looking ahead to the next election and how their political uncertainties eventually impeded their participation in the uranium cartel. Elsewhere, Bolivia consistently botched its participation in the international tin cartel largely because its governments were short-lived and typically laboring under tremendous pressure to deliver immediate economic results.[25] Likewise, ever since the 1920s, attempts to control the international rubber market have been plagued by the demands of small Malayan growers who live virtually hand to mouth and thus have never been in a position to abide by a longer-term view of their industry.[26] And Chile's participation in an international nitrogen cartel dissolved in 1932, when the government could no longer bear the vigorous criticism of its policy.[27]

[25] As John Hillman notes, "They could not afford the long time horizon which would allow them to pass over opportunities for immediate advantage for the sake of the general well-being of the cartel." See "Bolivia and the International Tin Cartel," p. 109.

[26] Finlayson and Zacher, *Managing International Markets*, pp. 109–18; and Richard Stubbs, "Malaysia's Rubber Smallholding Industry: Crisis and Search for Stability," *Pacific Affairs* 56 (Spring 1983): 85.

[27] Between 1929 and 1939, the government-organized nitrogen monopoly suffered from both declining profits and popular outrage against the perceived social consequences of monopoly. After a series of new governments, a president was elected in October 1932 on the specific platform of abolishing the nitrogen monopoly. Stocking and Watkins, *Cartels in Action*, pp. 138–39.

In a broader sense, the link between personal tenure and long-term commitment has become a recurrent theme in the popular press. American corporations, it is alleged, do not invest for the long term because American investors chase short-term gains from one corporation to another and American managers are particularly attuned to short-term performance measures such as current profits and stock prices.[28] American trade negotiators, meanwhile, are occasionally less concerned with winning at the bargaining table than with making the personal contacts that they will need once they are out of office.[29] The Japanese, by contrast, are said to benefit from a social and political commitment to lifetime employment. Because they know they will be in their ministry or corporation for the entirety of their professional lives, they have a personal interest in securing the long-term position of their employer.

For my purposes here, the point is simply that the shadow of the future needs to be understood at an individual and institutional level as well as at a systemic one. Even in the same external circumstances, not all competitors will have the same propensity to look far into the future and appreciate the long-term benefits of a cooperative agreement. Only certain kinds of competitors—those whose principal participants are in a particularly secure position—will be able to take the shadow of the future into account. To be sure, longevity is not the only criterion. In some cases the system may run independently of particular people, and individuals may also embrace a long-term attitude in the hope of influencing posterity or at least leaving their mark on it.[30] Nevertheless, it is hard to deny that individuals with the longest possible tenures will be most likely to appreciate the shadow of the future and to take it into account when weighing the benefits of cooperation against those of defection. For most of the others, it is their own—shorter and dimmer—shadows that will influence their calculations and shape their willingness to cooperate.

[28] These conclusions figure prominently in Michael Porter's recent project on competitiveness and investment. See Porter, "Capital Choices: Changing the Way America Invests in Industry," Executive Summary (Boston: Harvard Business School and Council on Competitiveness, 1992). See also "America's Investment Famine," *Economist*, June 27, 1992, pp. 89–90.

[29] This is the central argument, for instance, in Pat Choate, *Agents of Influence* (New York: Alfred A. Knopf, 1990).

[30] One might see President Reagan's last-ditch attempts at arms control in this light.

Riding Out the Slumps

Maintaining a cartel usually entails short-term costs. The producers must pay the opportunity costs of the unilateral action they resist, as well as the costs of restraint during times of depressed prices. Because even the most successful cartel will encounter occasional decreases in the price of its product, its members must have the financial resources to see them through the slumps. If the producers can afford to finance themselves during these hard times, they will be able to maintain the internal discipline of the cartel. If, on the other hand, their own resources are insufficient, they will be forced to expand their market share or undercut their partners, breaking the rules of the cartel and destroying its cohesion. When internal resources are scarce, the shadow of the future is rendered unaffordable, and cooperation becomes a too expensive luxury.

When the costs of cooperation become too much to bear, the competitor will be forced to defect. We saw earlier in this book, for instance, the extent to which Mexico and Peru were precluded from cooperating in the silver market by their overriding need for foreign exchange. Even though they understood the potential benefits of cooperation, their constant demand for exchange made them desperate to sell all the silver they could, regardless of its price or the prevailing state of the market. This sort of cost-related defection is a common problem in international commodity cartels and has been especially prevalent in cartels composed largely of Third World producers. The International Bauxite Agreement collapsed in the late 1970s, when the government of Jamaica needed to boost its income and thus signed a separate deal with the United States.[31] In the early 1980s the jute market fell when the price leader, Bangladesh, was suddenly forced to terminate its guaranteed price for growers because it could no longer afford to hold excess stocks.[32] In similar cases, any hope for cooperation in the international copper market was dashed in 1982, when Chile "continued to pump out metal, de-

---

[31] See Alan Litvak and Christopher J. Maule, "The International Bauxite Agreement: A Commodity Cartel in Action," *International Affairs* 56 (Spring 1980): 309–10. See also Finlayson and Zacher, *Managing International Markets*, p. 211.

[32] Finlayson and Zacher, *Managing International Markets*, p. 224.

spite low prices, in a desperate effort to bring in much-needed foreign exchange,"[33] and OPEC suffered a blow in 1981, when Nigeria, desperate for revenues to meet its spending commitments and debt burden, broke from the cartel and cut the price of its oil exports.[34] By contrast, when OPEC was at the height of its powers, one of the reasons commonly cited to explain its success was the tremendous financial resources of its members, particularly of Saudi Arabia, the leader of the cartel.[35] The notorious Medellin cocaine cartel is clearly supported by the vast personal wealth of its member families;[36] and du Pont's success in "managing" the international chemicals market during the early decades of the twentieth century was made possible in many ways by the substantial wealth of the du Pont empire and the du Pont family.[37]

In most of these cases, deep pockets correspond rather neatly with autonomy and long shadows. Regimes or corporations with the ability to ride out economic slumps seem also to have large amounts of centralized power. In my cases, the clearest example of this combination of resources is the former Soviet Union: not only did the Soviet state enjoy a high degree of control over its internal groups, but it also had the ability to incur occasional losses in its commodity trade without fearing either the economic or political consequences of the loss. If, for instance, an oversupply in the diamond market demanded a cutback in their sales, the Soviets could simply stockpile their surplus gems because, for all practical purposes, the costs they

---

[33] *Latin American Commodities Report*, January 14, 1983.

[34] See Peter F. Cowhey, *The Problems of Plenty: Energy Policy and International Politics* (Berkeley: University of California Press, 1985), p. 185.

[35] See, for instance, Stephen D. Krasner, "Oil Is the Exception," *Foreign Policy* 14 (Spring 1974): 78–79. The downside of this argument, though, is that if cartels are *too* successful in pushing prices above costs and if the members depend on a single commodity to provide the bulk of their foreign exchange earnings, then the temptation to defect will be particularly strong. See John E. Tilton, *The Future of Nonfuel Minerals* (Washington, D.C.: Brookings Institution, 1977), p. 84; and "A Confederacy of Cheats," *Economist*, June 10, 1989, p. 66.

[36] For a description of the cartel and its members, see Guy Gugliotta, *Kings of Cocaine* (New York: Simon & Schuster, 1989).

[37] On the du Ponts, see Alfred D. Chandler, Jr., and Stephen Salsbury, *Pierre S. Dupont and the Making of the Modern Corporation* (New York: Harper & Row, 1971). On du Pont's activities in the chemicals market, see George W. Stocking and Myron W. Watkins, *Cartels or Competition?* (New York: Twentieth Century Fund, 1948), pp. 83–91, 112–14.

encountered were minimal. The cutbacks never fostered any serious domestic opposition, as no specific group suffered as a result of them and the financial loss could generally be covered by gains in other sectors. Admittedly, there were also times when Soviet pockets became shallower and more constraining. In particular, when the Soviets faced a significant loss in hard currency revenues, they did have to put their short-term financial needs before any long-term market considerations. It is not surprising, therefore, that the Soviets were always less willing to cooperate in the oil and gas markets, which accounted for the lion's share of their export earnings.[38]

The Oppenheimer companies are also blessed with legendarily deep pockets. As mentioned earlier, the companies are "effectively bid-proof." Thanks to a series of cross-shareholdings and interlocking directorates, it is unlikely that even the steepest plunge in a company's earnings would make it susceptible to a hostile takeover. Moreover, the companies all benefit from a remarkably open flow of intercorporate funds; if one part of the empire is failing, the management can simply "borrow" whatever is needed from one of its sister firms. Finally, the entire empire is based on a monumental trove of hard assets. According to recent estimates, DeBeers, Anglo American, and their sister companies together control assets worth over $247 billion.[39] In simplest terms, then, the empire has whatever resources are necessary to ride out a slump or to limit its sales in order to sustain a cartel in any of its products. It is hard to imagine pockets much deeper than these.

RULES, INSTITUTIONS, AND TACTICS

The attributes listed above stem directly from the internal characteristics of the competitors. With the exception of deep pockets,

---

[38] Although the Soviets were vocal supporters of OPEC, their own actions in the oil market often ran directly counter to OPEC's policies. In 1973, for example, the Soviets praised the Arab embargo of oil sales to Europe even while they were taking the opportunity to boost significantly their own petroleum exports to Europe. See Marshall I. Goldman, *The Enigma of Soviet Petroleum: Half-Empty or Half-Full?* (London: Allen & Unwin, 1980), p. 89.

[39] Schmeisser, "Harry Oppenheimer's Empire," p. 42.

which is purely a resource-based concept, the other characteristics—autonomy, long shadows, and the ability to punish—are determined by the internal structures of each competitor and particularly by the internal position and relative power of the principal participant. In addition to these internal attributes, however, the cases also suggest that there are certain tactics that can facilitate the creation and maintenance of cooperation. Like the tactics often referred to by the institutionalists, these are "rules of the game," norms and procedures that all competitors can use to strengthen their cooperative ventures. These tactics depart from the institutionalists' recommendations, however, in several ways. Where the institutionalists urge openness and transparency, the record of successful cartels suggests secrecy. Where they suggest formal rules and codified norms, history seems to reward informal codes and unwritten agreements. And where they endorse inclusivity, my cases suggest the opposite. Overall, the tactics that emerge from this study are unfortunately much nastier than those put forth by the institutionalists. They are harsher and meaner and less forgiving. But where cooperation is really at stake, they may also be more effective.

Secrecy

The power of secrecy as a tool for cooperation is seen most strongly in the clandestine atmosphere that long surrounded the Soviet Union's many links to the Oppenheimer empire. Certainly this secrecy was always a necessity rather than a conscious choice. For obvious political reasons, neither side wanted to publicize the closeness of their relationship in the diamond and gold markets, and evidence of cooperation or even mutual restraint had to be hidden or denied. Nevertheless, the secrecy that was dictated by political circumstances seems also to have helped to smooth relations between these two strange bedfellows and to facilitate the cooperation that arose between them.

All negotiations between Soviet officials and South African executives were conducted with the utmost secrecy. They occurred not just behind closed doors but literally on tarmacs in the dead of night. This clandestine atmosphere no doubt made arrangements awkward at times. But it also meant that compromises could be worked out and concessions made without either side fearing that its "appease-ment" would be made public or that it would lead to similar de-mands from other trading partners. It is generally believed, for instance, that faced with the threat of Soviet dumping, Harry Op-penheimer granted the Soviets significant concessions in the dia-mond market in 1984. Assuming this is true, it is noteworthy that the bargaining that undoubtedly took place was never reported and the concessions never revealed. As a result, the cartel emerged un-scathed. Because the negotiations were secret, they did not raise un-certainties or cause speculation in the market. Because the terms of the agreement were never revealed, DeBeers's public image—and thus the foundation of the diamond cartel and the diamond mar-ket—remained unchanged and untarnished.

Similar, if less dramatic, evidence of the power of closed doors occurs throughout the empirical record of cooperation under anar-chy. Congressional scholars, for instance, have argued that bargain-ing in Congress was easier when committee sessions were closed and when the cloak of secrecy gave representatives the ability to make compromises and concessions without the fear of an immediate elec-toral backlash.[40] Likewise, describing the evolution of the Western economic summits, Robert Putnam and Nicholas Bayne have noted the success of the "Library Group," a small group of finance minis-ters who were able to meet discreetly and to keep their proceedings secret.[41] It is also generally acknowledged that the Seven Sisters, the legendary precursor of OPEC, was marked by the ability of its mem-bers to negotiate by themselves and behind closed doors.[42] In these instances, the principal participants were able to shield their activ-ities not only from their own internal factions but also from the gen-eral glare of public scrutiny. Thus the terms of their agreements were protected from both internal discontent over compromises made and external demands for reciprocal concessions.

By contrast, even though the members of the uranium cartel real-

---

[40] See, for instance, I. M. Destler, *American Trade Politics: System under Stress* (Wash-ington: Institute for International Economics, 1986), pp. 25–29, 57–86.

[41] Robert D. Putnam and Nicholas Bayne, *Hanging Together: The Seven-Power Summits* (Cambridge: Harvard University Press, 1984), p. 18.

[42] See Christopher Tugendhat, *Oil: The Biggest Business* (New York: Putnam's, 1968), p. 107.

ized the need for secrecy, they proved incapable of maintaining it. Their "secret" meetings were reported in the press the following day, and even one of the leading participants, the Canadian Ministry of Energy, Mines, and Resources, was releasing a constant stream of memoranda describing its activities. This lack of secrecy cannot be blamed on the mistaken idea that it was unnecessary. On the contrary, all participants knew how important it would be to keep the details of their arrangement hidden and to conduct their negotiations behind closed doors. As things turned out, though, one of the leading members of the would-be cartel was perpetually uncomfortable with the element of secrecy and forced by domestic constraints and underlying values to undermine it. In a similar incident, Putnam finds that "even though both the American and Iranian governments seemed to have favored an arms-for-hostages deal, negotiations collapsed as soon as they became public, and thus liable to de facto 'ratification.'"[43]

Overall, then, the record of secrecy is hard to resist. "Open covenants openly arrived at" may well be the normative choice for a democracy, and states may decide that closing the doors on their international negotiations is no longer politically feasible. Still, it is difficult to deny that, in the right hands, secrecy can be a powerful tool for enhancing bargaining and facilitating cooperation.

Exclusivity

Cooperation can also be enhanced, it appears, by strictly limiting the number of players in the game. Smaller numbers reduce the problems of collective action and limit free-riding. In less tangible terms, smaller numbers also create a more intimate environment, one in which the participants can generally come to know and trust one another. Smaller numbers will tend to create a club of sorts

---

[43] Putnam, "Diplomacy and Domestic Politics," p. 436. It is also interesting to note that at the height of the first full-scale Arab-Israeli peace talks, negotiators from both sides admitted that one of the major obstacles to their progress was the inability to negotiate in secret. As the *New York Times* reported, "It is now clear to all the parties that negotiations in the light of day, under the gaze of television cameras, are not the format for a breakthrough." See Thomas L. Friedman, "Arab-Israeli Talks: Slow, But Not Lost," *New York Times*, September 27, 1992, p. A12.

rather than a more formal institution. And as in any club, a small membership fosters a sense of exclusivity.

This sort of exclusivity emerges as an obvious and integral component of cooperation in the diamond and gold markets. Negotiations between any of the Oppenheimer companies and their partners are nearly always conducted in an intimate circle of associates, with any outsiders clearly excluded from "the club." In DeBeers and Anglo American especially, there is an evident sense of camaraderie that distinguishes the insiders and prevents any outsiders from coming in. Likewise, Soviet negotiations in these markets were reportedly conducted by the same individuals time after time and year after year. As a result, there was a consistency and predictability in all meetings between the Soviet officials and South African executives. There was even, it appears, a sense of friendship and mutual accommodation. The membership was exclusive, the number of participants limited, and the representatives from each side always knew with whom they would be dealing.

Exclusivity also has a considerable record of success in the broader political realm despite increasing demands for diverse and global institutions. The Concert of Europe was composed, for instance, of an "in-group of states . . . which displayed a high degree of homogeneity within itself";[44] and cooperation in the rescheduling of LDC debt has been led by a small group of creditors who know each other well and know that they will meet repeatedly in further negotiations.[45] Along similar lines, the Western industrialized nations have recently risked international censure by addressing some of their most pressing issues in smaller, self-contained groups such as the OECD, the G-5, the International Atomic Energy Association, and the Club of Paris.[46] Much of the current debate within the European Community on "broadening" versus "deepening" can also be seen as a debate on

[44] Edward Vose Gulick, *Europe's Classical Balance of Power* (New York: W. W. Norton, 1967), p. 19.

[45] See Charles Lipson, "Bankers' Dilemmas: Private Cooperation in Rescheduling Sovereign Debts," *World Politics* 38 (1985): 200–225.

[46] The G-5 is an informal group of the world's five leading economic powers. The Club of Paris comprises the leading holders of LDC debt. For more on the move toward smaller, more exclusive organizations, see Raymond Vernon and Debora L. Spar, *Beyond Globalism: Remaking American Foreign Economic Policy* (New York: Free Press, 1989), pp. 189–93.

the merits of exclusivity. Expanding the community's membership beyond the existing twelve means not only incurring the problems of higher numbers but also the complications of dealing with a much more diverse group of nations. Thus the "numbers" problem is likely to be far more a concern with regard to Poland and Hungary than with Switzerland, Austria, and Norway.[47]

Certainly, the European Community, like most other exclusive groups, continues to praise the virtues of international inclusivity and promises to open its membership to a greater circle of nations once they meet certain prerequisites of entry. For the moment, however, these groups are small, selective, and composed of like-minded nations and individuals. And they are working.

Informality

Finally, and perhaps somewhat paradoxically, cooperation in cartels also appears to be facilitated when procedures are informal and rules are unwritten. This does not mean that there are no rules or that violations will not be punished. On the contrary, it only means that informality may actually enhance compliance insofar as it allows for some flexibility in performance and does not demand that the sanctity of the entire agreement be called into question whenever a violation is suspected.

The diamond cartel, for instance, is a spectacular—although probably unique—example of the strength that can be derived from implicit rules and flexible regulations. There is remarkably little bureaucracy in the DeBeers network and no written rules; there are, instead, a series of understandings about the rules of the game and the powers that must be obeyed. The rules themselves are flexible and can be easily changed to reward good behavior, punish offenders, or adapt to the changing circumstances of the market. Gross violations, of course, such as the Zairian undercutting or the Israeli hoarding, will be punished—but punishment comes not from the breaching of a particular rule but from a total defection from the agreement. Small transgressions are allowed to occur without im-

---

[47] On this point, see "On the Way to the Forum," Survey, *Economist*, July 11, 1992, pp. 14–16.

mediate consequences and without calling the entire structure of the cartel into question. For all its secrecy and ostensible formality, then, the diamond cartel is actually a fairly flexible institution. And it is this flexibility, along with the other characteristics enumerated earlier, that has perpetuated the cooperation and the cartel.

Elsewhere, informality also appears as a useful tactic of cooperation. During the heyday of strategic arms negotiations, for instance, formal and precise rules proved particularly cumbersome. Repeatedly, U.S. and Soviet negotiators were forced to decide whether slight discrepancies in the number of weapons or troops deployed by the other side constituted sufficient cause to abandon an entire agreement. As a result, the negotiators tended to rely for the most part on their own informal rules and understandings.[48] Similarly, to avoid potential legal problems, the Final Act of the Conference on Security and Cooperation in Europe (CSCE) was explicitly *not* put into a legally binding agreement.[49] More generally, many international legal scholars have argued that international law exists, not in the formal technicalities of a "frozen cake of doctrine," but in a gradual and informal process of reformulation and consensus building.[50] The process of agreement, rather than the rules themselves, is what allows the system to function.

THE STRUCTURES OF CONTROL:
AUTHORITY, AUTONOMY, AND COOPERATION

The picture of cooperation that emerges from this study is not entirely pleasant. If the characteristics and tactics outlined above are accurate, then they suggest that cooperation is a rather harsh game to play and that not all competitors will be equally well suited for it. If they are to maintain their cooperative edge, competitors need to

[48] See Richard Burt, "Verification Arguments Aren't Only Technical," *New York Times*, April 22, 1979, p. 5; and James A. Schaer, "Verifying Arms Agreements: Promises, Practices, and Future Problems," *Arms Control* 3 (December 1982): 39–52.

[49] See Louis Henkin, *How Nations Behave* (New York: Columbia University Press, 1979), p. 14.

[50] For a classic argument along these lines, see Myres S. McDougal, "Law and Power," *American Journal of International Law* 46 (1952). See also Patrick Moynihan, *On the Law of Nations* (Cambridge: Harvard University Press, 1991).

be able to punish their external counterparts and constrain their domestic constituents. They need to operate in secrecy and bend the very rules they create. And to do these things successfully, it seems, competitors need a tremendous amount of internal autonomy and a tightly institutionalized structure of authority.

Extrapolated into the broader political realm, the success stories of this study suggest a strong link between international cooperation and internal authority. To perpetuate cooperation, a state must be able to deliver its promises and trust that its partners will do likewise. It must be able to prevent domestic groups from compromising its external agreements or from amending them to a point where they become virtually meaningless. It must be able to keep the players in the domestic game from constantly reshuffling the pieces on the international board.

This observation of a link between control and cooperation is not, of course, entirely new, nor is it necessarily as disturbing as it may initially sound. For years, scholars have argued that "strong" states are better able to manage their domestic constituencies and preempt any internal opposition to their external policies.[51] When control is concentrated in only a few hands, the government can avoid the pulling and hauling that defines politics in more open regimes and instead force its internal factions to accept whatever costs cooperation might impose on them. By contrast, "weak" or pluralistic regimes are in many ways hampered by their own freedoms. As authority is divided and checked, control diminishes and the implementation of any international accord becomes subject to the blocking efforts of affected groups and related agencies. The more inter-

[51] The classic works in this area include Peter J. Katzenstein, ed., *Between Power and Plenty: Foreign Economic Policies of Advanced Industrial States* (Madison: University of Wisconsin Press, 1978); Katzenstein, "International Relations and Domestic Structures: Foreign Economic Policies," *International Organization* 30 (Winter 1976): 1–45; Peter B. Evans et al., eds., *Bringing the State Back In* (Cambridge: Cambridge University Press, 1985); and Stephen D. Krasner, *Defending the National Interest: Raw Materials Investments and U.S. Foreign Policy* (Princeton: Princeton University Press, 1978). Like these works, this study also purposely avoids the question of whether "the state" can be regarded separately from the society that contains it. Instead, it focuses on the position of the top decision makers and their relations with the interests and institutions that surround them. For a detailed elucidation of the question of "the state," see J. P. Nettl, "The State as a Conceptual Variable," *World Politics* 20 (July 1968): 559–92.

nal groups there are and the greater opportunity each has to voice its claims, the harder it becomes for a nation's leaders to impose their own plans. Disgruntled groups will always have a greater incentive to organize than will satisfied ones. And whenever these groups see their interests at stake in an international agreement or feel that they are being forced to bear a disproportionate share of the agreement's costs, they are likely to organize and pursue redress through lobbying or other channels. The political arithmetic, therefore, is straightforward: the more opportunities there are for opposition, the tougher it will be to implement policies that impose costs. And because cooperation nearly always entails at least short-term costs, it will nearly always be difficult to implement and enforce in an open and competitive political system.

Lest this study be mistaken as an apologia for authoritarianism, however, let me stress that my point here is not about politics but about structure. I am not arguing that authoritarian states will necessarily be able to cooperate in the international arena or that democratic ones will be prevented from doing so. Rather, I am suggesting that there is something about the way in which authority is structured within the state that influences its propensity for external cooperation. This structural attribute is what I refer to as autonomy.

Autonomy is similar in many ways to what has been elsewhere described as state strength. It also corresponds in many instances with the centralization of power. The concept of autonomy that I am using, however, entails more than just state strength or centralized power. It is also categorically *not* equivalent to authoritarianism, even though the two may coincide. Instead, autonomy here refers to the ability of the principal participant in any external negotiation to implement the agreement it establishes without fear that it will subsequently be compromised by any other domestic interest, faction, or agency. For the state to act autonomously in any given negotiation or cooperative agreement, the principal participant must have the capacity to implement the policies agreed on at the international level. In practice, this means that the participant must (1) have clear control over the relevant policy area, (2) have the institutional means to require subordinates to follow through on whatever measures are necessary to enact the policy, and (3) have the ability to avoid, buy off, or quash dissent from other agencies within the state that may have competing interests. Autonomy is thus largely, though not entirely, a result of organizational structure.

This is not to imply, however, that autonomy can be equated with or guaranteed by any particular structure. Instead, autonomy as I describe it can be created through a variety of organizational forms. It can be imposed by a dictator or facilitated by a structure of carefully allocated responsibilities. It can emerge out of consensus as well as from coercion. In theoretical terms, the puzzle is to create the structures that will enable the state not only to issue promises at the international level but also to ensure that they can be implemented at home. In normative terms, the problem is how to create these structures without resorting to the unchecked control of authoritarianism. And on this score, as we shall see, the prospects are not nearly as bleak as they may initially appear.

THE STRUCTURES OF AUTONOMY

Centralization of Power

On the surface, the most obvious way to establish autonomy is to centralize all power within the state.[52] If all power is in the hands of one person or shared among a small number of people and if there are simply no other organized groups, then there will be no channels through which opposition to the center's policies can arise. Whoever controls the state in a centralized or unitary system will also be able to control the passage of laws and the direction of policy.

In its classic form, the centralized state is an absolute monarchy, with all powers bestowed on a ruling family and its offspring. Examples of this model include not only the feudal monarchies of Europe and the East but also the modern-day kingdoms of Saudi Arabia and Kuwait. Power in these systems, whether derived from religious authority, military force, or some combination of the two, is absolute. The state *is* the monarch, and the monarch determines the external

---

[52] Or as Paul J. Quirk explains, "Cooperation is easier with a simple and closed decision-making process—one that has few independent decision-making units, a small number of individuals directly involved in decision-making, and limited publicity." See Quirk, "The Cooperative Resolution of Policy Conflict," *American Political Science Review* 83 (September 1989): 918.

policy of the state. When the emir of Kuwait signs an international accord, he does not need to consult with his pollsters back home or worry that his commitment will be modified by a subsequent process of domestic ratification.

In a less dramatic way, power can also be centralized in a situation short of an absolute monarchy. It can be centralized by the force of a military junta as in Guatemala, by the repression of a totalitarian apparatus as in Stalin's Soviet Union and Hitler's Germany, or even by the constitutional delegation of responsibility as in France and (arguably) modern-day Japan.[53] Although the extent of central control varies widely among these states, they are all characterized by a relative weakness of competing claims for authority and a relative dearth of channels through which opposition can be routed. And in this regard, they should all be well positioned to commit themselves at the international level and thus to participate in cooperative accords.

In the case of commodity cartels, this certainly seems to have been true with regard to the Soviet Union and South Africa, the countries that sponsored the best cooperators in my survey. Despite the ideological rift that divided them, these two countries were remarkably similar before 1989 and unusually good models of a completely centralized political system. Both, of course, were characterized by extreme forms of social and political control—Stalinism in the Soviet Union and apartheid in South Africa. Both had an overarching ideology that denied power to large segments of the population and vested it instead in a narrow ruling coalition. In both, the bulk of the economy was controlled either by the state or by vast conglomerates with close links to the state.[54] Both these economies, moreover, were fundamentally dependent on maintaining access to a vast reserve of

[53] France is generally heralded as exemplifying the "strong" state. See, for instance, John Zysman, "The French State in the International Economy," in Katzenstein, ed., *Between Power and Plenty*; Zysman, *Governments, Markets, and Growth* (Ithaca: Cornell University Press, 1983); and Ezra Suleiman, *Politics, Power, and Bureaucracy in France* (Princeton: Princeton University Press, 1974).

[54] For a fascinating discussion of these parallels by a Soviet academic, see Kamil Vsevolodovich Ivanov, "South African and USSR Economies: Unexpected Parallels," *Mirovaya Ekonomika i Mezhdunarodnye Otnosheniya*, November 11, 1990, pp. 77–87. Translated and reprinted in *Joint Publication and Research Service*, February 13, 1991, pp. 18–24.

natural resources. And getting these resources out depended on a constant supply of cheap and pliable labor—provided by apartheid, as by the Soviet gulag. If this labor had been any more expensive, it would have robbed the Soviet and South African producers of the economic stability that they did, in fact, enjoy and that allowed them to adopt a long-term perspective. To a large extent, therefore, the economic success of the Soviet trading agencies and the South African conglomerates must be attributed to the political repression that defined their societies.

But repression alone was never what gave these two groups their cooperative edge. Rather, what allowed them to cooperate so successfully was an all-encompassing structure of control. Both the Soviet Union and South Africa were, for all their moral and political atrocities, models of what Samuel P. Huntington describes as "effective" political systems.[55] Both countries had extremely strong political institutions and an extensive network for regulating political conduct throughout all levels of their societies. They had distinctive ideologies that defined the goals of the state and created a long-standing aura of legitimacy for the government. Clearly, these countries were never well governed in ethical terms, but they were effectively and extensively governed. They were not just dictatorships held in place by repression but complex hierarchies of power in which repression was only one of many structures of control.

By itself, the centralization of power is not sufficient to create autonomy.[56] Rather, even in a system of indivisible and undisputed power, autonomy also demands that the rulers be able to disseminate their power throughout the state and compel the obedience of their people. Just as Huntington's model of political development relies on the creation of institutions to govern participation in the state, so too does autonomy require an organizational structure that brings the ruler's policies down to the lowest levels and channels

[55] Samuel P. Huntington, *Political Order in Changing Societies* (New Haven: Yale University Press, 1968), pp. 1–92.

[56] Similarly, in the conclusion to a recent study on the relationship between domestic politics and international cooperation, Peter Evans finds evidence that "highly restricted franchise and lack of formal checks on the power of the chief executive do not necessarily lead to executive autonomy." See Evans, "The Interaction of International and Domestic Politics: A Synthesis of Findings and Prospective Generalizations," in Evans, Jacobson, and Putnam, eds., *Double-edged Diplomacy.*

compliance back toward the center. Autonomy means having the ability to implement policy as well as the prerogative to make it. Many states are characterized by an extreme centralization of power. But most of these states are not capable of making credible commitments or joining in successful international accords. States such as Liberia or Panama or Haiti simply do not have the internal means to deliver their external commitments. They have no effective way of disseminating policy choices or enjoining the participation of their people. Their rulers may have control of the apparatus of the state without necessarily having the capacity to do anything with this power.

To create autonomy, therefore, even absolute power has to create an organizational structure to support it.[57] "Strong" states such as the Soviet Union and South Africa were able to cooperate in the international arena not because their leaders had the prerogative to determine policy but because they had the institutions, hierarchies, and legitimacy that allowed them to deliver their promises.

Decentralized Power and Divided Responsibilities

If maintaining autonomy is a complicated task in a centralized state, it is an even more delicate endeavor in "weak" or fragmented states. When power is divided among competing entities and factions proliferate, it becomes increasingly difficult for any agency to deliver its external commitments. In nearly every instance there will be forces within the state that have some interest in blocking an international agreement and some means by which to do so.

But even if autonomy is scarce in competitive political systems, it is by no means absent. There remain plenty of ways to create autonomy within the confines of a fragmented democracy and much evidence that fragmented democracies can indeed cooperate at the

[57] Even the power of medieval monarchs came largely from the highly sophisticated organization of feudalism. With its elaborate structure of rights and responsibilities, feudalism enabled monarchs throughout the premodern world to reach down into their populations and implement policies of conscription and taxation. See Douglass C. North, *Structure and Change in Economic History* (New York: W. W. Norton, 1981), pp. 126–32. In his description of this period, North also compares the late Middle Ages to an oligopoly, one characterized by "periods of collusion interrupted by eras of cutthroat competition" (p. 138).

international level. Some of these cases—the World Health Organization, the International Postal Union, Interpol—fall so close to the pole of harmony that internal autonomy is not even an issue. If all parties stand to benefit from an agreement and the interests of all domestic groups are relatively homogeneous, then it is unlikely that any significant domestic opposition will arise. In these cases the principal participant can act with autonomy, and cooperation will proceed apace.

In other cases, fragmented states will often facilitate autonomy by ceding certain realms of authority to the exclusive jurisdiction of a particular agency. In the United States, for instance, control over interest rates is firmly in the hands of the Federal Reserve system. Although the Fed is by no means authoritarian, it is autonomous. It has clear legal hold on its responsibilities, there are no competing claims on its power, and it has the capacity to implement its policy through an extensive regional network. The Fed can deliver. Because its authority within the United States is explicitly described and largely uncontested, it is able to move nimbly abroad and issue credible commitments and believable threats.[58]

Less dramatically, the bulk of responsibility for U.S. security policy has long been vested in a Department of Defense characterized by clear lines of authority. Although other agencies of government have related authority (the National Security Council, Central Intelligence Agency, and Senate Armed Services Committee), they generally leave day-to-day responsibilities in the hands of the Pentagon. And even when the Pentagon participates in interagency task forces or working groups, representatives from agencies with competing interests generally defer to the Pentagon on clear-cut issues of national security. Thus even though it is just one bureaucratic player in

---

[58] For an account of how the U.S. Federal Reserve system was able to initiate a major international agreement on capital adequacy ratios, see Ethan B. Kapstein, "Resolving the Regulator's Dilemma: International Coordination of Banking Regulations," *International Organization* 43 (Spring 1989): 323–47; and Peter C. Hayward, "Prospects for International Cooperation by Bank Supervisors," *International Lawyer* 24 (Fall 1990): 787–801. For a more general (and somewhat extreme) discussion of the autonomy of the system, see William Greider, *Secrets of the Temple: How the Federal Reserve Runs the Country* (New York: Simon & Schuster, 1987). Greider argues that the position of the Fed constitutes "the crucial anomaly at the core of representative democracy" (p. 12).

an open democracy, the Pentagon still maintains a specific realm of authority that is only rarely challenged by other domestic groups. This authority in turn enables the agency to move relatively freely on the international level and to enter into agreements on behalf of a much broader and more diverse constituency. In general, it seems, when issues are narrowly defined or demand a certain level of technical expertise, the relevant agencies are usually able to enter into international agreements without worrying about subsequent internal opposition. It is no surprise, then, that many of the most successful international agencies—for example, the International Atomic Energy Association (IAEA), the International Telecommunications Satellite Organization (INTELSAT), and the European Center for Nuclear Research (CERN)—are also the most technically oriented. It is also not surprising that technical cooperation has been one of the hallmarks of integration within the European Community.[59]

When issues are not highly technical or narrowly defined, it becomes considerably more difficult for decentralized states to carve out spheres of autonomy. Some issues, such as trade or macroeconomic policy, affect such a diverse array of interests that most democracies refrain from yielding complete authority to any specific agency. Certainly this is the case in the United States, where the division of power and the balancing of factions lies at the very foundation of the country's political system.[60] Yet even here, in what would appear to be the toughest of cases,[61] it is still possible to create

[59] See Axel Krause, *Inside the New Europe* (New York: Harper Collins, 1991), esp. pp. 110–25; and Martin Mruck, "Is Science Going European?" in Brian Nelson, David Roberts, and Walter Veit, eds., *The European Community in the 1990s: Economics, Politics, Defense* (Oxford: Berg Publishers, 1992), pp. 152–58.

[60] For evidence of the fragmentation that characterizes the formulation of U.S. trade policy, see Stephen D. Krasner, "U.S. Commercial and Monetary Policy," in Katzenstein, ed., *Between Power and Plenty*; I. M. Destler, *Making Foreign Economic Policy* (Washington, D.C.: Brookings Institution, 1980); and Stephanie Lenway, *The Politics of U.S. International Trade* (Boston: Pitman, 1985).

[61] Some authors, most notably Thomas C. Schelling and Robert Putnam, contend that freedom from domestic pressure actually weakens a state's international bargaining position. Without denying the logic of this argument, I would assert that success at the bargaining table is not the same as successful cooperation. In fact, the same interest groups that may serve as convenient threats during the bargaining phase of an agreement may subsequently undermine this agreement during the ratification phase. See Putnam, "Diplomacy and Domestic Politics"; and Schelling, *The Strategy of Conflict* (Cambridge: Harvard University Press, 1980), p. 28.

structures that grant principal participants at least a modicum of authority.

For example, one powerful means of precluding domestic opposition is to bring all potential opponents into the negotiating process *before* an agreement is struck. If the various parties can have their concerns addressed early in the game and if the necessary side payments can be arranged, then affected groups will be more likely to define their own interests in terms of an international settlement rather than in opposition to it. Even when interests are potentially in conflict, principal participants can occasionally preempt the conflict by integrating these groups into the earliest stages of the negotiating process.

During the course of the U.S.-Canada Free Trade Agreement of 1988, for instance, U.S. negotiators were careful to garner domestic support for their positions before they actually cemented them with their Canadian counterparts. Technical proposals were circulated to representatives of the industries most likely to be affected by them; the most obvious opponents of the agreement—softwood producers—were granted a side payment in the form of countervailing duties; and to ensure broad support in Congress, "small but meaningful concessions" were made "to protect interests near and dear to legislators' hearts."[62] Similarly, when the U.S. State Department sought to commit the United States to an International Coffee Agreement that ran contrary to the interests of U.S. coffee traders and roasters, it went directly to industry leaders, soliciting their advice and bringing them into the process in the role of "business statesmen." As a result, the industry supported the agreement out of an apparent sense of public duty, and Congress ratified an international commodity agreement that explicitly was not in the interest of its own domestic industry.[63]

At a more general level, the preemption of opposition is a key element of the "fast-track" approach to trade policy. By bringing the

---

[62] See Clyde H. Farnsworth, "How Congress Came to Love the Canada Free Trade Bill," *New York Times,* June 4, 1988, p. E4. See also the account in Raymond Vernon, Debora L. Spar, and Glenn Tobin, *Iron Triangles and Revolving Doors: Cases in U.S. Foreign Economic Policymaking* (New York: Praeger, 1991), pp. 21–53.

[63] See Stephen D. Krasner, "Business Government Relations: The Case of the International Coffee Agreement," *International Organization* 27 (Autumn 1973): 495–516.

relevant interest groups into the negotiating process from the start, U.S. administrations have, in effect, been able to reverse the sequence through which checks and balances are customarily exercised and to minimize the chances that international trade agreements will be significantly altered during the ratification phase.[64] Once the concerns of affected groups have been embedded in an institutional framework, it appears, their checking and balancing is likely to be more restrained. Rather than undermining the international agenda of the principal participant, erstwhile opponents may even rally to its cause. Once again, then, organizational structure proves critical in shaping the autonomy of the principal participant. If the lead agency in any outside negotiation is to forestall the inevitable constraints of a system built on divided interests and overlapping authority, it must create an internal structure that draws the opponents into the process and converts them whenever possible from spoilers to supporters.

Admittedly, this conversion will not always be possible. Groups may refuse to be drawn into the process or to make concessions when their own interests are directly at stake. European farmers, for instance, have repeatedly refused even to come to the bargaining table of the European Community, knowing full well that any movement toward economic integration is likely to dismantle the subsidies on which they have come to depend.[65] In cases like these—and there are many—compromise may not be possible. But still there are ways in which internal barriers to implementation can be lowered. Even when principal participants are unable to assuage the opponents of an international agreement, they may be able to counter them with a more powerful coalition of their own.

For many proposed international agreements, there tends to be a silent majority of groups who stand to benefit but are not so concerned about passage that they feel compelled to lobby. When these silent groups are mobilized into an active coalition, however, they can overcome even the most concerted opponents of a deal. Re-

<hr>

[64] For a more general discussion of the fast track and its benefits, see Destler, *American Trade Politics*, pp. 62–69; Vernon and Spar, *Beyond Globalism*, pp. 197–201; and Robert A. Pastor, *Congress and the Politics of U.S. Foreign Economic Policy* (Berkeley: University of California Press, 1980), pp. 136–85.

[65] See Krause, *Inside the New Europe*, pp. 218–22.

sistance to the U.S. foreign aid program, for instance, has constantly been overridden by a ragtag coalition of development academics, agricultural exporters, and the Pentagon.[66] The vehement opposition of Canadian labor to both the U.S.-Canada Free Trade Agreement and the North American Free Trade Agreement was balanced by the combined forces of Manitoba wheat farmers, Alberta oil producers, and Ontario exporters.[67] And even European agricultural interests have been unable thus far to stop the momentum toward regional liberalization.[68] Sometimes, of course, coalitions mobilize by themselves, and the fight between the opponents and advocates of an agreement is the usual pace of politics in an open democratic state. In these instances, the principal participant can be seen simply as the beneficiary of a large domestic "win set."

Often, however, win sets are made, not born. Often, the principal participant will play the role of deal maker, bringing diverse groups together and forging from them a common position.[69] These combinations can be explicit organizations or the quiet result of behind-the-scenes bargaining. What matters is that they be pulled together during the negotiation phase of an agreement so as to afford the principal participant the autonomy needed at the bargaining table.[70]

Autonomy, then, is by no means incompatible with democracy, any more than it is equivalent to authoritarianism. In both systems, and indeed in all political systems, autonomy is largely derived from the structures of control that prevail in a given issue area. This con-

[66] See the account in Vernon and Spar, *Beyond Globalism*, pp. 141–64.

[67] See Fakhari Siddiqui, ed., *The Economic Impact and Implications of the Canada-U.S. Free Trade Agreement* (Queenston: Edwin Mellen Press, 1991), p. 26.

[68] The closer the European Community moves to majority voting, the more it removes the possibility that any disaffected national group will be able to hamstring policy making in the community. See "Power Games," *Economist*, July 22, 1989, p. 39.

[69] This seems to have been what happened during the Tokyo Round of GATT negotiations, when a surprising coalition of free-trade interests was cobbled together under the consummate leadership of Robert Strauss. See Destler, *American Trade Politics*, pp. 65–68; and Gilbert Winham, "Robert Strauss and the Control of Faction," *Journal of World Trade Law* 14 (September/October 1980): pp. 377–97.

[70] This kind of internal consensus-building seems to describe quite accurately the usual process in Japan, where government officials typically engage in protracted internal discussions before presenting their position at the international level. See, for instance, Richard J. Samuels, *The Business of the Japanese State* (Ithaca: Cornell University Press, 1987), esp. pp. 285–90. Interestingly enough, it is also apparently an integral element of the corporate culture at Anglo American.

trol can come from many sources—coercion, jurisdiction, persuasion, side payments, or the all-encompassing reach of a bureaucratic hierarchy. But it has to come from somewhere. Without it, the principal participant will be left without any means of delivering the commitments made at the international bargaining table. And thus without it, the prospects for cooperation are substantially diminished.

WEIGHING THE COSTS

Ultimately, the decision to cooperate is a distinctly political act. In each of the markets studied here—and indeed in all situations involving a small number of powerful competitors—cooperation was made possible by the configuration of the competitors and the structure of the system in which they were operating. The process by which this possibility became a reality, however, was a political process. It entailed a continuous series of deals, compromises, and concessions, and the outcome was dependent on the political circumstances that either constrained the principal participants or gave them freedom to bargain, make commitments, and accept and impose costs. Exogenous factors may compel or constrain cooperation; internal structures will either facilitate or impede it. But the final act of cooperation can only emerge from a conscious decision and a political process.[71]

If the argument of this book is correct, moreover, the very act of cooperation may require a political configuration that some states simply will not abide. Many states, and the United States foremost among them, could probably enhance their prospects for coopera-

---

[71] In discussing the "state strength" literature, both Putnam and Peter Gourevitch argue that it is apolitical, that it "suggests that the type of relation predominates, hence the identity of the governing coalition does not matter" (Gourevitch, p. 903). What I am arguing here, however, is not that internal structure categorically determines the ability of a state to cooperate but rather that these structures are a key intermediate variable that has been overlooked in much of the international relations literature. Saying that structures matter in no way implies that politics does not. See Putnam, "Diplomacy and Domestic Politics," pp. 431–33; and Gourevitch, "The Second Image Reversed: The International Sources of Domestic Politics," *International Organization* 32 (Autumn 1978), esp. pp. 902–7.

tion by centralizing power to a greater degree or creating more agencies akin to the Federal Reserve system or Japan's MITI. The point, though, is that the benefits of cooperation may in many instances not be worth the costs. Every time a nation confronts the question of cooperation, it also confronts a series of questions about its own political values. It has to decide whether this agreement is feasible, given the constraints of the state's political structure, and whether it is in keeping with underlying national values. In striving to maintain the cooperative edge, states need constantly to weigh the rewards that cooperation can bring against the price they may have to pay to make themselves capable of it.

In a different context, George Kennan once argued that the internal organization of the United States was at least partly to blame for the protracted tragedy of World War I.[72] Had the United States mobilized itself earlier, he suggested, had it clothed its efforts in a realistic perception of the interests at stake, and had it refrained from making the war a moral struggle that could only end with total victory, then perhaps things would have been different, and the train of events that led inexorably to World War II might never have been put in motion. In the same breath, however, Kennan also acknowledged that the peculiar characteristics of the American political structure that had permitted these mistakes to occur were, simultaneously, the values for which both wars had been waged. To Kennan, the fact that these characteristics were at the core of the American political system did not exonerate the United States. "History does not forgive us our national mistakes," he wrote, "because they are explicable in terms of our domestic policies. If you say that mistakes of the past were unavoidable because of our domestic predilections and habits of thought, you are saying that what stopped us from being more effective than we were was democracy, as practiced in this country."[73] At the same time, though, the fact that mistakes had occurred did not mean that the political system had to be eliminated or even drastically altered. Rather, "hoping and praying" that

---

[72] George F. Kennan, *American Diplomacy, 1900–1950* (Chicago: University of Chicago Press, 1951), pp. 50–65.
[73] Ibid., p. 65.

American democracy would continue, Kennan was urging a heightened self-awareness and caution. America should not feel obliged to renounce its democratic system simply because the system acts to constrain it at the international level, but neither should Americans assume that their system comes without costs. Whether the domestic benefits are worth the international costs varies with specific issues and in the end becomes something that only the people can decide.

This book reaches a similar conclusion. International cooperation does not come easily or without a domestic price. If nations are ever to cooperate in an anarchic world, they must begin by acknowledging the limits of their own internal structures. They must gauge whether their structure affords them the power and the flexibility they will need at the international level and then decide whether the expected benefits of the cooperative endeavor will compensate for the domestic costs of implementing it. The internal approach helps us to understand not only why cooperation is so difficult to attain but also why, occasionally, it may not even be worth the price.

Methodology of Case Selection

To narrow the scope of the inquiry to a manageable size, this study looks only at international raw materials markets. Specifically, as in a previous study conducted by Fiona Gordon-Ashworth, I was concerned here with "attempts to regulate *primary* as opposed to *manufactured* goods at the *international* as opposed to *national* level."[1]

To select the specific cases, I referred to the five structural variables emphasized by most economic analyses of cartels: high concentration, small fringe, high barriers to entry, nonsubstitutability, and nondifferentiation. At the outset, my objective was to specify the raw materials commodities that, according to these structural criteria, *should* be most conducive to the formation and perpetuation of either cartels or producers' agreements. The commodities, compiled from the United Nations Conference on Trade and Development (UNCTAD) commodity list, the Commodities Research Bureau commodity yearbook, and the U.S. Bureau of Mines yearbook, were selected for their "fit" with each of these five factors. As Table 1 shows, nearly one hundred various commodities were checked and eliminated when they were found to deviate from any of these factors. The first two criteria, market concentration and the size of the production fringe, were the primary test by which most of the commodities were eliminated from the list. Once a market was found to have a four-country concentration of less than 50 percent or more

[1] See Fiona Gordon-Ashworth, *International Commodity Control: A Contemporary History and Appraisal* (London: Croom Helm, 1984), p. 3.

Table 1. Concentration of production and number of fringe producers

Product	Concentration	Fringe	Product	Concentration	Fringe
Aluminum	51%	6	Molasses	37%	7
Antimony	75%	2	Molybdenum	89%	3
Apples	55%	8	Nickel	63%	9
Arsenic	61%	5	Nitrogen	54%	6
Asbestos	84%	3	Oats	65%	5
Barite	47%	9	Olive oil	83%	3
Barley	47%	7	Oranges	71%	6
Bauxite	69%	6	Palm oil	80%	0
Beryllium	99%	0	Peanuts	73%	3
Bismuth	79%	5	Peat	99%	0
Boron	98%	0	Perlite	82%	4
Bromine	90%	2	Petroleum	49%	9
Cadmium	46%	10	Phosphate	76%	4
Castor beans	83%	3	Platinum	99%	0
Cattle	57%	5	Potash	79%	4
Cement	43%	8	Rapeseed	69%	4
Chromite	76%	4	Rayon	58%	4
Clay	65%	5	Rice	69%	5
Cobalt	86%	5	Rubber	81%	2
Cocoa	69%	4	Rye	85%	2
Coffee	58%	7	Salt	45%	9
Columbium	99%	0	Sheep	61%	7
Copper	47%	10	Silver	62%	4
Corn	68%	4	Soybeans	92%	0
Cotton	67%	4	Sugar	33%	7
Cottonseed	69%	1	Sulfur	60%	7
Diamond	75%	1	Sunflowers	62%	8
Diatomite	78%	5	Talc	57%	6
Feldspar	61%	7	Tallow	65%	8
Flaxseed	88%	1	Tea	64%	4
Fluorspar	56%	7	Thorium	99%	0
Gold	74%	5	Tin	54%	5
Graphite	62%	5	Titanium	82%	4
Gypsum	41%	7	Tobacco	57%	5
Honey	50%	4	Tungsten	67%	3
Iodine	99%	0	Uranium	70%	2
Iron ore	64%	5	Vanadium	75%	2
Lead	48%	10	Vermiculite	99%	0
Lime	52%	9	Wheat	54%	6
Magnesium	89%	4	Wool	65%	4
Manganese	74%	3	Zinc	50%	9
Mercury	79%	5	Zirconium	96%	0
Mica	86%	2			

Notes: Concentration: four-country share of total world production. Fringe: number of outside producers in command of more than 2 percent of the total world market.

than five outside producers in command of more than 2 percent of the total market, it was considered to be relatively competitive and therefore unlikely to spawn any cartels or producers' agreements.

All the markets that did emerge as highly concentrated were then also examined in accordance with the three remaining criteria of nonsubstitutability, high barriers to entry, and product homogeneity (see Table 2). Because measurements of these factors are considerably more subjective, qualitative rather than quantitative assessments were used, and determinations were based on commodity summaries prepared by the Bureau of Mines. Generally, a commodity was deemed nonsubstitutable if there are no known substitutes for its primary use. It was considered to have high barriers to entry if any initial investment in the market entails either extremely high costs or the discovery and acquisition of a rare material. And all single-element commodities (such as titanium or mercury) were deemed nondifferentiated. A slightly less definite ranking with regard to any of these criteria moved the commodity down to a "moderate" position in that particular category. Any commodity that failed to meet all three of these tests was eliminated from the final list. But because the qualifications applied here are admittedly more subjective, some commodities are included in the final list that do not meet the tightest test of all three factors. Nevertheless, the markets listed in Table

Table 2. Structural criteria of cartelization

Product	Nondifferentiation	Nonsubstitutability	Barriers
Antimony	●	○	X
Arsenic	●	○	X
Asbestos	●	X	X
Beryllium	●	●	●
Bismuth	●	●	●
Boron	●	○	●
Bromine	X	X	X
Castor beans	X	○	○
Cattle	X	X	○
Chromite	●	●	●
Clay	X	X	X
Cobalt	●	●	●
Cocoa	X	X	X
Columbium	●	X	●
Corn	○	X	○
Cotton	X	X	○

Table 2. (Continued)

Product	Nondifferentiation	Nonsubstitutability	Barriers
Cottonseed	X	●	○
Diamond	X	●	●
Diatomite	X	○	○
Flaxseed	X	○	○
Gold	●	●	●
Graphite	●	X	X
Honey	○	○	○
Iodine	●	X	X
Iron ore	●	●	●
Magnesium	●	X	X
Manganese	●	●	●
Mercury	●	X	●
Mica	X	X	X
Molybdenum	●	●	●
Oats	X	X	○
Olive oil	○	○	X
Palm oil	○	○	X
Peanuts	○	○	○
Peat	X	X	○
Perlite	X	○	○
Phosphate	●	●	●
Platinum	●	●	●
Potash	X	●	X
Rapeseed	X	○	○
Rayon	○	X	X
Rice	X	X	○
Rubber	X	○	X
Rye	●	X	○
Silver	●	●	●
Soybeans	X	X	○
Tea	○	X	○
Thorium	●	●	●
Tin	●	X	●
Titanium	●	●	●
Tobacco	X	X	○
Tungsten	●	X	●
Uranium	●	●	●
Vanadium	●	●	●
Vermiculite	●	○	●
Wheat	X	X	○
Wool	X	X	○
Zirconium	X	○	X

● - Conducive to cartelization
X - Moderately conducive to cartelization
○ - Nonconducive

Table 3. Commodity markets most conducive to cartelization

Beryllium	Iron ore	Thorium
Bismuth	Manganese	Tin
Chromite	Mercury	Titanium
Cobalt	Molybdenum	Tungsten
Columbium	Phosphate	Uranium
Diamond	Platinum	Vanadium
Gold	Silver	

Note: Derived directly from Table 2. Includes all commodities that ranked highly conducive in at least two of the three categories and at least moderately conducive in the third.

3 can reasonably be described as markets with similar structural characteristics and are markets that, according to structural criteria, should prove similarly amenable to the formation of cooperative agreements between the largest producers.[2]

[2] Most wide-scale economic analyses of international cartels and collusion rely on similar structural criteria to identify cartels and potential cartels. See, for instance, Paul Leo Eckbo, *The Future of World Oil* (Cambridge, Mass.: Ballinger, 1976); Arthur G. Fraas and Douglas F. Greer, "Market Structure and Price Collusion: An Experimental Analysis," *Journal of Industrial Economics* 26 (September 1977), pp. 21–44; and Carl Kaysen and Donald F. Turner, *Antitrust Policy: An Economic and Legal Analysis* (Cambridge: Harvard University Press, 1959).

Index

AEC. *See* U.S. Atomic Energy Commission
AECB (Canadian Atomic Energy Control Board), 105, 130
Agfa-Gevaert (company), 182
Alaska, 144, 157
Alcoa (company), 223
Alt, James D., 25n
Aluminum market, 222–23, 235
Anglo American Corporation of South Africa: as DeBeers' sister company, 75, 102; and diamond cartel, 51, 52; and gold, 143, 150–56, 164–66, 168, 170–71; internal structure of, 222, 225, 241; power of, 76n, 77, 143, 150–56, 221–22, 229–30, 237; RTZ links to, 100, 101, 102, 130. *See also* Oppenheimer family
Angola, 64, 87
Anthony, Michael, 101, 112
Antwerp (Belgium), 59, 62, 70, 71, 72
Apartheid: development of, 148–50, 155, 247–48; Oppenheimer opposition to, 77; Soviet opposition to, ix
Arab-Israeli peace talks, 240n
Armenia, 157
Arms control agreements, 32n, 129n, 224, 243
Artels, 172
Association of Tin Producing Countries, 5n
Austin, Jack, 99–100, 103–6, 134, 135–36
Australia: diamond mines in, 52, 53n, 68n; domestic constraints on cartels in, 128, 132–33; gold in, 139, 144; nuclear power opposition in, 88, 125,

130, 132; perception of future in, 233; and silver, 181, 197; uranium in, 91, 94–95, 102, 108, 129n; uranium cartel in, 88, 90, 104, 107, 109–11, 114, 128, 131, 222. *See also* Mary Kathleen Uranium Ltd.
Austria, 242
Authoritarianism, 33–34, 220, 223–24, 238, 243–49, 254. *See also* Internal structure
Autonomy, 17, 245–46, 249, 254–55. *See also* "Autonomy of competitor"
"Autonomy of competitor," and internal structure, 14–20, 24–25, 41, 73–82, 170–71, 218–24, 236
Axelrod, Robert, 21

Bain, Joe, 36
Banco Central (Mexico), 211–12
Bangladesh, 235
Bank for Foreign Economic Affairs (Soviet Union), 169
Bank of England, 163
Bargaining: and cooperation, 17, 28–34, 217, 218–19, 238–40, 249–54; between DeBeers and Soviet Union, 65–74, 82–83, 239. *See also* Exclusivity; Flexibility; Secrecy
Barlow Rand (company), 152
Barnato, Barney, 49n
Bayne, Nicholas, 31n, 239
Belgian Congo, 54
Belgium. *See* Antwerp
Bland-Allison Act (U.S.), 194
Boart (industrial diamonds), 62–63, 67, 79–80
Bohr, Niels, 93